Winfrid Alden Stearns

Labrador

A Sketch of Its People, Its IIndustries and Its Natural History

Winfrid Alden Stearns

Labrador
A Sketch of Its People, Its iIndustries and Its Natural History

ISBN/EAN: 9783337025960

Printed in Europe, USA, Canada, Australia, Japan

Cover: Foto ©Andreas Hilbeck / pixelio.de

More available books at **www.hansebooks.com**

LABRADOR,

A SKETCH OF

ITS PEOPLES, ITS INDUSTRIES AND ITS NATURAL HISTORY.

BY
WINFRID ALDEN STEARNS.

BOSTON:
LEE AND SHEPARD, 47 FRANKLIN STREET.
NEW YORK: CHARLES T. DILLINGHAM.
1884.

PREFACE.

IN presenting to the public the following journal sketches of the country of which they treat, the thought that I am writing of a region so new and so little known, though so near to us, together with the pleasure which I have experienced both in my travels and in the preparation of this account of them, will furnish a sufficient excuse for the undertaking. Although so little has been known or written about Labrador, yet it is a region not a thousand miles away from us, and one which bears a most important relation to the fishing interests of this continent.

The knowledge of this region, which is within reach of the public, is to be found only in the pages of an old-fashioned document, of two volumes, now out of print, and almost unknown save to large libraries, entitled "Cartwright's Journal;" in Hind's "Labrador Peninsula," 2 vols., and in occasional articles in some magazine or newspaper. If I have added some new and interesting matter to our present knowledge of this subject, my labors will not have been in vain.

My first trip to Labrador was during the summer of 1875, when I collected largely in all the branches of Natural History, and especially in Botany, finding, with the assistance of the Rev. Mr. Butler, the then missionary to this region, many new and rare plants. This number has since been enlarged and a catalogue of them, as of collections in several other branches of Natural History, published in the sixth volume of the Report of the National Museum, at Washington. In September, 1880, I again visited the coast and remained studying the region and collecting until September, 1881. During this time I had abundant opportunity for investigation. In the summer of 1882 I made my third trip, starting from Boston with a company of about a dozen fellow-voyagers, and proceeded nearly to Harrison Inlet.

I would tender most cordial thanks to several of the officers in charge of various posts of the Hudson's Bay Company where I visited, who gave me much help in my investigations: as also the courteous Magistrate at Bonne Esperance, Mr. Wm. H. Whiteley, with whom I spent a great part of my time while on the coast.

Hoping that there may be found enough of value and interest to counterbalance the many too obvious defects, I submit these pages to those who may be interested in such researches.

Respectfully,
WINFRID A. STEARNS.

Amherst, July 14, 1884.

CONTENTS.

	PAGE
Preface	iii
Introduction	1-7

CHAPTER I.
PHYSICAL GEOGRAPHY OF REGION.
Survey of Labrador — Elementary physics — Physical geography   9-26

CHAPTER II.
STARTING ON THE JOURNEY.
Trip to Labrador — Arrival at Montreal — Arrival at Quebec and description of the city   27-38

CHAPTER III.
QUEBEC TO GREEN ISLAND.
Our stay in Quebec — Starting for Berthier — Berthier — Off for Labrador — Bunking in — Island of Orleans — Islands and channels — Sunday — Other islands — The Saguenay — Fog again   39-51

CHAPTER IV.
GREEN ISLAND TO BONNE ESPERANCE.
The weather — *Beluga borealis* and other huge animals — A sundog — Birds — The rusty blackbird — Bradore hills — Varieties of rocks — Coast line about St. Augustine — Reaching Bonne Esperance — Old Fort island — Eider ducks — Other birds — Garden vegetables — Hay — Raised beaches — Labrador dogs — Searching for driftwood   52-66

CHAPTER V.
BONNE ESPERANCE.
Bonne Esperance — Esquimaux river and island — Caribou island — Entering Bonne Esperance Harbor — Vessels in the harbor — Their nationality — Activity of place — Religious character of people — Chapel and Mission house — Residence of Mr. Whiteley, magistrate — Nescopies — Store and shop provisions — Money — Trade — A trading story   67-75

(v)

CHAPTER VI.
NATURAL HISTORY: TOPOGRAPHY OF COUNTRY.

Raspberries — Weather — Hudsonian chickadee and other birds — Black fly — Topography of country — Old Fort bay, physical features and surroundings — Superstitions concerning the raven   76–96

CHAPTER VII.
OLD FORT: INVESTIGATIONS.

Indian tents — New fields for research — Visit to the Indians — Seals' flesh — Dogskin boots — Cattle food in hard winters — *Coptis trifolia* — Spruce partridge — Inland — Hypothesis of Aurora — Little auk — Signs of a wreck — Ascent of western arm of the bay — Wreck of the Edward Cardwell — Picking up lumber — First snowstorm of the winter   97–118

CHAPTER VIII.
A LABRADOR HOME.

A Labrador home — Houses — Where erected — Stage — Shop — Stable — The house — Papering — Family — Occupation of its members — Out-of-door life   119–131

CHAPTER IX.
A GALE: KOMATIK, RACKETS, ETC.

Dinner off fresh meat — Credit and shiftlessness — A Labrador snow-storm — Wind — Preparing for storm — Storming hard — Firewood — Storm increases — Sleepless night — Another day of it — A grand sight — Violence of wind and wave — Destruction of stage — Calmer weather — Beautiful ice scene — End of storm — Thanksgiving day — Komatiks and rackets   132–151

CHAPTER X.
WINTER SCENES AND OCCUPATION OF PEOPLE.

Trip up the river to the mission — Ice pictures — Bad walking — To the old Fort — New scenes and bad walking — Pleasant Sunday — The return — Journal — A komatik ride — Christmas gathering — Wood cutting — Work for the evenings — Making sealskin boots, mittens, and other needful and fancy work   152–171

CHAPTER XI.
WINTER SCENES AND AMUSEMENTS.

New Year's day — How to walk on rackets — "Fish, dogs, and seal," the general topics of conversation — Obtaining skeletons — Larch poultices — "Small talk" — Low temperature — Deer stories — Trapping — Indians — Up the river — At the mission — Harnessing the puppies — A racket walk . . . 172–190

CHAPTER XII.
OLD FORT TO L'ANSE AMOUR.

80° in winter — Trip eastward — Starting — Esquimaux river and island — Salmon bay — Bradore bay — Caribou island — Five leagues — Middle bay — Belles Amour — Over Bradore hills — L'Anse Dunes — Blanc Sablon — L'Anse Coteau — L'Anse Clair — Forteau — Amour 191–213

CHAPTER XIII.
A TRAMPING EXPEDITION.

Canadian porcupine — Picking fall berries in spring — Carrying wood to summer quarters — Anticipating Fourth of July — Summer quarters in winter — Capsized — Fox hunt on rackets — A mile of soft snow without rackets 214–220

CHAPTER XIV.
MOVING OUT.

Preparing the summer house to live in — Moving out — A spring rescue — Seals on ice — Larks — A home scene — Spring duck shooting — Repairing the boats — Visit to the Indians — Indian canoes — Netting nets — Labrador mail — Natural scenery of Labrador — Repairing canoes — Visit to Esquimaux graves — Ornithological notes 221–238

CHAPTER XV.
FROM BLANC SABLON TO MINGAN.

Blanc Sablon again — Northern limits of the bittern — Return along the coast of Natashquan — Spring scene in Red bay — Other places — St. Mary islands — Cormorants — At Natashquan — Rambles about the place — Appearance of the birds — The dark day — Arrival at Mingan 239–253

CHAPTER XVI.
MINGAN TO OLD FORT ISLAND AGAIN.

Mingan and surroundings — Hudson's Bay Companies' buildings — Mingan river — Indians of this region, their habits, religion, etc. — Montagnais and Nascopies — The Indian trade at the various places along the north shore — Romaine or Olomanosheebo — Natashquan again — French steamer and salmon freezing — Jewelry peddler — Agwanus, Nabasippi — Terns and gulls — Cod fish " schooling "— Esquimaux Point — Indian names, etc. : St. Genevieve island, Watcheeshoo, Manicouagan, Saddle Hill, Mt. St. John, Washatnagunashka bay, Mushkoniatawee, Pashasheeboo, Peashtebai — Shooting at the Fox islands — Mutton bay, Great Mecattina islands — Old Fort island again at last   254–272

CHAPTER XVII.
HOMEWARD BOUND.

Affairs at Old Fort Island — The fishing season — Thunder storm — Arrival of vessel which is to take us home — Our trip in her to L'Anse Loup — Scenes at intervening places — Off for home — Double reefed fore and main sails — Island of Anticosti — A hurricane — Quebec and home   - • - - - 273–279

CHAPTER XVIII.
THIRD TRIP TO LABRADOR.

Third voyage: summer of '82 — Puffin-shooting — Dredging — Bad weather — Main boom breaks — Chateau and Temple bays — Places of interest — Mines and minerals — Aurora and phosphorescence — Icebergs — Fox harbor — Battle island — Indians and Esquimaux — Indian vocabulary — Square island — Dead island — A water garden — Triangle harbor — Homeward bound — Notes on Dutch and Esquimaux settlements.   -   280–295

INTRODUCTION.

LABRADOR: ITS DISCOVERY AND ITS LOCATION.

THE coast of Labrador is well known to you all, as it figures on your maps and on your charts. There are probably very few who do not recollect this little oblong plateau as it appears thus jutting eastward into the Straits of Belle Isle from an almost desolate, and on your maps plainly colored, portion of inhabitable northern North America. If there should be those to whom this location is as yet unfamiliar, let them refer to their geography, and then, following the river St. Lawrence as it flows to the Gulf, and the Gulf as it flows through the Straits of Belle Isle, they will readily find, just before entering the narrowest part of the Straits, the coast of Newfoundland on the right and that of Labrador on the left of this portion of the Gulf.

A section, and that the most easterly, of the Canadian Province of Quebec, is usually included with Labrador proper in the term, generally applied, of "Labrador." As a part of this Province it has its mails, though irregular at best; while its seat of government is in Quebec.

Of Labrador a certain writer has said, perhaps as truly as the times (by which I mean the explorations of science and survey) will permit, that "it is an immense peninsula extending over an area of four hundred and fifty thousand superficial miles, and bounded by the Atlantic, the Gulf of St. Lawrence, and Hudson's Bay."

Of this part of the coast there is a considerable division of opinion, as in fact of other neighboring parts, as to the people who first discovered it, as well as of the origin of the name.

It is not the place here to enter into a discussion of this question nor yet to call up all the points in the arguments in favor of or against any particular hypothesis. The fact that as yet we know little enough of these interesting points of inquiry, which, while they answer for individual effort and research, will hardly be necessary in such a place as this, will therefore limit us to what we do know.

We do know of the contention among both French and English as to the discovery of Labrador by Sebastian Cabot in 1496, and its exploration soon after by the Portuguese Corterell, who is said to have named it. We do know that Mr. Samuel Robertson, who has given this matter his most careful attention and who has perhaps searched more thoroughly than any other man in the country for the real facts bearing upon this subject, in his excellent article read before the Literary and Historical Society of Quebec, dated January 16, 1841, gives us the summing up of what are the results of his labors. From them we learn that "the universal tradition of the coast," and which his inquiries seem to verify and establish, is "that one Labrador, a Basque whaler, from the kingdom of Navarre in Spain, did penetrate through the Straits of Belle Isle, as far as Labrador Bay, sometime about the middle of the fifteenth century; and, eventually, the whole coast took the name from that bay and harbor."

There is very little doubt, as far as circumstantial evidence goes, that the coast here, as in the neighboring places, was visited by the Norsemen in the tenth century; but they left no signs of colonization by which we can prove it.

There were some remains of buildings, also instruments discovered, that were supposed to be of later and Esquimaux origin, but these, Mr. Robertson thinks, can be proven of Basque origin. In all probability, therefore, Labrador was discovered by Basque fishermen and whalers before the discovery of Cabot, and before Christopher Columbus discovered America. We know that the French carried on fisheries along the coast of Newfoundland earlier even than the year 1500. In 1532 Jacques Cartier, *with Bretons for pilots*, visited this coast, and as early as 1506 a chart of the Gulf had been published. Besides all this the Welsh and Irish, as also the Icelanders, put in the claims of being early visitors. Thus the difficulties of origin increase rather than diminish.

The first established colony in Labrador was at "Brest," now Bradore. It was founded about 1508, was a trading post, contained the residence of the Governor and other officers, and, it is said, contained "200 houses and 1000 inhabitants in winter, which latter were trebled in the summer." Thus you will see that very early this was an important trading post, though it gradually lost its importance, and soon dwindled to a few houses whose inhabitants were settlers, who took what they could find as they found it, and were without law and government, as one might truly say.

You will understand that this settlement at Bradore was not a permanent one, that is, dependent upon other settlements on the coast; but was one, so to speak, complete in itself for the purpose of carrying on fisheries at that place, while the greater portion of the coast had neither been much settled nor much explored; consequently, at the time called the Conquest, when the Esquimaux were nearly exterminated from these districts, and when the owning foreign monarch began to cut up this almost thriving colony into special grants to his favorites, its prosperity began to decline. Though at first the fish, whale, and fowl were everywhere abundant, a slow but perceptible decrease of these productions tended also to dishearten the colony; and a natural unfavorableness of the coast, being then, as it now is, a mass of granite rock, as also the severity of the climate, combined with a dread of extermination, to scatter them completely. You will now also understand why, if Labrador was once in a way to become a popular fishing station, it broke up rather than increased in its settlements and thus possible future growth. Having thus broken up, you will see why it has remained waiting for the energy and determination of Americans to combine with the sturdy *hold on* of the English, who have now gained possession of the coast and added it to their already important Canadian and Newfoundland Colonies, to open it again to the world as a fishing post, when centuries shall have restocked its waters.

As Labrador looks upon the charts, one would easily imagine that it was a vast expanse of lowland, and one almost plain peninsula extending into the sea as a continuation and part of the British Provinces, and auxiliary, perhaps, to the territory of the Hudson's Bay Company. In point of fact this latter case is partly true and partly false. It is indeed a part of the British possessions, and it is also a part of the Hudson's Bay Company's territory; at least there are several trading posts of that Company placed occasionally along its shores, and the Company own considerable land located about and around each such post; yet it forms but a small part of that Company's productive ground, which is much farther north, and extends a considerable way into the interior of the country, thus approaching the great bay which bears the name of that hardy, early pioneer and explorer who discovered it, as also the river of that same name which here takes its rise. At one time Labrador *was* a small part of these the best fur regions of the world. Then many trading posts were established, of which the most important, perhaps, at least of that portion of the coast of which I shall speak more at length presently, was at St. Augustine, near the St. Augustine river, and only a few miles — so to speak — from the principal settlements in this section about Esquimaux river, and Bonne Esperance the seat of local government. It was only at a late day that this post was abandoned as a trading station, and, unless recently resupplied it is no more a permanent authorized station of the Company. Though the post here has been formed but a few years, new ones are being so constantly made — or rather abandoned ones resupplied — and old ones broken up, that it is impossible to keep an exact and satisfactory account of them all.

The portions of Labrador which I visited are contained within the easternmost extremity of the Province of Quebec, and the westernmost part of Labrador proper, comprising an included distance of about five hundred miles, in which extent of coastline I have visited nearly every harbor of importance. In describing two or three of these locations a sort of idea may be obtained of what is to be seen elsewhere along the coast, as the simple inhabitants differ little in customs and manners.

The line which divides these two portions of territory is established in a direct northern route from the settlement of Blanc Sablon, which is only about twenty miles from Bonne Esperance, the residence of Mr. William H. Whiteley, the magistrate for this part of the coast.

Of course the trading post of St. Augustine was not the only one on the coast. It was simply the only one which the people within a radius of fifty miles recognized as available for uses of immediate trade, while yet a licensed station. From St. Augustine almost to the head of the St. Lawrence River, many places such as Tadousac, Port Neuf, Goodbout, Seven Islands, and Mingan; Natashquan, Musquarro, Romaine, and perhaps others, were regular posts of the Hudson's Bay Company, and, together, formed a chain of the most important localities along the coast, all of which belonged to the Eastern division of what is known as the Montreal Department, which, with the Northern, the Southern, and the Columbian Departments, form the four portions into which that great Company is divided. As the southwesternmost of these posts is not far from Quebec, a sort of central station for most of the trading of this region, one can see quite easily that the settlers along the coast are not so far from communication with civilization, especially in summer, as one would at first imagine; though in the long winter months when the bays and harbors are frozen over so that no vessels can approach, and no boats can sail from post to post, to the stranger at such a time on these ice-bound shores the prospect seems dreary enough. In the winter, travelling is mostly on foot, shod with the racket as it is called, a sort of padded or rather wicker snowpad; or on komatiks or sledges drawn by dogs which can go over the high hills, lining the very coast, with safety and often with great speed. Yet Labrador in as low a latitude as it is, compared to what is beyond, and as near civilization as it is compared to what is beyond, though pleasant for a short time in summer, is sufficiently dreary in winter. No wonder that at such a time a stranger feels that he has reached the limits of civilized warmth, so to speak, arising from his own country, home; while he is surrounded by the icy arms of the far north stretching continually downwards and outwards!

We have seen now that Labrador was discovered—no matter by whom—at a time very nearly contemporary with the discovery of Columbus, if we exclude the probable claims of the Norsemen; that it was once an important fishing station whose development was in every way hindered rather than helped; that its relation to the Hudson's Bay Company's trading territory was a very near though not absolutely necessary one, as far as that company was concerned—since the agents of that Company always ran more or less opposition to the Quebec and Halifax traders; that its relation to the Province of Quebec was that of a perfectly natural northeastern dependency or addition; and that Blanc Sablon, situated as it is at the entrance of the Straits of Belle Isle, was so evident and natural a division between this and the Newfoundland dependency of Labrador proper, that it ought not to be difficult to understand where the one ended and the other began.

In Anspach's "History of the Island of Newfoundland," 1827, p. 323, the reason for annexing Labrador to Newfoundland is given as follows:—

" The coast of Labrador, although discovered by Cabot, was very little known until the latter part of the last century, when the progressive increase of the Newfoundland fisheries induced the British Government to extend them to this coast, by annexing it to the government of that island, in the year 1763. The native inhabitants of those parts were included in the regulations which were, at the same time, forwarded to the Governor of the colonies, to prevent the different tribes of Indians from being in anywise molested or disturbed in the possession of such territories as, not having been ceded to or purchased by the Crown of England, were reserved to them as their hunting grounds. All settlements, formed either wilfully or inadvertently upon such lands, were to be immediately given up; nor were any such lands for the future to be purchased from the said Indians, but in the name of His Brittannic Majesty, at some public meeting or assembly, of said Indians, to be held for that purpose by the Governor or Commander-in-chief of such colony within or near which they should lie. The trade with the said Indians was declared free and open to all British subjects who should take out proper licenses for that purpose.

This union of the coast of Labrador with Newfoundland, by placing the former under a jurisdiction which could, from local circumstances, more effectually than any other, provide for the maintenance of order and the due administration of justice in those parts, tended materially to increase its importance as a fishery without any injury to the fur trade, both being perfectly compatible. When this arrangement was altered in 1774, and the jurisdiction of the Governor of Newfoundland was reduced to its former limits, a superintendent of trade, appointed by the Governor-General of the Four British Provinces, and responsible to him, used to reside at Labrador. This measure, which appeared to have had for its principal object to encourage the fur trade, must have proved very prejudicial to the fishery, and the source of much disorder and irregularity. The re-annexation of the coast of Labrador and adjacent islands to the government of Newfoundland, in the year 1809, was consequently a measure extremely favorable to the interests of the trade and fisheries."

With a proper understanding, then, of the region visited, I will proceed with the narrative of the expedition, trusting that a greater part of it may be of general interest to the reader.

CHAPTER I.

Survey of Labrador — Elementary Physics — Physical Geography.

THE most complete, in fact the only real, survey of Labrador ever made, was in 1832 and 1834, by Capt. H. W. Bayfield, R. N., F. A. S. He was assisted by other parties, though perhaps none of them were so thorough as was that of Capt. Bayfield — at least he is quoted as authority to this day — and I found that our vessel, by following the directions of his admirable chart, entered and left many an opening of but sufficient size to admit the passage of our vessel, with perfect safety; showing that the soundings were for the most part taken correctly, and that comparative quiet had remained in regard to subsidence of waters or elevation of land during the lapse of a period of nearly forty years. Though the change of level of the water itself, or the variation in depth, would have been but slight in so short a time, yet the fact that so many of the soundings remained unchanged gave us additional proof against the rising or sinking of the land at that place. Comparing Capt. Bayfield's chart, therefore, with our own soundings, we obtained very favorable and often important results. 'Previous to a short account of some of the physical phenomena of this region, let us rehearse a few of the elementary principles of physical geography necessary for their clear understanding.

For the purposes of science and convenience, the earth is traversed by imaginary lines running in all directions about and around it. The equator is a great circle passing around the earth from east to west and is equidistant from each of the poles. The meridians are great circles passing around the globe from north to south, crossing the equator at right angles and meeting at the poles. The parallels (of latitude) are smaller circles parallel to the equator. The tropics, marking the highest latitude receiving the vertical rays of the sun, are situated twenty-three and one-half degrees both north and south of the equator. The polar circles are situated (to correspond with the tropics) twenty-three and one-half degrees, the one north of the south pole, and the other south of the north pole, and are the limits of light when the sun is vertical at the tropics. The ecliptic marks the apparent path of the sun from tropic to tropic, and as it continues around the earth requiring three hundred and sixty-five days for the sun to pass to its end it divides the seasons and days, hence the weeks and months of the year. Latitude is the distance from the equator to the pole, measured in either direction: thus there are ninety degrees of north latitude and a corresponding number of degrees of south latitude; the length of a degree of latitude is sixty-nine and one-half miles. Longitude is the distance east or west from any given meridian measured on the equator; the length of a degree of longitude is also sixty-nine and one-half miles. The relative difference in longitude between two places marks, also, the difference in time between those places; for since there are 360° degrees around the earth traversed in twenty-four hours, one hour of time must correspond to fifteen degrees, or four minutes to one degree. When, therefore, a place is so many degrees from any given locality, it is easy to see what will be the difference in time between these places; if east the time is slower, if west faster than the given time at the given place.

Applying other simple laws we find that the nautical mile is equal to one and one-sixth English miles: or there are sixty of them to a degree of latitude; it is therefore natural to compute distances in nautical miles by applying the latitude as a measure of distance.

Though these remarks may not now seem in place, their suggestion will become evident at once in measuring distances without the use of a regular scale of miles, the degrees and minutes of latitude answering every purpose.

Waves have been defined as the "alternate rise and fall of successive ridges of water." They are formed by the action of the wind, or the disturbance of the balance of equilibrium in the surface of the water itself. Waves vary in their rapidity of progress, their extent, and their height and breadth, according to the area of water in which they occur, its depth, and the force and direction of the wind; being smallest in small bodies and largest in large bodies of water. The wave movement primarily is that of simple oscillation, or of repeated risings and fallings without apparent forward or backward motion of any kind; thus a chip thrown upon a surface of water affected by such motion retains its position while rising and falling as the water of that area rises and falls. Such is the case if the surface of the water is at apparent rest and there be no wind. Let the wind arise, or the sea be affected by currents, or both, and there arises a complexity of wave phenomena at once interesting as it is difficult to study with any degree of satisfaction. The other kind of wave motion is called the wave of translation. It is a long, solitary line of crests, such as would be formed by the pushing forward of a mass of water over and above the level of the surrounding water; it progresses slow or fast according as the depth about is great or small. The typical wave of translation is the tide wave. The phenomena of the rise and fall of the tide are too well known to have escaped the attention of the ordinary individual. They are produced by the action of the sun and moon, primarily of the moon alone, upon the surface of the earth. They occur with regularity in all great bodies of water, and consist of the rising and falling of that body of water effected as a whole, at periods of nearly six hours apart, with a few moments of calm at the end of each period. The period of rising water is called flood tide, and the highest elevation of flood tide high water; while the period of falling water is called ebb tide, and the lowest ebb tide low water. The period of time between the highest or lowest tide to the next tide of the same kind, or between one high tide and the next high, or one low and the next low tide is twelve hours and twenty-six minutes. Hence, as there are two such periods in a day, and only twenty-four hours in that period, high tide occurs fifty-two minutes later each successive day. In a month's time this very nearly coincides with the period of a lunar month, and in fact we find that the highest tides occur at such a time as answers to the new and full moon, and the lowest at the change of first and third quarter. In a table of tides, therefore, the tide, if marked for new moon at a certain place, will answer for every new moon at that place throughout the year and following seasons. Thus in a book of sailing directions, a table of high and low water, or rather of spring and neap tides, gives the height of water or time of occurrence of the highest spring tide (when the moon is exactly at new and full) at any time of any year; and also the height of water and occurrence of any neap tide (when the moon is at exact first or third quarter) at any time of any year.

The interval between is easily determined by taking the time of highest or lowest water, and for each day subtracting fifty-two minutes from said time. Thus by means of these tables navigators can always tell high or low water at any day or any time of the day for any year, at any place mentioned in these tables; or they can by marking the spring and neap tides make a table of their own, that, if their reckoning is correct, will answer equally well for other parties as for themselves. But a few words of explanation as to the reason of high and low water. I have said that both sun and moon have their influence in the tide of our larger bodies of water throughout the globe. The influence of the moon is about three times that of the sun. The moon attracts both land and water; one can easily see that the movable particles of the latter will respond to this magnetic force much more noticeably than the almost immovable particles of the former. The rising of the crest of water, directly under the centre of influence of the moon at full or new, causes of course a depression at the sides, being greatest at the centre of this non-magnetic attraction; thus the centre of attraction will be distant from the centre of depression by 90°. To restore the equilibrium the water must fall to a crest on the opposite side of the earth equal to that of attraction beneath the moon.

The same law will hold good with regard to the sun. Therefore when the moon and sun are in a line with the earth and each other, the greatest elevation will occur, as it does at new and full moon; and when the moon is farthest from the sun, the attraction of the sun will be exerted on the line of depression 90° from the line of greatest elevation, which is always beneath the moon, and attract that portion to the corresponding depression of the other portion, so that the moon exerts its least influence upon the water beneath it and the tides are the lowest; these occur at the 1st and 3rd quarter. The action of tides may be thus briefly described; we then come to local variations in height of tide. Thus if the sea beach of any given surrounding is low, and the tide has free access to all parts at once, one can easily see that the tides of that place will be moderate in height and depth and least liable to change, while if the surroundings are narrow and confined and the sea is obliged to force itself against high cliffs and into narrow passages the accumulated waters must form an abiding place by raising the level of the water to that of the nearest open basin, which often causes the tides to rise to the extraordinary height of forty, fifty, and even sixty feet above ordinary level. In that narrow arm and clifted channel of the sea, the Bay of Fundy, this remarkable phenomenon actually occurs. At the head of the bay the tides are eighteen to twenty feet high; here the highest springtides occasionally reach seventy feet. Marine currents are so influenced by local irritation that it would be difficult to describe them, but let us notice a few of the most important ones:—

It is pretty generally conceded that a constant current sets out of the Gulf between Newfoundland and Cape Breton, in a southeasterly direction. This is changed more to the southward by a current entering the Gulf from the Straits of Belle Isle. There are other minor currents due to prevailing winds at the time that affect the waters, but, unfortunately, they have not been studied with sufficient care to define them. There is, however, no doubt about the northern current, and the huge masses of ice often transported through the Straits would alone prove its existence, coming as they do with their large area of surface directed against a strong opposing southwest wind and even thus reaching the eastern point of Anticosti before finally disappearing. The current bearing these masses is, however, very irregular, being weak at times and very swift at others. In following this most important current I must give the words of the original survey, as simpler than any I can invent, and more truthful than any non-discoverer can give. " After entering the Gulf the current runs along the north or Labrador coast at the distance of two or three miles from the outer islands, leaving a narrow space in-shore in which the streams of the tide, when uninfluenced by winds, are tolerably regular. Passing outside of Mistanoque, the islands of Great Meccatina and Southmaker's Ledge, it pursues a direction given to it by the trending of the coast till it is turned gradually to the southward by the weak current which is often found coming from the westward between Anticosti and the north coast, during westerly winds, and which is set off to the southward from Natashquan point. The united streams continue their southern course at a rate diminishing as they become more widely spread, and which seldom exceeds half a knot, and, finally, joining the main downward current out of the St. Lawrence, of which an account will be given immediately, they all pursue a southeast direction towards the main entrance of the Gulf, between Cape Ray and the island of St. Paul. It is this current from the northward which is felt by vessels crossing from off the Bird rocks towards Anticosti: and which, together with neglecting to allow for the local attractions of the compass, has been the principal cause of masters of vessels so often finding themselves, unexpectedly, on the south coast. Many shipwrecks have arisen from this cause near Cape Rosier, Gaspé, Mal bay, etc." The same authority adds, further on, as an explanation of the irregularities of current near the north coast of the Gulf, that " both these currents, viz., that from the northward, and the main downward current of the St. Lawrence, are modified by the tides, but in a way directly contrary ; for the northern current, in through the Straits of Belle Isle, is accelerated by the flood and checked by the ebb, while the other is accelerated by the ebb, and checked by the flood tide. These modifying causes, viz., the tides and winds, give rise to various combinations and consequent irregularities, in the direction and strength of these streams which it is extremely difficult at all times to estimate." The idea, then, that in so narrow an area as that occupied by the Straits, and the Gulf and River St. Lawrence, the main currents are constantly diverted by counter currents and inconstantly influenced by wind and tide, shows the truth of my words when I say that navigation in these waters, especially when impeded by adverse winds and weather, and enveloped in the thick fog so characteristic of these regions, is anything but easy, even to the experienced seaman ; many are the tales of horror, at which the heart sickens, known only too well to be true, that might be told of Anticosti, as well as other prominent places along the south shore especially of the St. Lawrence. Among the causes influencing the current, especially in the river are the spring freshets, annually descending the small streams, and pouring their bodies of water into the St. Lawrence. Here, of course, the accumulation of winter's snow and ice, thawing, descends in the shape of an accumulated mass of fresh water and makes its influence felt far into the river. Then, too, the tide of the sea reaches far up the river and is also often mistaken for a current in the river itself. All these agents, acting in more or less harmony, often produce a current of three and even four knots an hour, decreasing in velocity as it approaches the Gulf. There are also great differences in strength and direction of flood and ebb tides, that frequently produce strong ripples on various parts of the coast, and differing according to locality, so that unless a seaman has studied local phenomena carefully, he will be entirely deceived as to the proper course to pursue to keep his vessel from running aground upon the numerous sandbars here present. It is safe to say that the river St. Lawrence, from Quebec to the Gulf, is one of the most difficult of our large American rivers to navigate in all seasons, with continually varying wind and weather. The

Gulf is sufficiently difficult for large vessels, while the river is perhaps still more so for medium sized crafts.

Next to the currents the winds are perhaps the most varying cause of assistance or hindrance to the navigator in these same portions of the water. During the greater part of the season " the prevailing winds," says our best authority upon this subject, " are either directly up or directly down the estuary, following the course of the chains of high lands on either side of the great valley of the St. Lawrence." This appears to be in the main true, though the same author tells us that "westerly winds do not appear to be so much guided in direction by the high lands, excepting along the south coast." Winds varying from west-northwest to north-northwest frequently blow for days in succession, accompanied by weather in every way fine and beautiful; then the wind will often turn and blow from corresponding easterly points as long again, bringing cold, wet, foggy weather, and more or less rain. The easterly winds prevail in spring; the southwest — especially in the Gulf and at the opening of the Straits — in the summer, and the westerly in the autumn. The north and south winds occur only occasionally, in the winter months the northwest and northerly winds prevailing. Strong gales of wind are of frequent occurrence especially in the Gulf, in autumn; generally speaking, however, all winds subside more or less at dusk, to be followed by light off-shore breezes during the night. It will be seen, therefore, that the winds are perhaps more regular than might be expected from the nature of the locality; a good navigator will soon learn to depend upon the weather, and even in a measure foretell it with accuracy. Let him be in whatever part he may of the gulf and river St. Lawrence, a careful study of the sailing directions will lead him, except in unusual weather, to pretty safe and sure conclusions as to what the morrow will be, and plans laid upon these conclusions seldom fail of realization.

Besides and next in importance to the currents, and the winds, the marine barometer is indispensable in determining the weather, and guiding one's course both by day and night, here as in other

THE BAROMETER.

great bodies of water. A few moments only will serve to give a proper idea of this most important instrument.

A barometer is an instrument used for ascertaining and measuring the weight of the air or more strictly speaking of our atmosphere. It was invented in 1643, when Torricelli was making his examinations as to the reason why water ascended in pumps to the height of thirty-two feet, and there remained. Taking a glass tube some four feet in length and closed above, he filled it with mercury and reversed the open end in a basin of that same substance. The column sank to a level of 27.5 inches and there remained. Comparing the column of water with that of mercury he found them to be to each other in height in an inverse ratio of the specific gravities of these two substances; that is, a column of mercury 27.5 inches high would balance a column of water 32 feet; and both would remain the same, while the pressure of atmosphere from outside upon the open basins of mercury and water in which the columns were inverted remained the same. In 1646, at Rouen, one Pascal repeated this experiment, and further proved that while one column of mercury remaining at the bottom of a mountain underwent no change, a similar column taken to the top of the same mountain was reduced in height by several inches by the diminution of pressure, while it regained that same height, and corresponded with the one left at the bottom of the mountain when brought down. By this means he proved the possibility of measuring heights by the variations of the barometer, for thus the tube of mercury was named. Boyle, in 1666, discovered that the atmosphere was elastic and compressible, and Mariotte that the density of the atmosphere was in proportion to the weight with which it was compressed. The layer of air nearest the earth was heaviest and sustained the weight of all the rest of the atmosphere above it and each succeeding stratum was lighter and lighter. *Aqueous vapor* is the amount of water evaporated and held in suspension in the atmosphere. As evaporation is promoted by dry air, wind, a diminution of pressure, and heat, the quantity thus held in suspension depends upon the temperature. Since "heat expands the gaseous portion of the atmosphere, the spaces between its particles are enlarged and their capacities for containing moisture augmented. Still further we know that "aqueous vapor is highly elastic; its elasticity, which increases with an increase of temperature, has been determined by Dalton, and its force measured by the height of the mercurial column it is capable of supporting. Aqueous vapor, raised to 32° Fahrenheit, exerts a pressure on the mercury equal to 0.2 of an inch, at 80° to 1.03 of an inch, at 180° to 15.0 inches, and at 212° to 30.0 inches, — a pressure equal to the pressure of the whole atmosphere at the level of the sea." The amount of vapor existing at any time in the air is determined by an instrument called the hygrometer. By means of this instrument we obtain the *dew-point*. When the readings of both thermometer and the hygrometer are alike, the temperature of the dew-point is the same as that of the air; the air is then saturated or full of moisture. Quoting further from our generally accepted theory, we say that "it is chiefly in the nights and early mornings of the winter months, that the atmosphere is saturated with vapor, or that vapor is at its *maximum* of elasticity for the temperature. In our climate, vapor never attains its greatest elasticity at a high temperature; for if in the summer months the atmosphere becomes saturated it is caused by a declination of the heat, which, contracting the spaces between the particles of the air, squeezes the vapor contained in them closer, and thus brings its elasticity to a maximum for the temperature to which the air has fallen. It was upon the changes of temperature in the atmosphere that Dr. James Hutton founded his theory of rain. He considered rain to be formed by the mixture of two strata of the atmosphere of different temperatures, and each stratum saturated with moisture. The mean quantity of the vapor contained by the two strata before the mixture being more than the mean heat of the two (after the combination), the excess is precipitated." The principal causes of variance in the weight of the atmosphere are moisture and heat; the variation is greater in polar than in tropical countries, and in mountainous than in more level regions. We can now understand the importance of the use of the barometer in determining the weather, especially in such a country as is found along the coast of Labrador. Barometers are of two varieties: the common mercurial, where the air acts directly upon a basin of mercury in which the inverted column of that same substance is placed; and the aneroid, where the atmosphere acts upon a metallic box, from which the air has been exhausted, and by its pressure communicated by a system of levers acts upon the needle to register the amount of variance; this is possible, since the column of mercury is counterbalanced by the weight of the atmosphere. For a barometer to be of the greatest use it must be read in connection with the direction of the wind, and the temperature of the air, as shown by the thermometer. The hours in the day when it stands highest are at 9 A. M., and 9 P. M.; and it is usually lowest at 3 A. M., and 3 P. M. These hours, therefore, are the best for making observations and are generally used by scientific men generally the world over.

The following table of rules will be found to apply in nine chances out of ten, for the correct use or reading of the barometric needle.

Rising barometer with south wind,— fine weather.

Sudden rise, wind N. or N. N. W., in broken cold weather, — rain or snow and sometimes nightly thaws.

Rapid rise after S. W. gale and rain,— clear sky and sharp white frost.

Steady high pressure, wind strong W.,— high temperature and very little rain.

Steady high pressure, wind strong E.,— lower temperature and sharp frost.

Falling barometer, with N. wind,— cold rain and storms in summer, deep snow and severe frost in winter.

Falling barometer, wind S.,— more or less rain.

Falling barometer, wind N. W.,— cold rain in summer, severe frost in winter.

Falling barometer, high S. W. wind,— increasing storm.

Steady and large fall, wind E.,— wind S. or heavy snow or rain.

Sudden and large fall, wind W.,—violent storm N. W., or N.

Great fall during frosty weather,— thaw continued with S. or S. E. wind, and returning frost if S. W. wind.

Lowest depressions, wind S. or S. E.,— much rain and severe gale.

In general: a rapid rise gives a violent wind; continued fall, continued wind.

Great depression in summer,— storms, wind and rain, thunder and hail.

Rise with S. wind,— high temperatures.

Mercury unsteady,— air in electrical state.

No great storm sets in with a steady rise.

N. and S. winds are the origin of our greatest storms.

W. winds blow mostly at night.

E. winds calm at night, blow by day.

There is least wind at sunrise and sunset, and most wind at 1 or 2 P. M.; wind with the sun fine; wind against sun mercury falls, bad weather generally.

Meteors are not common during low temperatures; the Aurora borealis has been seen at all heights of the barometer. It has been noticed and recorded that, "the finest and most beneficial state of the atmosphere, more especially as regards the health of man, is with a uniform pressure at the mean height of the climate varying from 29.80 to 30.00."

A poetic barometrical rhyming table which lately came to my notice reads as follows:

> "When rise begins after low,
> Squalls expect, and clear blow;
> Long foretold long last,
> Short notice, soon past,
> First rise after low
> Foretells stronger blow."

Still another comes to mind:

> "When the glass falls low,
> Prepare for a blow;
> When it rises high,
> Let your kites fly."

A great many other foretellings of weather are known in one shape or another, but it is not the province or purport of this work to be a prophetic indicator of the weather, but simply to explain some of the most common and important physical phenomena of the region about Labrador: hence a few of the usual combinations of thermometer and barometer readings, which may generally be relied upon with a tolerable degree of accuracy in guiding the mariner along these coasts, where, in summer, travelling is by water and a fair day is predicted as far ahead as possible.

The combinations of the clouds are also great indicators of weather and affect the barometer more or less indirectly. The *cirrus* is seen at all seasons of the year and at all heights of the barometer; it has a slow motion in fair and a rapid one with falling barometer in foul or stormy weather. The *cirro-stratus*, not unlike the cirrus of which it is a peculiar condition, is the forerunner of a falling barometer with wind or rain. Sometimes it appears after a rapid rise in the mercury; then also rain generally follows soon. The *cirro-cumulus* comes with a rising barometer and is a warm weather cloud. The *cumulus* is seen chiefly in spring and summer; it is seen in showery weather with the cirro-stratus, and in hot weather alone or with other clouds. "If during a fine morning this cloud suddenly disappears, and it be followed by the cirro-stratus with the wind backing to the south, the mercury falls, and rain soon follows. The cumulus is a day cloud; its greatest density keeps off the too scorching rays of the noonday sun; it usually evaporates an hour or two before sunset. When it increases after sunset, and shines with a ruddy, copper-colored light, it denotes a thunder storm." The cumulus is seen with a rising barometer generally. The cumulo-stratus appears much like the cumulus, indicating sudden changes of wind, thunder squalls, and even hail. It tends to raise the mercury. The *stratus*, in the words of the same authority above quoted, "is formed from the sudden chill of certain strata of the atmosphere, which, condensing the vapor contained in them, renders it visible in a misty cloud or creeping fog. Calm weather is essential for the formation of the stratus; it is frequent in fine autumnal nights and mornings. It obscures the sun until his rays have raised the temperature of the air sufficiently to evaporate it, when it gradually disappears and leaves a clear, blue sky. The stratus deposits moisture, is called the night cloud and is most frequent from September till January. When the temperature, from radiation or other causes, sinks below 32°, we find it fettered with icy spiculæ upon trees and shrubs and sparkling in exquisite frost work upon all nature." It is not known to affect the barometer much either way. The *nimbus* is seen during showers : it is not seen with the barometer at great heights. A study of *vapor point* would be of great interest to one desiring to pursue this subject further; and there are plenty of books on Physics and Physical Geography for those who are thus inclined, not to waste useless space and time here upon definitions. One point further, however, before we leave the subject :—

We see, therefore, that the rising or falling of the barometric needle corresponds with the pressure of the atmosphere. This pressure is due to changes of temperature, moisture and wind. To show that the barometer is more of an instrument than appears upon first sight, and must be studied in itself without reference to the words marked upon its face, a clause from one of our scientific college text-books of natural philosophy tells us that "the practice formerly prevailed of engraving at different points of the barometric scale several words expressive of states of weather : fair, rain, frost, wind, etc., etc. But such indications are worthless, being as often false as true : this is evident from the fact that the height of the column would be changed from one kind of weather to another by simply carrying the instrument to a higher or lower station." The measuring of heights by the barometer will be spoken of in another place. It remains but to speak of the dew-point, and the resultant forms of water manifested. The dew-point is "the temperature at which vapor, in a given case, is precipitated into water in some of its forms." The amount of vapor in the air is expressed by its *tension* or elastic power, and its *humidity*, or " its quantity present, as compared with the greatest possible amount at that temperature." When the air is colder than the temperature of the dew-point, the surplus amount of vapor is condensed by the amount of difference of pressure, and the result is dew, frost, fog, etc. The first deposition is dew; then, according as the radiating body is acted upon with greater or less amount of temperature, we have frost; then fog, which becomes clouds of different kinds, forms, and shapes; these in turn condense and precipitate rain, which pressure still forms into a spray called mist; and this, crystallizing, gives us, first hail, then sleet, and finally snow in all its perfection of microscopic crystals.

Before closing my remarks on the barometer a few quotations from the Sailing Directions will serve to give you a good idea of the use of this instrument, or rather of the use it may be if carefully and properly studied. "The barometer has a range of from 29 to 30.5 inches in the Gulf and River St. Lawrence during the navigable season, and its changes accompany those of the winds and weather with a considerable degree of constancy. The fluctuations of the barometric column are much greater and more frequent there than in lower latitudes, and sudden alterations, which in other climates would be alarming, may occur there without being followed by any corresponding change either in the wind or in the weather." The most practical part is still to follow, and expresses the pith of all that can be said thus concisely : "But the navigator should not be inattentive to these minor changes, as a constant attention to the instrument can alone enable him to appreciate those decisive indications of the mercury which seldom or never prove deceptive."

Quoting further from the same source, of the fogs it says: "they may occur at any time during the open or navigable season, but are most frequent in the early part of summer; they are rare, and never of long continuance during westerly winds, but seldom fail to accompany an easterly wind of any strength or duration. The above general observation is subject, however, to restriction, according to locality or season. Thus winds between the south and west, which are usually clear weather winds above Anticosti, are frequently accompanied with fog in the eastern parts of the gulf.

Winds between the south and east are most always accompanied with rain and fog in every part. E. N. E. winds above Point de Monts are often E. S. E. or S. E. winds in the Gulf, changed in direction by the high lands of the south coast, and have therefore, in general, the same foggy character. Winds of considerable strength and duration are meant here, which probably extend over great distances. Moderate or partially fine weather winds may occur without fog at any season, and in any locality. In the early part of the navigable season, especially in the months of April and May, clear weather N. E. winds are of frequent occurrence, and they also sometimes occur at other seasons in every part of the Gulf and River St. Lawrence. "The fogs sometimes last several days in succession and to a vessel either running up or beating down, during their continuance, there is no safe guide but the constant use of the deep-sea lead, with a chart containing correct soundings.

"The fogs which accompany easterly gales extend higher up into the atmosphere, and cannot be looked over from any part of the rigging of a ship. They, however, are not so thick as those which occur in calms after a strong wind, and which are frequently so dense as to conceal a vessel within hail, while the former often, but not always, admit the land, or other objects, to be distinguished at the distance of half a mile or more in the daytime.

"The dense fogs which occur in calms, or even in very light winds, often extend only to small elevations above the sea; so that it sometimes happens that when objects are hidden at a distance of fifty yards from the deck, they can be plainly seen by a person fifty or sixty feet up the rigging. In the months of October and November, the fogs and rain that accompany easterly gales are replaced by thick snow, which causes equal embarrassment to the navigator."

I have frequently proven the truth of nearly every statement contained within the above quotation.

One other subject remains to be spoken of, and that but briefly: It is the ice of the Gulf of St. Lawrence and the Straits of Belle Isle. It is very fortunate for us that the admirable work done by Bayfield along this part of the coast remains as a monument to his thoroughness of exploration and the study of the phenomena of this region. His well chosen language often supplies to us the lacking power of expression in descriptions of this kind, and we take his words in preference to our own. On this subject, also, he remarks: "In spring, the entrance and the eastern parts of the Gulf of St. Lawrence are frequently covered with drift ice, and vessels are sometimes beset with it for many days." I have seen a vessel in the spring of the year closed in on all sides by ice that formed during the night augmented by drift, and obliged to stay there the remainder of the week until the sun broke the surrounding crust and the wind dispersed the drift. Again he says: "Being unfitted for contending with the danger, they often suffer from it and are frequently lost; but serious accidents from this cause do not occur frequently, because the ice is generally in a melting state from the powerful effects of the sun in spring. In the fall of the year, accidents seldom occur from ice, except when the winter commences suddenly, or when vessels linger imprudently late from the temptation of obtaining high freights." Several instances have occurred where boats and small vessels have thus lingered late and been overtaken by the breaking up of previously formed and solid ice by the sun's rays, on some warm day, and thus been carried off into the Gulf, or wrecked on some of the islands or more dangerous portions of the surrounding coast. In the fall when the ice from above breaks up and is taken by the current through the Straits of Belle Isle, ships often run into large floating bergs that are lying about here and there in the water, and directly in the way of navigation, and are either crushed by the falling of the berg upon them, if it be a tall and large one (for it must be remembered that from two-fifths to nine-tenths of an iceberg remains under the water, and that, gradually worn away by abrasion and the warmer waters of the current, it has become so brittle that a jar easily displaces it and therefore causes the remainder to assume a different position —by which I mean that the whole structure falls—and thus doing damage according to its size); or, again, a vessel going with her usual speed may run into a solid block of ice, where indeed the current would be otherwise unimpeded, and cause much damage in this way. In spring the water is covered with what, in Labrador, is termed *sheshe* ice; this is a thin mass of *slob* (another expression used here) that has formed by frost or snow, or a combination of both, during the night, which in the morning when the sun comes up breaks up and goes floating about in the water, often attaching and carrying away with it still other pieces of stray ice, and becoming generally dangerous. Small boats, that are at this season numerous, since the dog sleds can no longer be used, often get entangled in these masses, while a turn of the weather brings cold that cements them into the ice which forms an impassable barrier to further progress. The boat cannot urge a way through it, and the foot cannot yet walk on it, the craft drifts at the mercy of the tide, the currents, and the wind, and is often carried out into the Gulf, or thrown in contact with the shore, while woeful tales of starvation are known to be only too true from this as other like causes. The ice causes another sort of damage here, which is a source of great annoyance. Large numbers of pieces of ice are found at the first breaking up of the bays and waters, until August, and often even later. I have known a piece to strand on some fishing ground, and with a rising tide go on its slow but in a measure almost irresistible way directly through the well laid nets of the fishermen, carrying them off bodily into the sea. Of course this cannot be helped, yet I have witnessed this spectacle, with the unfortunate fellows thus loosing their net, from the shore, unable to do anything with them to recover the lost property. Navigation in the Gulf and River St. Lawrence is usually closed the first of December, and remains so until the first of May; even after that, drift ice in large quantities is liable to occur for a month more.

CHAPTER II.

Trip to Labrador—Arrival at Montreal—Arrival at Quebec, and Description of the City.

IT was in the early part of September that I first formed the idea of a trip to Labrador, where I hoped to remain during the winter months, and the following season. I had been working hard during the previous year, and forming an idea that a trip to Labrador and a study of the natural history of that region would be of great use in the determination of the variety of species and their geographical distribution in migration in the study of New England Natural History, I determined to profit by an opportunity offered and start for the coast.

Knowing that the last vessel left Quebec for Labrador sometime during the above mentioned month, a letter and a telegram apprised us (myself and two friends who also wished to go) that we must start for Quebec at once if we wished to reach this means of conveyance before it was too late. My letters reached me on Thursday the 9th of the month, and this gave but two days to prepare for a journey of over a thousand miles, and an absence of at least a year in the cold region of the North, since I must leave by the late train on Saturday night to be in time to reach the vessel which the letter said would probably start Tuesday from Quebec.

The suddenness of the decision which I had thus formed will be seen when I say that many of my friends saw the news first in the papers before even my letters reached them, though I had written as soon as it was possible after deciding. Intending to purchase the greater part of my supplies in Quebec, I put in my trunk only such things as I needed, adding a few simple medicines, since I was going to a place where there were no doctors, and, bidding my home and friends the usual form of parting, was at the station promptly for the train.

Travelling by night is at no time pleasant to the majority of people whose occupation takes them from place to place, and it is often especially unpleasant where the nine o'clock evening train is a slow mixture of a very few passenger and a great many freight cars, whose fastest gait is an amble, and its stops frequent and of long duration; while the interior of the most inhabitable of the cars upon the passenger list is at best a dim, cloudy, close atmosphere of condensed and accumulated dirt and soot and bad breath,—said interior looking as if it had seen neither pure air nor water since the day of its first appearance on the road up to the present. Such as it was we were all soon seated, as comfortably as possible, having waved our hands at our friends on the platform, feeling that the car was really in motion and we were being surely drawn towards the north and away from home. It was then that I had my first opportunity for reflecting: first, that I was leaving home for a new and comparatively little-known region, second, that I might have left the very things that I should most want and need and taken things that would be of comparatively little or no use — though there was really little to fear on that score;—and third, as to the prospect of outliving the fierce winter of such a region as that to which we were going.

I did not long trouble myself with these reflections, however, as the hurry, excitement, and constant bustle of the past two days had left me considerably fatigued, and so turning over an empty seat behind, and arranging myself in the most comfortable position possible where the seats are hard at the best, I composed myself to sleep. I say to sleep, but I should much better have said to try to sleep; no doubt the excitement of the previous days rendered it a more difficult matter than it would have been had the journey been longer contemplated. Thus I dozed away and caught an occasional nap of short duration throughout the night, until we reached St.

Albans somewhere in the small hours of the morning. After a little refreshment, and a short stay here, not long enough, however, to enable me to get much of a glimpse of this queer old Canadian and American town, yet with plenty of time to secure the latest New York and Boston newspapers, the train which was to take us to Montreal arrived; and soon we were whirling off in the direction of that place, comfortably seated in a car whose atmosphere was a pleasing variation from that of the car we had so lately left, in that its purity was its main attraction. We had now daylight before us, and though still rather tired and sleepy, could at least vary the monotony of our trip with the natural objects that presented themselves to our gaze through the car windows. An officer soon awakened those disposed to slumber with the intelligence that we were crossing the line and must soon submit to having our baggage inspected. I thought it very kind of him to give us notice beforehand of this most important event, and also most kind of the inspector when he appeared, and most indicative of his ability to judge of human character by the face, that he gave us so little trouble with our bundles. These contemplations, however, did not long deter me from another attempt at a nap, and once more settling myself down I tried to sleep.

As our train went along slowly it was sometime before we reached Victoria bridge spanning the St. Lawrence below Montreal; after a long rumbling through this covered bridge, whose little skylights far above the head on the side of the building shed but a feeble occasional gleam, we emerged into the light again only to pass along through low flats of land or near high walls of buildings, both of which seemed equally the abodes of poverty and dirt, and reached Montreal two hours late since we were due at 8 and it was then 10 A. M. Here our trunks were inspected with the same kindness that our bundles had been in the cars —mine not being opened at all— and we were soon rumbling over the stones to the hotel where an abundance of good warm substantial food soon revived us again. It is quite unnecessary to enter into a description of this old-fashioned place, as that has been too often done and to a much better advantage than anything I could say with my present knowledge of the city, confined as it is to a day only, and that too a Sunday, when none of the places of interest to the visitor were open, and the long lines of huge, gloomy stone buildings frowned upon pavements, and churches, especially that massive structure, the Notre-Dame Cathedral alone, were the scene of flocking multitudes.

Early the next day, at about seven o'clock, we were aroused from our sleep and told to get ready at once as the train for Quebec, and the one on which we intended leaving, started from the other end of the city at about half-past seven, a truly cheering bit of news. Hastily dressing and descending to the hotel parlor I found my friends just hurrying down from their room, and together we went to the clerk to inquire if breakfast was ready; to our surprise it was not, but soon would be. Here was a long delay of five or ten minutes before the door to the breakfast-room was opened, and we were summoned to table just as the coach drove up to the door bringing us word that we were probably already too late to catch the train; but breakfast must be eaten, and some six minutes were lost again which made the driver sure we were too late, while it assured us that we had had just enough hot steak and coffee to make us wish for more.

Nothing could be done, however, but to pay an exorbitant hotel bill and urge the coach off at its fastest gait for the depot at the other end of the town. We had six minutes, I think, in which to accomplish our journey of about a mile over the hardest of pavements, and in a vehicle that tossed about from side to side threatening every moment to upset as we fairly steamed down the streets, rattling as if our life depended on the amount of noise made, and bouncing about in a manner calculated to digest what little nourishment we had taken before our ride was half completed.

We reached the door of the station on the minute, purchased our tickets, received our checks from the driver, who had left his team at eminent risk of its running away to procure them, and stepped on the train as it was just moving from the depot.

STOP FOR LUNCH.

Travelling by rail is at no time pleasant when the train is a slow one, and the prospect of an all day's trip a pretty safe one. I do not mean to enter into the subject of conveniences or inconveniences of such travelling, but true it is, that one can often make one's self comfortable or uncomfortable, as one desires, when placed under such circumstances. Desiring the former, as by all means to be preferred to the latter, I took off my tall hat and, much to the apparent envy (I flatter myself judging from their looks) of several persons around me, drew from my pocket, and adjusted on my head, a soft, brimless, smoking cap, while I lay back in the seat, head to the window and feet on the extreme end of the cushion and against the handle bars, and read my book. Oblivious to all around, I continued to peruse the before mentioned volume till our noon stop at a long-platformed, spacious-roomed station. Finding, here, that it would be an hour or more before the train was made up that was to take us on to Quebec, or rather Point Levis, as we were on the Montreal side of the river yet, I took a hasty lunch in the refreshment room and then started off in the direction of the river which here flowed gently by not far off, at the right of the railroad track. The water was quite shallow at this place, and long banks of sand extended here and there in points as far as one could see. I thus walked easily half way across the stream, stepping cautiously over rills and damp and soft places, until I came to the main channel of the water. As far as I could see, both up and down the stream, these low sand flats extended fully half way across the bed of the river; exposed now, though probably a part of the year several feet under water.

Dead shells of various species of *Unio*, and *Anodon*, common to fresh water rivers farther south and west, were everywhere in abundance. I gathered several distinct species, all of which probably live in the river in great numbers.

But time progressing, I unwillingly relinquished my pleasant acquaintance with these attractive natural surroundings of a place, none too well known natural-history-wise, and pocketing my specimens started for the station. To the amusement of several gentlemen of the, perhaps, loafing profession,—though I may be doing said gentlemen a great injustice, for which I beg many pardons, not intending my remark as an insult, but rather using the word in place of any knowledge of the occupation of said persons who were strangers to me,—whose inquisitiveness led them to assemble about me and ask various questions, I emptied my pockets on the sill of a window of the station house and proceeded to do the specimens up carefully in papers that I might the more easily carry them, and having placed them in a satchel, I began to look about me for the train. Before long it approached the station, and after standing still in front of the door for half an hour or so, during which time we transferred our portable luggage and ourselves to a comfortable seat near the rear of the last car, it slowly started off, and again we were on the move.

The train was a slow one, and after occupying half of the afternoon reading I spent the greater part of the remainder of the trip on the rear platform watching the nature of the country through which we were passing. The air was cool and clear, and vegetation and foliage still wore their summer dress, but in place of the usual moist feeling which New England air possesses, the words dry and crisp seem to express, to me at least, the condition of earth and air in this "cold temperate" region of the globe. Standing thus and enjoying the comfort and ease with which the car slowly proceeded through the varied scenes along the passage, the shades of evening approached, and as darkness came on, passing through the outskirts of what was apparently a manufacturing village, by day the scene of industry, but now a confusion of shops, sheds, wharves and buildings, as seen thus in the darkness of night, we came at last to the celebrated Port Levis.

It was night when we reached this ancient military station, and being in great haste to see to the transporting of our luggage to the ferry boat which was then waiting for us and the other passengers who were to be transported to the Quebec side, there was no opportunity of going about the place at all with the view of examining its huge fortresses of military fame, and of which we had read, as well as its other attractions of merit; we could simply reflect on the immense cost of warfare, and of the reported expenditure of some millions of dollars in the construction of the three forts here represented, as well as their maintenance, and which, defending the lower harbor and city of Quebec, rendered the place famous. If my memory serves me, it was in 1759 that the lower town of Quebec was bombarded from the heights of this town by General Monckton, at the time the English captured the former place and reduced it to an English Province. Hastily recalling these events the boat is quite ready to leave, and we are soon settled and pursuing our way accompanied by the dash and splash of the paddles as heard from outside, and the nearer plunge and spit of the engine as it drove the machinery, while the fires below roared and crackled, and the boat shivered from stem to stern as she urged her way forward in the dark waters which sent billows of foam on either side of the prow, to reflect an instant in some light either from the vessels near by, or the lamps on the opposite shore.

The scene that presented itself to us as we stood thus on deck looking out into the twilight about and beyond was one of strange fantasy, you might almost say: above, on our left, dark frowning heights were illuminated with lamps that sent their rays in many directions penetrating the darkness, while all about us the solitary lights of vessels lying at anchor glimmered from a darkness, which occasionally reflected a darker outline of the vessel to whose light we were nearest. We wove in and out of these until, rounding the cliff, the full blaze of the lower town shone upon us, and showed the confusion of a low-roofed housed city on the left, and a river full of boats, vessels, and ships of all kinds and descriptions on the right; thus we approached the landing.

I had chosen the deck of this little ferry steamer for my outlook upon the city, as I could then have plenty of air, and be free from the crowd below. The boat was small and substantially built, rather cramped for standing or sitting room, and inconvenient; besides, the body of the lower part was an open receptacle for bales, boxes, and bags of luggage which nearly filled it, and the passengers' rooms small and full of angles and corners; everywhere a strong smell of closeness overladen with tobacco smoke filled the air, and moving about was attended with a great deal of difficulty. Congratulating myself that I had secured as airy a place as anybody, and viewing the scene as I have attempted to describe it, we slowly made the landing and were in Quebec.

The lower city of Quebec presents very few attractions by night to a stranger; the streets and the sidewalks are narrow, while both are muddy and slippery at this season of the year, especially if it has lately rained. The cooped-up feeling that it gives you to land in one of these narrow alley streets and find that you know nobody and nobody knows you, that you don't know where to go and a dozen cab drivers and hotel porters all say that you are going with them, is a peculiar one and best appreciated by anybody that has been in such a place and obliged to decide immediately what to do, or have it decided for him by having his baggage and himself suddenly ushered into a cab and the door shut,— this is anything but pleasant. Though I did not undergo this last experience literally, it was so near becoming such that the cab started off with the luggage; while, after a few inquiries and some complicated directions, I started off to find the wharf at which the vessel destined to convey me away was moored. My companions and myself went together and after travelling through various streets and turning down many side alleys, all of which presented the same dirty, narrow, and contracted general appearance, bestrewn with plenty of mud and nearly solitary, we approached a shed-like opening on the opposite side of a very dirty street, through which we passed and emerged on a long wharf, on either side of which were vessels closely packed and in process some of lading and some of unlading. Not knowing which one contained the object of our search,—the captain, with whom we had not yet even taken passage,— we hailed a man standing by and inquired of him; from his reply, only given after the question had been repeated in French, we found the vessel, aroused some of the crew, and put to them our inquiries for the captain and learned that he was probably at the hotel to which our luggage had been taken. There being nothing to do but to go back again and find the hotel, we started off in no very pleasant spirits at the failure of our expedition. Pursuing the way in silence we again reached our stopping place, found the captain, engaged our passage, settled all the preliminaries, and were soon washed and sitting down to a spread table with the prospect of a comfortable, hot meal of the best the place afforded, in which we were not deceived. The grossness of describing a meal, unless it is an exceptionally good or an extremely poor one, is so obvious that I will not enter into the details of ours, but, simply using the novelist's phrase say, "we ate as only hungry persons eat with a savory and hot meal before them." I retired quite early after supper being rather tired with the excitement of the previous day's journey, and determined now that we had reached Quebec, and knowing that we had all the next day before us, to make up for my lost quota of sleep of the previous nights.

Morning came at last and with it I sprang from my bed, quickly dressed myself, and descended to the hotel office. The night had been a good one for sleeping, the air was cool and the temperature outside such that windows could be safely kept open all night. I had slept soundly, not waking once to the best of my recollection till morning; and now, refreshed and enthusiastic for a day's pleasure trip about the city, I took my cap and went out for a short stroll before breakfast which was not yet ready.

As a rule I do not believe in introducing borrowed matter into a work that pretends to be an account of original journey and exploration narrative, but as occasionally the already published accounts of well known places visited on such excursions, from the pens of accurate writers, are so much more complete than could be given by any passing stranger, that, considering myself such a stranger, and finding in a little volume of guidance through the city of Quebec a most excellent account of the progress and growth of that city, I will venture to give the same in extract, as it may contain matter new to many and interesting to all :—

"In 1534 Canada was discovered by Jacques Cartier, of St. Malo, in France. The name is derived from 'Kanata', an Indian word signifying 'a collection of huts.' In 1535 Jacques Cartier made a second voyage and made friends with Donnacona, the chief of Stadacona, where Quebec now stands. Stadacona is Algonquin, while Tiontirili is Huron, both meaning 'the narrowing of the river;' the St. Lawrence being less than a mile wide opposite the city. Jacques Cartier wintered in the river St. Charles and called it St. Croix. His winter quarters were near the present residence of Mr. Park Ringfield. In 1540 he made a third voyage and built a fort at Cape Rouge and also visited Hochelaga, now Montreal. In 1608 Champlain arrived at Stadacona, and landing his followers founded the city of Quebec. No satisfactory explanation can be given of the meaning of the word. The city has been besieged five different times. In 1629 Champlain was obliged to deliver up everything to Sir David Kerkt; but by the treaty of St. Germain-en-Laye, Canada was restored to France, and Champlain returned as Governor of the colony. In October, 1690, Sir William Phipps appeared before the city and demanded its surrender of Count de Frontenac who refused; after a harmless bombardment the English retired. In 1711 another English fleet under Sir Harendon Walker sailed for Quebec, but was nearly destroyed by a storm in the Gulf of St. Lawrence; for these two last deliverances the little church in the lower town was called Notre Dame des Victoires.

"On the 25th of June, 1759, Admiral Saunders anchored his fleet and transports, with General Wolfe and the English army on board, off the Island of Orleans, then called Isle de Bacchus. The troops landed on the Island on the following day, near the church of St. Laurent and marched to the west end from which position they could view Quebec; the French army under Montcalm, consisting of about 13,000 men, was encamped on the opposite shore of Beauport. General Monckton, with four battalions, occupied the heights of Levis from which position he bombarded the city and laid it in ruins. General Wolfe then crossed to the mainland, to the east of the river Montmorenci, and on the 31st of July attacked the French and was defeated with a loss of 182 killed, 650 wounded, and 15 missing. After some delay the English fleet sailed past the city and on the 14th of September landed his troops at Wolfe's Cove, scaled the famous heights of Abraham, met the astonished Montcalm and defeated him. Wolfe died on the field in the moment of victory, and Montcalm, killed also, was buried in the Ursuline Convent. The city was surrendered to the English on the 18th of the month and General Murray with 6000 men was left as a garrison,— the former was also Governor. The fleet with Wolfe's body sailed for England in October. On the 28th of April the next year a French army of 10,000 men, under De Levis, appeared on the Plains of Abraham and met Murray with 3,000, sickness and death having reduced the number. The English were obliged to retire behind the fortifications of the city, but on the 15th of May, an English fleet under Commodore Saunders, arrived with reinforcements, and compelled the French to retreat. At this time Quebec became an English colony.

"In 1775 Quebec was again threatened. General Arnold, with a small American army, arrived on the heights of Levis by the Chaudière valley and on the 14th November landed at Wolfe's Cove; soon General Montgomery took command; the attack was unsuccessful though much property was destroyed just outside the town, while Montgomery was killed and Arnold wounded.

"In 1837 Quebec suffered a rebellion within its own walls. The militia were called out and the city placed under military rule but nothing of consequence occurred. One night, however, there was heard a loud ringing of bells, and it was said that the rebels had risen and would sack the place. The cause of all this alarm was, nevertheless, very simple—the singeing of a pig in the Hotel Dieu Nunnery Yard. In the following year Messrs. Teller and Dodge, two American sympathizers imprisoned with three others in the Citadel, escaped; four of them let themselves down from the flagstaff bastion, and Teller and Dodge passing the city gates reached the U. S.

"In 1832 and '34 Quebec was visited by the Asiatic Cholera. In 1834 the Castle St. Louis was destroyed by fire. On May 28, 1845, the whole of St. Roche was burnt; on June 28, the suburbs of St. John and St. Louis were also burnt; the loss by these two fires was over $2,000,000, the insurance and subscriptions of aid amounting to $900,000. In 1846, in the month of June, the Theatre, formerly the Riding school attached to the Castle of St. Louis, was destroyed by fire during a performance when the building was crowded,—fifty-five persons lost their lives. In 1853 the Parliament houses were burnt down, when a large library and museum were destroyed. The sittings of the House were transferred to the Church of the Grey Sisters near Gallows Hill (which had not then been consecrated); this also burnt down, when the sittings were held in Music Hall in Louis Street. In 1867 the Province of Quebec was granted a colonial government, with the seat of the Province at Quebec."

CHAPTER III.

Our stay in Quebec — Starting for Berthier — Berthier — Off for Labrador — Bunking in — Island of Orleans — Islands and Channels — Sunday — Other Islands — The Saguenay — Fog again.

I WILL not attempt to give a description of my feelings at being in this ancient city, nor yet will I give an account, which would be much inferior to many former similar ones, of the sights I saw and the impressions they left upon me ; all this has been done so often by others that the charm of novelty would be lost, and it would prove only a waste of time and words thus to attempt to describe, from a stay of only a few days, that which would need weeks to see properly. I will therefore hasten to say, that the brief stay here was spent in the continual pleasure of evening rambles about town, combined with the necessity and in truth unpleasantness of making daily purchases for a year's sojourn in a country about which I knew very little ; yet the pleasure, counterbalancing this unpleasantness, so far exceeded it, that I remember the former while forgetting the latter. The walks about the Terrace, of a calm, clear evening, both before and after the lamps were lighted, displayed the lower city and harbor — the former with its rows of roofs, for they were the only parts of the houses visible, and the latter with its countless masts and water-vehicles from the boat to the man-of-war, of which three lay swinging at the end of their cables just near the channel over against the opposite shore, the whole scene presenting a silent witness to the industry of the day ; then the view of Point Levis from the walls of the upper city ; and a trip around the city itself,—all these are pleasures to be remembered ; and I shall remember them with a fresh delight whenever I recall the circumstances that caused me to start upon this Labrador trip, for the invigorating air of new scenes and a new climate.

Friday, in the evening, we started from the hotel, with our baggage, for the vessel. Arriving there we deposited our effects on the wharf, whence they were speedily transported to the deck; then the trunks were taken to the hold and the bags and boxes to the cabin of the vessel, and we stationed ourselves to wait for the captain, as we expected him to start that night. After waiting several hours, and some after dark and consequently past supper time,—which fact I mention since our dinner had been taken early and it was now fast getting late,—he arrived in a great hurry, and then we learned that the vessel must wait until high tide (it was then low and we could see the muddy bottom near the vessel), which would not be until about three next morning, before leaving; the ladies of the party not caring to sleep in so exposed a situation, the captain kindly invited us to the hotel, where we all went with him, partook of an oyster supper, and passed the night quite comfortably. The vessel started in the morning for Berthier, where we were to meet her the next day noon by a little steamer that runs from Quebec and makes that place one of its stopping stations. The night's rest had refreshed us and the next morning, quite disconsolately, we wandered about the streets of the lower city, and the wharf whence the steamer was to leave, waiting for the time of departure, which came slowly. It was market-day, and the streets, especially the square about the market, were crowded with all sorts and nationalities of people buying their week's provisions; we watched them for a long time, and were especially amused in noticing the people who failed to catch the ferry boat that landed not far from us. Some ran for it and, leaping, caught it, but others running for it failed to catch it; and as the boats alternated with each other every fifteen minutes, there was always some one in a state of frenzy with the retreating ferry for a fault for which he alone was to blame; there were several old women with large baskets, evidently returning home from market; two or three priests; and a number of other people who were successively left by the retreating boat,—some expressing their indignation while others, like ourselves, contented themselves to wait their turn. At last, twelve o'clock, and our captain, came; and the steamer started. We slowly passed along the channel, watching the scenes on either bank, and, leaving the city with its confusion and the harbor with its abundance of crafts of all kinds, we steamed into pure waters, clearer atmosphere, and the rocky borders of the mighty St. Lawrence. On our left we presently passed, if I remember rightly, the famous falls of Montmorency— at least we saw a precipitous mass of dashing, struggling waters, that looked the mighty cascade that it probably was—while a short turn soon brought us to the Berthier wharf. Our vessel was at the wharf receiving her last cargo, in the shape of potatoes and several kinds of fresh vegetables, for her voyage, and as it would take several hours to complete the loading we accepted the captain's kind invitation to visit his home and dine there with him. Berthier is a small French Canadian village, situated on the southern side of the St. Lawrence, and very nearly opposite the eastern extremity of the island of Orleans; it is about fifteen miles from Quebec. The long wharf built for the accommodation of freight and coal, extending far into the water, had several vessels lying at each side, either being or waiting to be loaded, and though the coal dust was everywhere under foot, and in the air flying in our faces, we forced ourselves through it and soon reached a cleaner footing and much purer air. A walk up a rather long slightly sloping hill brought us to the principal street, along which low roofed, yet small and cosey looking houses, for the most part clean with white paint, not yet ugly from exposure, with their corresponding barns — mostly unpainted — extended on either side where the open fields on the right near the water, and high hillocks of granite on the left, back of the houses, had not established a prior claim. As neat a house as appeared, on this apparently one streeted township of about fifty houses—if the town was really no larger than it seemed—was that of our Captain, and we passed a quiet time both before and after a hearty, homely meal, until about dusk, when we started for the wharf again taking a cut across the meadows in the direction of the water, having seen very little of the town itself, though enough to commend it as an old fashioned, curious place, well worth visiting and investigating. Soon the wharf was gained; a boat waiting bore us to the vessel, which by this time had finished her loading and was lying at anchor out in the channel, and with a dim twilight at our backs, a lighthouse in front of us, and a bonny breeze to shape our course, we hoisted sail and bade farewell to the last landing this side of "The Labrador," whither we shaped our course. We were at last really moving. The vessel was really gliding along under the pressure of the wind towards that region so prominent on the eastern part of northern North America, yet so little known, called the plateau of Labrador, or, as the people themselves call it, as I have above quoted, "The Labrador."

It is by no means an easy matter to arrange four persons, let us say for example two men and two ladies—though it makes very little difference as to the number and sex when even a single person is, so to speak, unceremoniously deposited in a small cabin of a small sailing vessel, and shown a small bunk in which to sleep, scarcely big enough for one yet the usual abode of two *able bodied* (?) seamen—in such contracted compartments as those we were about to occupy: how the affair was brought to a happy termination I cannot tell. Our voyage would last about a week, our accommodations for that time *multum in parvo*, and with a more literal meaning than we had ever before imagined that the words could possibly convey. Our trunks were expelled from the cabin and confined to the hold; our bags were insufficient at best to meet our wants; the matter was thus ludicrous as well as provokingly uncomfortable and inconvenient. While we were enjoying ourselves on the outside of the cabin, watching the stars, the dim outlines of the shores in the darkness around, and the darker yet sparkling water — sparkling from the reflection of the stars — the ladies were somehow preparing affairs below; soon they joined us, and we together sat watching, we could hardly tell what (the custom usually seems to be when starting on a sea trip, to spend the first evening on deck), until the lateness and chilliness of the hour reminded us of our berths below, and descending the narrow stairs or steps of the cabin we sought them and were soon wrapped in slumber in spite of the uncomfortableness of our contracted and narrow box-beds.

I will not describe either the ship or the accommodations provided for us while we traversed the St. Lawrence to our destination; the latter would be too personal a matter,—though it was the best the place afforded,—and the former, hardly differing from the thousand water conveyances, of similar shape and size, too trivial and uninteresting to be worth mention here. Four of us, who were together bound for the same place, made the best and freest use of both ship and accommodations, while the sociality usual on shipboard prevailed with great harmony. In so small a vessel we could not but take an interest in all that occurred, and in all the crew, and they, no doubt, took full notice of all we said or did; while the wonder expressed in their faces whenever I at least met them seemed plainly to say, why are you going to such a place as Labrador? to which mute question I reserved the probable and veracious answer —I hardly know myself, why. Now that we were fully started upon our journey, the chart, the directions for sailing, and what we did and saw occupied our chief attention, and as we pursued our way we studied these diligently.

In going to Berthier by the steamer we had passed the Island of Orleans, that curious, oval island only three miles outside of Quebec that so nearly fills the river at this point. It lies like an egg in the very centre of the stream with only a narrow pass on either side, and while its length is full eighteen miles, its width is scarcely five. The north shore being rather flat and muddy with more or less rocky outline, the south shore with its sandy beach and few rocky points presents the best and most used channel for vessels going to and from Quebec. From a central elevation of some three hundred and seventy-five feet the land slopes to the rather steep banks around it. We did not see much of the beautiful gardens and places which are said to occupy the southern slope of the island, neither did we see the little churches of St. Lawrence and St. John though standing near the shore, since we had no one to point them out to us. The two lighthouses, that of St. John village with its white revolving flash every half-minute, which is visible ten miles, and that of St. Lawrence village with its fixed white light visible eight miles, would also have escaped our notice, as we passed them in the daytime and not the night, but that the white towers seen from the wharf attracted our attention. On leaving Berthier a small fixed light on a little island, known as Belle Chasse Island, guided us towards the entrance of that part of the channel known as the Middle Traverse. Leaving the North Channel, separated from our route by a shoal of rocks and reefs on the north, and the South Traverse, similarly separated on the south, we pursued our way, by this time guided by the fixed light on the western end of Crane Island, which with Goose Island, forms a very narrow, meadowy, and muddy strip of land, some fifteen miles long between us and South Traverse, until we had safely passed the dangerous shoal in the centre of the Traverse; then, coming into clear open water, we saw the light boats of St. Roque on our right, and Isle aux Coudres on our left as we sailed easily and pleasantly along the now safe passage before us. Soon the captain with the chart showed us our position, and a hasty glance as we passed this little island, about twice as long as it is broad ($5\frac{1}{2}$ miles by $2\frac{1}{2}$), lying snugly tucked away in a baylike enlargement of the north shore, revealed but a glimpse of Notre Dame Church steeple as we passed to the open water beyond. Here we came for the first time upon the open river, a distance of about eleven miles across from Mal Bay (which is ninety miles from Quebec and noted for its salt-water bathing and trout fishing, the sports of its summer visitors, who are often quite numerous), with its bold, rocky point on which a light is situated while the shoals are only a quarter of a mile from shore on the north, to Rivière Ouelle, with its summer pleasure grounds and hotel only ninety-two miles from Quebec on the south bank of the St. Lawrence; only a little below which point, this hilly region of earthquakes bears the name of Les Eboulements. But it is now Sunday, and the ladies have fixed their abodes, and with fair winds and a good run we compose ourselves to the first real rest that we have had since leaving home eight days before. We read and doze in the bright, warm sun like dogs, or cats, or insects, insensible to all save the inspiration of rest and the enjoyment of ease.

At sea on board a vessel there are two counteracting influences at work to render Sunday—especially if it come as ours did on the next day after setting sail—either a day of rest or a day of unrest. In the latter case, to one who would not attend any place of divine worship, even were he at home and on shore, the desire to be quiet is drowned by a deluge of worldly activity that waits and longs for the morrow that his conscience may be easy in pursuing his own pleasures, and so the hours pass heavily, and "the longest day I have known for a perfect age," as it is often aptly styled, comes to its close, with no refreshment to the mind, and thus a continued increase rather than decrease of the bodily infirmities; since the real health of the body is, in a certain measure and to a greater extent than perhaps we imagine, dependent upon that refreshment of mind, from a spiritual source. In the former case, it is different. A day of rest means, in every sense of the word a day of rest, mentally and spiritually, hence, more or less directly, bodily. While many thousands enjoyed this rest in attending church at their homes this beautiful Sabbath day, we enjoyed it in indulging our own thoughts of rest, quiet, and all good things, while bathing in a flood of bright, warm sunlight; while watching the almost calm surface of the now sun-reflecting water; and while reading or conversing with each other on pleasant topics, yet in no mere sensual manner.

Night came soon enough, and if the day had been quiet and peaceful, the evening, with its moon full at yesternight, was much more so. After an almost perfect day we retired to rest. The clear sky remained throughout but part of the night and then gave place to clouds; the calm, warm, almost hot weather turned them to mist, fog and then rain; the west wind to east southeast.

We awoke Monday morning with an uncomfortable feeling

of dampness all about us, of chilliness within us, and an atmosphere of thick, sticky saltwater —and especially St. Lawrence saltwater noted for its nature as described—above, around, and on all sides, enveloping the vessel and shutting out earth and sky and water. We were in the miserable arms of a light attempt at Newfoundland fog, to us a most admirable display of those qualities so inherent to the atmosphere about and around all parts of the Gulf of St. Lawrence. If this was a taste of what was to come, no wonder that they were noted the world over; and one could readily believe the old saying that "the inhabitants of Newfoundland use their fog for cloth, cut it with scissors, and make shirts and breeches of it." The vessel, of course, was obliged to anchor. Once during the day we tried to proceed, but, unable to do so, we anchored again, this time off Green Island, to which place several of us went to examine the hunting, while the crew searched for dry wood—a hard thing to find—to burn. We had passed, up to this time, several noticeable places both on shore and in the shape of islands close to us; and as it is well to know the important items of interest connected with places thus visited or passed by the tourist, let us see what has escaped us. On our right, directly opposite Mal Bay, the group of Kamouraska islands just hides the village (with its little church, hotel, and other buildings) by the same name. As a pleasure resort it is noted in Quebec and the neighboring regions for its fresh, country-like appearance, as are most of the villages on the south shore of the river, and its excellent bathing. A little farther on the same side, the Pilgrims—whence the name I cannot tell—another smaller group (five small islands), about six miles further eastward, are quite interesting in a scientific point of view. They are quite near the land and connected by reefs dry at low water. Though small at best, the largest of these islands, nearly two hundred and ninety feet high, is well wooded. Still but a short distance farther east are the three small, steep islands called the Brandy Pots. The most northern and largest, being half the height of the largest of the Pilgrim group, and also partially wooded, is often visited at the fine spring of water on its southwestern extremity, which spring dries only in the warmest weather. About and around nearly all of these islands reefs and rocks are everywhere visible. I am not confident that we passed through the narrows between the Pilgrims and Hare Island Bank, but think that we did; at any rate, when about opposite Rivière du Loup we had Hare Island on our left. The two oblong islands called Hare and White, the latter just east of the former and very much smaller, with their reefs, which are quite extensive, are about twenty miles long; of their nature I was unable to judge. I was much interested in spying the distant horizon of Rivière du Loup, formerly so much frequented by the fashionable of Canada — as well as elsewhere — a village of great attractions I am told; while not far from it Cacouna, hardly a hundred miles from Quebec, the now favorite resort of the people of Canada, with its many elegant establishments and cosey summer residences graces this part of the coast. Many sportsmen take pleasant fishing trips and frequent baths in the chosen resorts and not cold waters about here; while the temperature, they tell me, is delightful. It is not long — not twenty years ago — since this place was of comparatively little account and notice, with only a rocky peninsula some four hundred feet high to commend it to the scientist, hardly the tourist. It is now a fashionable resort.

We had hesitated for some time as to whether it were best to anchor where we at last did, or by Red Island just on our left, named from the color of its soil and rocks, which is a low, flat island of little importance, when we decided in favor of the former place. At any rate I remembered that we were opposite the noted and far famed Saguenay river, the largest on this part of the coast, rising in lake St. John, about ninety miles directly west from the river's mouth. A place of so much interest and importance needs better words than I can give, having never even seen it, so I will copy from another author, though it is not my purpose to give you other peoples' adventures and descriptions as a rule.

In describing the mouth of the river, which is full of shoals and reefs, he says: "Saguenay river has an entrance between Vaches point on the northeast, and Lark point composed of low clay cliffs on the southwestern side, from each of which dangerous reefs project into the St. Lawrence. These reefs leave an entrance into the Saguenay only three-quarters of a mile wide, though nowhere less than ten or eleven fathoms deep."

He then goes on to say, "That this extraordinary river, which was imperfectly known until the late surveys, is as remarkable for the great volume of water which it brings down to the St. Lawrence, as for the enormous depth of its bed, which is fully one hundred fathoms lower than that of the St. Lawrence. It comes from the lake St. John, and at Chicoutimi, a trading post of the Hudson's Bay Company, which is sixty-five miles above its mouth, it becomes navigable, and six miles above which, to the rapids, the tide ascends. To point Roches, fifty-seven miles from the St. Lawrence, and eight miles below Chicoutimi, it is navigable for the largest ships, and up to this part there is no danger in the river; the shores consist of steep precipices, some of the headlands rising more than a thousand feet in height.

"The current runs down with great force, the ebb tide varying from three to five knots according to the breadth of the river, which is from two-thirds of a mile to two miles. *Tadousac*, which is on the eastern shore, is about one and one-half miles, within the entrance of the river, and was formerly the principal post of the French for trading with the Indians. It now belongs to the Hudson's Bay Company. The harbor is abreast the settlement, and is well sheltered:" but for the scientific value of the facts it would be needless to add that "a heavy anchor should be cast close in shore on account of the eddies which sometimes set into it from the river.

"Fronting the mouth of the river there is a kind of bar upon which are twelve, twenty, and twenty-eight fathoms, but immediately within the depth increases to above one hundred, and a little farther up to one hundred and fifty fathoms. The current setting strongly over the bar, meeting with the spring ebbs of the St. Lawrence, causes breaking and whirling eddies and ripplings; and these streams opposed to a heavy easterly gale cause an exceedingly high, cross, and breaking sea in which no boat could live. On the flood at such times, there is no more sea than in other parts of the river. A fixed white light is exhibited from Lark islet; the tower is a square white building; the light is thirty-five feet above high water, and visible ten miles. Two range lights (fixed white) are shown on the western side of the entrance to the river; one eighty-two feet above high water, on point Noir, distant one and a half miles from Lark islet lighthouse; the other one hundred and seventeen feet above the sea and distant from it about six hundred yards, and are for the purpose of leading vessels clear of Prince shoal, Bar reef, and Vaches patch, and visible nine miles." A curious fact, besides all this nautical description above quoted, appears from the description of another writer who says: "At spring tides a large body of water passes over the Chicoutimi shoals (at a very rapid rate during ebb tides), and falling suddenly into deep water seems to strike downward at once, leaving but a slight current on the surface." The Chicoutimi river enters the Saguenay about sixty-five miles from the mouth of the latter. Further on he adds: "The strong flood tides over the bar, at the entrance of Saguenay river, falling suddenly into deep water, may also contribute to a certain extent to check the strength of the surface-current of the river." A singular fact appears that *at Tadousac was built the first church in Canada.* I understand that it is still standing.

I have not forgotten that it is Monday morning, a damp, foggy day—for which reason we find ourselves anchored near Green island, by whose reefs it is most dangerous to pass except in clear weather; thus it happens that we take the boat and are rowed to the island on our first gunning expedition. We find the island low and rocky, with occasional sand patches on the southern shore: on the east some half a mile long, narrow rocky points, almost reefs, are above high tide, while rocks and shoals are distributed quite abundantly all around the island. Not three miles north and a little east of Green is Apple (or Pomme as the French call it) island; between the two is a reef of slate rock, visible at low tide. The passage, at high tide, between these two islands, is but very shallow at best, and not fit for vessels to go between. From a square white tower on the northern part of the island, a fixed light, sixty feet above the sea, and visible fourteen miles, shines by night. We heard the half hour gun, from this same quarter, during the fog — it is also fired during dense snowstorms — all the time we were anchored; and far into the night its heavy and loud boom echoed to our ears with a dull thundering roar. Our hunting, not as successful as it might have been, brought several species of birds to our notice, but our wet clothes called for more attention than our birds, for the time being, while we dried ourselves as well as we could under the circumstances. The next morning as the fog cleared away the clink, clink, clinkety clink, of the anchor chain, as all hands heaved at the patent windlass, sounded merrily (it was about six o'clock) on the otherwise quite still air, and before long we were dashing along with a breeze that had by this time nearly cleared the air of fog, though it was soon on us again as thick as ever; but we were past the dangerous shoals and in free water, so we kept on our course, and let the thick fog come on again. Little we cared for it although we kept the old tin fog horn, with its toot-toot-toot, and tootety toot, going all the morning. A vessel's fog horn is an old fashioned institution, and consists of a tin horn similar to that used by venders of fish, yeast, and other articles of street commerce; or by the noisy college student in his rows between classes or his midnight music, of horrid notoriety, at home. The main difference is that the tin is unpainted or unvarnished, and the whole horn shorter and less clumsy. Any one can blow it, and on this particular morning, any one did. It lay upon the deck of the cabin, and while it was the special duty of the man at the wheel to "tend it," as is sometimes said, everybody that came around had his or her turn at it. It acts as a warning to other craft that we are around and coming, while all vessels use one in a dense fog. We had started from Quebec with a consort, in the shape of another vessel, supposed to be a slower sailer than ours, of similar size and lading, bound for the same ports with us. In fact one captain owned both, and was on a trading expedition down along the coast. In the thick fog we had lost her: supposing her to be still behind us the continued sounding of the fog horn, more often than otherwise necessary, was to let her know where we were. Imagine our surprise when, on the lifting of the fog for a few moments, we just saw the vessel in the dim distance ahead, and not behind us; she had got ahead, and kept so, for the rest of the voyage, outsailing us; we could not and did not catch her at all until near our second stopping place at Bonne Esperance, nearly eight hundred miles from Quebec.

CHAPTER IV.

The weather — *Beluga borealis* and other huge Animals — A Sundog — Birds — The Rusty Blackbird — Bradore hills — Varieties of rocks — Coast line about St. Augustine — Reaching Bonne Esperance — Old Fort island — Eider duck — Other birds — Garden vegetables — Hay — Raised beaches — Labrador dogs — Searching for drift-wood.

WEDNESDAY, September 22. The weather to-day was cold and chilly, but clear; the wind blew strong west-southwest. I made a reckoning of both thermometer and barometer, and found that throughout the day they ranged as follows: at 8 A. M., ther. 51, bar. 28.45; at 12 M., ther. 57, bar. 28.50; at 4 P. M., ther. 51, bar. 28.57; and at 6 P. M., ther. 50, bar. 28.52. This is an average pleasant day in this locality. We are now about opposite Point de Monts, and swiftly approaching the Gulf. With a fair breeze the vessel flew along the water sending clouds of spray way over the side of the prow. Although there was quite a breeze the surface of the water a little way from the vessel was quite even. We saw plenty of porpoises of both the black and white varieties. The latter are very abundant in the waters of this region, and about this part of the coast. From the river Saguenay to the west end of Anticosti, they abound more or less frequently at all seasons in open water. This is the *Beluga borealis* of Lesson, and according to Professor Tenney, "A specimen of this animal about ten feet long, and weighing about seven hundred pounds, was kept in a tank in the Aquarial Gardens, Boston, for about two years. He was quite docile, learned to recognize his keeper, and would come and take food from his hand. He was trained to the harness, and drew a young lady in a car prepared for the purpose." Occasionally a large whale would be seen in the distance spouting high columns of water, but none came very near to us. The captain informed me that at times they did appear close by the side of the vessel. The Grampus is also occasional here, but they are much more abundant farther north. At one time during the day several horse mackerel appeared by the side of the vessel, and amused us for a time as they kept up with her, swimming abreast and in perfect line with each other. They would dash through the spray, appearing and disappearing with surprising readiness; but we soon lost sight of them. The captain told us that about this part of the coast he was almost always followed by a party of four or five of these huge fish. As the strength of the wind was spent, I stood looking over the prow of the ship, watching the most perfect rainbows formed in the water by the shining of the sun through the spray as it dashed from the sides of the vessel. Occasionally I thought that I could detect a second bow behind the other (ahead of it I mean), but it might have been the optical delusion caused by my straining my eyes by too much and too close looking. Of course nearly everybody on board is to-day suffering from the usual *mal de mer* accompanying sea voyages, as too many know at their own cost.

Thursday the 23rd. The fine breeze of yesterday kept up all night, and brought us a long distance on our way; in the morning the breeze calmed down, however, and left us a cool and balmy though cloudy day, with only occasional glimpses of sunshine. The captain foretells stormy weather from the appearance of a sundog this morning. These solar appearances are supposed to be caused by the presence in the air of minute six-sided ice crystals, which refract and decompose the rays of light passing through them; they are seen usually at a visual angle of 22°, and are quite frequent in the polar regions of cold countries generally.

Friday the 24th. This was another such a day as yesterday. The morning finds us not far from the island of Great Mecattina, with a fair breeze pressing us onward. In the morning one of the species called pigeon hawk (*Hypotriorchis columbarius*) flew about the vessel several times, and at last lit upon some portion of the mast. These birds are quite common here all along the coast, and it is not at all rare to see them accompany a vessel, now lighting upon it and now again making a short flight seaward, for a distance of many miles. I also saw a small owl, but could not tell the species—unless perchance it was our common *Scops asio*—that acted in much the same way, alighting frequently upon the masthead. About noon a rusty blackbird (*Scolecophagus ferrugineus*) alighted upon the deck of the vessel and remained with us some time. As we were very near the land, and somewhat of a fog existed at the time, he might have mistaken us for some portion of land. I found afterwards that this bird had a summer breeding range all along the coast here as far as L'Anse au Loup, at which latter place a resident, Mr. Fred. Davis, informed me that the bird occasionally built its nest in his woodpile—the people there are obliged to cut enough wood at one time to last the year around; thus there is always more or less of a pile about in the summer season—and his boys called it quite common there. This, I believe, is the only species of blackbird that regularly remains so far north to breed; the cow and red winged blackbird, and the purple grakle, though extending quite far north and east, being hardly more than of occasional occurrence. The rusty blackbird, as you remember, is generally regarded as an unsocial and retiring bird; here it is the reverse, and its nest is not unlike that of a small robin with many sticks outside, and its eggs about 3 or 4, bluish white with spots and dashes of light brown. It feeds upon seeds of various plants and a few insects. Strange to say, they are here frequently kept as cage birds, and their cunning, and power of mimicry of song, something rather remarkable. I have seen it in confinement, and found it to keep admirably. At evening we anchored in calm water at the mouth of the large rigoulette, not far from St. Augustine, and had the satisfaction of passing the night, at least, in calm water: there was really some satisfaction in sleeping off the confusion of the four previous days of rough weather.

The coast all about these parts presents the same rocky aspect.

I have visited nearly all the important harbors from Natashquan to Blanc Sablon, and find the same general appearance in the surface geology, and a similar rocky contour in every place thus visited. Bold masses of rock rear themselves as hills from five to seven hundred feet in height; except the three Bradore hills, which are here called "the mountains," and attain the height, as marked upon the charts, of 1264 feet for the highest, and 1135 for the second, while the third is of nearly the same size as the second. It is rare that the coast line itself presents, anywhere near the water, a spot large enough upon which to build a house and have the foundations rest upon an upraised seabeach, or any kind of earth. Some of the houses are built on part rock and part earthy patches, while the majority are built directly upon a rocky layer which sometimes appears within a few inches of the surface.

The rocks here present the same general character of coarse granite or gneiss, that is formed chiefly of feldspar in great excess. Occasionally, especially the farther down the coast one goes, the mica is in excess, and several localities give an abundance of good sheet mica that might almost be worked with profit were it not for the distance that it must be transported over land, or rather over rocks. The rock is for the most part syenitic gneiss; that is, hornblende takes the place of mica, and the feldspar, which is usually orthoclase, as far as I was able to ascertain, is of both white and flesh-colored varieties. The hornblende is of a greenish-black color, and often present in large crystals, but so embedded in the mass of surrounding rock, as, with the fact of its extreme brittleness, to render it impossible or nearly so to extract them. I did not visit the Bradore hills, but they are said to be of gneiss of this same general character. Quartz does not seem to be abundant here. I have several times had an elderly resident of the coast speak to me of a "vein of marble" running through the rock not far from his house, but upon examination had it proven, as I had previously anticipated it to be, a vein of quite poor quartz. It is not my purpose, however, to give here a general dissertation upon the geology of this region,—that must be left to those better qualified to do it; a few general remarks may be of value however.

The waters about St. Augustine, as all along the coast to a greater or less extent, are crowded with large and small islands, that have been severed from the coast at some remote period, and which now present narrow, winding, and more or less dangerous passages for vessels or small boats, according to their depth. At this point, and for a distance of some twenty or thirty miles up and down the coast, is a most interesting and remarkable feature. It seems as if the whole coast region had received a lateral and perpendicular pressure, that pressed these islands into the sea; as if a large number of small card blocks, placed side by side, had been pressed from three sides so that they burst out upon the fourth. From the mouth of the Kecarpwei river to that of Shecatica bay, the strict coast line presents the following peculiar shape; at point

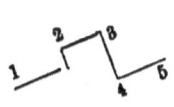

1, we find the Kecarpwei river entering the sea by a narrow channel between the islands; at 2 the St. Augustine river enters in a similar way; and at 3 the Carkewetchepe also. At 4 is the headland promontory of Shecatica bay upon its northeastern side; while from there to *Baie des Roches* (5) the coast is more or less indented by small bays, and deep fiords extending in a north-northeast by south-southwest direction. The almost square patch of water between the St. Augustine and Carkewetchepe rivers, is filled up with the small Main island, Large island, and Sandy, Cumberland, and Dukes islands in the northeast extremity, while River island, at the mouth of the St. Augustine river, fills the eastern end of the figure. Along the line of coast from 1 to 2, is first Inner, and directly southeast, with only a small passage between, Outer island; while southwest of Inner is Long Island. All these islands are separated from the land and from each other by narrow strips of water as I have stated, and these passages receive the name of *rigoulettes* (from the French word *rigole*, a trench or gutter), and are thus called by the inhabitants. The passage between

Inner island and the land is very small, and has received the name of "little rigoulette;" between Inner and Long islands is a passage leading into the sea; between Long island and the mainland is a passage which really is a continuation of "little rigoulette," but there is no passage for vessels at this extremity which lies opposite the mouth of Kekarpwei river. I mention this as you will see that upon our return trip we passed the opening to the sea and ascended this narrowest part of the rigoulette nearly to the mouth of the river, in an early foggy morning, before finding that we must retrace our steps; but that, with a description of the scenery, which was something very lovely, will occur in its place. Between Inner and Outer islands, occurs "big rigoulette," the general passage for coasting vessels into the channel seaward, just ahead of the opening of St. Augustine river and River island. As we did not remain long at St. Augustine, and did not go ashore at this time, there was no opportunity to examine the region carefully.

There were plenty of birds flying about in all directions over our heads, and others swimming in the waters around us. The herring gull (*Larus argentatus*), and great black-backed gull (*L. marinus*), were very abundant but very wild, especially the latter. The eider ducks (*Somateria mollissima*) were frequently to be seen with their broods of young just ready to fly sporting in the water all around us, or flying from point to point of land at our left, while numerous "pigeons," or black guillemots (*Uria grylle*), swam about us on both sides. We amused ourselves by firing at these latter birds, and watching them dive almost at the flash of the gun. We soon sailed by them all into the open water again, where, looking over the side or prow of the vessel, the many shaped and colored acalephs or jelly fishes lay swimming along with the lazy flappings of their gelatinous-like disks. Although not an expert in the subject, I am sure I detected several species here apparently common that I have not seen in our home waters, though I may mistake. What surprised me the most was finding these delicate and apparently easily destroyed animals in these cold northern waters at this time of the year in such abundance.

We anchored here for the night, and in the morning continued our journey, the destination of which was about fifty miles farther down the coast.

Saturday the 25th. About 11 o'clock, A. M., we reached Bonne Esperance safe. Mr. William Whiteley, who resides here, and is the magistrate of the coast, met us and invited us to his house. Here we met a charming English-American family, and were cordially entertained by them; but as both the people, their work, and this place will be more fully described farther on, I will not now linger upon its attractions. In the afternoon we took a boat to Old Fort island, a small island, though the largest for some miles around, and were soon being piloted through the narrow passages so dangerous to those not fully acquainted with their shoals and concealed rocks, to the latter named place. I will leave the general features of this place, also, to be described later in a little sketch entitled: A Labrador Home. Here I have given an outline of the general style of living in this region, as well as a description, also, of Old Fort island, the place where we found ourselves at about five o'clock the same evening, and where I remained for some time studying the general appearance of the region, and making frequent excursions in various directions to examine the peculiarities of the locality in which I found myself placed. It was, I assure you, quite pleasant to be on shore once more.

Monday the 27th. This morning a party of us went out in a boat for a short sail, taking our guns with us. The water was full of birds, especially ducks and auks, as well as the other birds that frequent this region in such abundance, and of which I shall speak in other places; while my attention was called particularly to the "sea duck," of which we shot several from flocks that chanced to fly near enough to us. As the sea or eider duck is one of the peculiar residents of this region, a few remarks upon it, collected from the experience of my year's observation may not be uninteresting, so I give them. The sea duck, as it is here called, and by the word here I mean all along the coast from Mingan—if not from Quebec—to Red bay, perhaps beyond the Straits of Belle Isle, is the eider duck of the naturalist, and the *Somateria mollissima* of the scientist. The first specimens we obtained were shot Sept. 27, the above date, and were young birds. We saw a great many small companies of birds scattered here and there about the harbor, but they were generally, at this season, composed of old birds and their broods of young; the latter were now large enough to kill and are excellent eating. In hunting these birds, especially the old ones, one is obliged to proceed with the greatest caution. A good sighted hunter will detect a flock or a single duck, in rough water even, at a great distance — this is probably due to the fact that living in a region where one must depend so much upon eyesight, that sense is remarkably quickened — at the same time the duck will also perceive the hunter almost as quickly as it is seen. When the duck sees the suspicious object it reaches its neck to its full extent and takes a long, though quick sight; if the hunter sees this movement he knows that he is detected; if he at once remains perfectly still, the duck is often outwitted, since not seeing the object move, it supposes that it is some stone or piece of wood before unnoticed, and continues its feeding; should the hunter move visibly ever so little, the bird takes fright and is off at once. In a clear day a person peering cautiously over a slight eminence can see, especially if the water be tranquil, a flock of ducks often a couple of miles seaward. A patient hunter will then conceal himself near some chosen feeding ground, imitate the call of the male bird, and decoy a flock or single bird quite close and within shooting distance. The call is whistled, and sounds like the single, double, or triple call of a snipe, repeated several times in a sort of guttural tone, if such an expression may be applied to a whistle; after every few times there is an extra low and another similar high note which rounds off the whistle with that peculiar effect so often practised by small boys in trying to roll the tongue, and which enters into the call of so many of the water birds. At low and falling tide the ducks assemble in large colonies on their feeding grounds where the water is shallow and the kelp and muscles thick, — generally at evening and in the early morning; at such times they will sit upon the rocks and remain there until urged or driven off; their sight and hearing seem then to be marvellous, and the slightest noise sends them off into the water. I have seen them in midday thus sunning and resting themselves, but they are so watchful that it is rare that you can get near enough for a shot at them. They dive at the flash of the gun. I have fired at them at a rather long gun-shot off, and seen them dive while the shot struck the place they occupied a second previous.

An experienced hunter when on shore will get as near to a flock or single bird as possible without alarming it, wait patiently for it to dive, as it so often does while feeding in apparent safety, when he will run ahead to some shelter nearer the object of his desire, repeating the operation until he regards himself sufficiently near, and then, remaining standing with his gun at his shoulder, fire at the unconscious bird when it rises from some long dive, generally killing it. In the fall, when a brood of young ducks is surprised it is quite easy to secure a large number, though the old birds generally escape by flight and swimming under the water; they accomplish this latter act with ease, and often pass long distances before appearing to the surface for fresh air. In the open water, a flock of old birds when approached will separate and swim or fly in different directions, while the young cluster, and thus expose themselves directly to the hunter's fire. The best way to pursue both young and old birds is to drive them into some angular indenture of the surrounding islands or land, and then wait for them to appear on the surface of the water after their long dive. The boat stationed too far away for them to swim clear of it, the hunter has every chance for bagging his game. I have noticed that wounded birds do not swim far, about eighteen inches to two feet, below the water; both bill and head are extended forward in a straight line. The old birds will often swim over a quarter of a mile, if not a full half, in extent, beneath the water without appearing for air. As far as my experience goes the birds are rather tame in the winter season, or at least in the extreme late fall; they huddle together in close bunches of from fifty to several hundred birds, and I am informed that an old hunter once fired into a cluster thus gathered and bagged fifty-nine birds with a single discharge of his gun, a common large bore fowling piece. Occasionally old ♀ birds in full heat will be shot that have the back and wing coverts edged with deep rusty brown, and often very deeply so; other birds, smaller, (young) at the same season of the year will have the feathers, particularly of the breast, edged with deep gray; young birds generally have the top of the head darker and the neck much lighter. In some old birds the whole plumage will be unvaried and of a dark brown color. Large flocks are usually made up of a number of small family broods of from five to seven birds that unite from some common cause, and then pursue some common flight until scattered from other causes. The usual feeding grounds of the eider duck are shallow waters over a bed of seaweed or mud, at some rods from land on its south, southwest, or west side. They feed principally on mollusks, barnacles, and a variety of marine animal life, with an occasional piece of seaweed such as may be obtained in the shallow basins of accumulated débris, and on the land-wash. In summer the ducks breed in large numbers on the islands about the harbors, and though their numbers are fast decreasing there are still colonies of them, making their nests of down from their own breasts, beneath some overhanging grassy clump, and laying from three to five olive colored eggs. The people here rob the nests several successive times during a season, while the female continues to lay eggs in the hopes of securing enough to hatch her brood. When setting, the eider duck remains upon her nest until the very last moment, and then forced, takes a rapid flight a short distance off, and does not appear again — at least I have not noticed it — until the intruder has gone away. To what extent the males assist the females in the matter of incubation I did not succeed in finding out positively, that they do so to a limited extent I cannot doubt. They remain in the region until the last waters of the bays freeze over, and are then seen no more until spring returns and thaws the ice, when they appear in company with the king eider (*S. spectabilis*), and the Pacific eider (*S. V-nigra*) — which also are found in immense flocks, but distinct from, that is not mingling with, the others.

We here shot several other species of birds; the titlark (*Anthus ludovicianus*), sandpipers of the species known as the white-rumped (*Tringa bonapartei*), as also the sanderling (*Calidris arenaria*), all of which were more or less abundant. As the afternoon proved rainy we remained in the house and amused ourselves as best we could until bed-time.

Tuesday the 28th. To-day we were out shooting almost all day; we obtained several of the species of plover known by the many different names of blackbellied, whistling field, beetlehead, ox-eye, bull-head, and here by the queer title of Quebec curlew: it is in fact the *Squatarola helvetica* of the scientist. I found this bird in small flocks more or less abundant all along the coast at most of the different places visited from Quebec to Blanc Sablon. It was generally rather wild, and, wading deep into the water, fed on the small sea animals that it could there capture. Its flight was low and rather short. I went out before breakfast this morning to make an attempt on the small beach birds that abounded in a cove of the sea not far from the house, and was successful far beyond my most sanguine expectations. The great dish prepared from these small but delicately flavored little birds, is to fry them in their own fat. Out of several good sized flocks I managed to procure, I think, eighty-seven birds, which, carried home, were soon sending up their savory odor from the frying-pan. Rain in the morning obliged us to stay within doors. Here it rains about one-half the time; it is foggy and uncomfortable weather for nearly the other half, leaving but a short season of sunshine, and there is seldom anything like hot weather. If the thermometer goes up to 70° it is *hot*, while the usual temperature is from 45° to 60° in summer, and as low as often to freeze the mercury in winter. Mercury freezes at about 40° Fahrenheit.

As it came off pleasant in the afternoon we had abundant opportunity for walking about the island, enjoying the prospect as well as seeing the sights. In a little corner of the yard our host had started a small garden, but as its care depended upon his own personal labor at the height of the fishing season, when every spare moment was occupied in the business of the hour, or one was indulging in rest, it had fallen rather out of use. The plants grown were of the varieties often found in similarly situated little corner gardens, and consisted of turnips, cabbages, and potatoes. The latter, of the species known as "Early Rose," were very small; while the turnips had turned out here as they do so often elsewhere along the coast, rather small but very good. Of the cabbages, the best that can be said of them is that they flavored an occasional soup. Onions are rarely raised here, I saw only a few. The soil is generally too sandy, being usually an elevated sea beach, to grow much upon, and the vegetables suffer in consequence. The great reason why farming is not made of more account here is the fact that so few people have their houses where there is abundance of soil proper for such work, and also the fact that they can purchase quite fresh articles in the fall from the Quebec traders, at almost as low prices as if they procured them in Quebec itself.

Many of the people along the coast keep cattle, and the family with whom we stayed possessed two heads besides numerous goats. The cow gave fine milk, and a good generous amount of it, as did also the goat; the cream was thick and sweet, and the fresh butter made twice or three times a week was really most excellent. The cattle are fed upon a rather coarse, though sweet grass, which grows in abundance on the level flats of the islands about. In the fall it presents an appearance quite like that of a field of stunted grain, since it is of a brown color and quite high, with light tassels hanging drooping downward and stirred with every breath of wind. Several species are very common and combined from excellent hay: with *Poa pratensis*, we find both *Hierochloa borealis*, and *Elymus mollis*, though the first mentioned one is without all doubt the most excellent grass or hay here for the cattle. The majority of the low grass grows in thick matted clumps, this is undoubtedly because it is not cut sufficiently often to produce a large and thinner variety; it is much like our "rowen," however, and seems to answer nicely for the cows. In the summer there is plenty of first class feed, and good pasturage anywhere. The cattle are let out to graze at will; when evening comes they are sought after among the dells and vales of the neighboring region and driven home. It is often no slight job to find them when they have strayed for several miles over hillocks, across plains and open stretches of meadows that lead to a succession of elevations and depressions, when perchance they have rounded on their tracks and are quietly grazing not far from the house in some entirely opposite direction from that in which they started out. Strange to say the grass comes up here quite early in the spring, and is grown some length before even the snow has become melted, so that there is good grazing even in early spring.

A curious fact remains to be spoken of: in digging in the garden I was informed that at the distance of about three feet under ground the sand contained abundance of shells similar to those now growing alive on the beach a few rods away, and which belong, I believe, to the species *Mytilus edulis;* a little further front, along the same sand ridge, nearer the shore,—or land-wash as the expression is here,— these same shells appear on the surface, or at least so very near the surface, that comparing the several lines of demarcation there would seem to be a fair amount of evidence that either there had been a gradual subsidence of the waters about this part of the coast, or that the land had gradually risen, allowing the sea to heap up a succession of beaches over which the sand had been blown from above until they had been covered, as they are at present, and overgrown with vegetation.

It seems not unlikely that one or the other of these actions has taken place. In several different places along the island, and in several of the islands, there appears to be this same peculiar sand structure overlying what were apparently once old beaches of the sea.

A few words only here, about the dogs of Labrador. Upon our first stepping on shore we were met by a troop of about fifteen dogs. These dogs are of mongrel breed between the Esquimaux, the Newfoundland, and the various species imported here from other regions. They are used to draw the sledges in the winter, and are as valuable to the inhabitants as horses are to us, yet a worse set of snarling, barking, and generally fierce and also unhospitable animals, it would be hard to find. They feed on blubber and any food that they can obtain in the winter, which has been previously banished from the odds and ends of what can be made no use of in the house; while in summer they are never fed, but allowed to roam at will and find what they can along shore and around the island; they fight incessantly, while, unlike our dogs, should one get undermost, the rest will turn upon him and worry him to death. The people are thus frequently obliged to arise even in the middle of the night to save the lives of their animals, or their numbers would rapidly decrease. They are by far too valuable animals to lose so easily.

Wednesday the 29th. Another rainy day has prevented our doing much outside of the house, and we must be contented to remain within doors. I have been struck with the very unusually large amount of bread that is used all along the coast. It is in reality "the staff of life," in these parts at least. It is raised with a yeast made from the spruce. The fine tender twigs of the young plant are taken, and being boiled in water made into a regular spruce beer. The beer will keep fresh about a week in summer time, and nearly all winter. When fresh it is an excellent drink and much used here in place of water, which, poor at best, is usually taken from ponds, and rarely from springs or running water; these ponds are the result of the melting of large bodies of snow that drain into the low mud flats, often with rocky bottoms, which abound everywhere, high and low: a fair evidence that successive elevations were at one time much nearer the sea-level than they are at present. When a moderate amount of this beer is mixed with a cup of molasses it forms a yeast-like substance, or raising mixture, which fully equals our ordinary raising compounds. The beer itself has a peculiarly bitter taste, from lack of any article in the boiling to counteract the natural taste of the spruce; it makes a very palatable drink, however.

Thursday the 30th. To-day I succeeded in obtaining a specimen of the *Limosa hudsonica*, the hudsonian or black-tailed godwit, also called the ring-tailed marlin. It is a rare bird, even in these regions. It was the only one I obtained on the coast. It was at the time flying rather high up in the air, and with the irregular flight of the spotted sandpiper. Its note, uttered while in the air, sounded more like the squeak of a mouse than anything else I can name. From its rarity I give the dimensions as I took them. Length from end of bill to tail 16 inches; end of bill to toes 18.50; extent 28; wing 8.75; tail 3.25; bill 3.25; unfeathered tibia 1.13; tarsus 2.50; hind toe and claw .50; middle toe and claw 1.65. It was a ♂ and had the gizzard full of gravel and nearly digested matter. The people tell me that it is occasionally seen in fall, but that it is rare. Audubon speaks of it as "rare along the Atlantic district in spring and autumn. Breeds in the barren grounds of the Arctic seas in great numbers." It seems to be confined to the more middle interior parts of the Arctic regions, and the majority of writers whose works I have seen speak of it, as I have generally found it, as rare along the Eastern Atlantic and Gulf coast generally.

Friday, Oct. 1. To-day has been occupied in procuring firewood. A number of the men who live upon the island started off with their boats for a tour along the shore after drift-wood. The wood collects in the coves everywhere about the islands as well as the bays of the mainland, and is eagerly sought after by the people who, in many cases, are obliged to go a considerable distance otherwise for their supply; it is brought in boat-loads to the shore close by the house, the wet material spread out to dry in the sun, while the remainder is sawed or chopped up for immediate use. In this way any old wreck or pieces of vessels that have floated ashore are soon spied out and secured; limbs and branches of trees, as well as boards that have fallen off from vessels and floated ashore are all serviceable, for if clogged with wet they will generally soon dry when exposed to the sun away from the water. Old boats are also found occasionally; all this apparent old rubbish is of value, and shows that very little is lost in the economy practised on these shores.

Saturday the 2nd. To-day we visited Bonne Esperance and passed the day with Mr. and Mrs. Whiteley in a very pleasant manner. As the locality presents some very interesting features of surroundings, as well as some attractions in itself, it may be well to give a general description of the place.

CHAPTER V.

Bonne Esperance — Esquimaux river and island — Caribou island — Entering Bonne Esperance harbor — Vessels in the harbor — Their nationality — Activity of place — Religious character of people — Chapel and Mission house — Residence of Mr. Whiteley, magistrate — Nescopies — Store and shop provisions — Money — Trade — A trading story.

BONNE ESPERANCE, or Good Hope as it would be called in English from a simple translation of the words from the French, is a small island lying off the Labrador coast about opposite the mouth of Esquimaux river, and a little to the right of it, in very near latitude 51° 24' north, and longitude 57° 39' west. It is quite a small island, and lies within a few miles only of the mainland, with several other islands all somewhat smaller than itself around it, principally between it and the shore. About three miles on the northwest, Esquimaux island nearly fills the mouth of the Esquimaux river, and is the largest of the small islands on this part of the coast. This was undoubtedly one of the chief seats of the Indian and Esquimaux, as well also as of the French and Indian wars. A large number of graves were supposed formerly to exist on the island, while an occasional one is still to be found there, though it is of course impossible to say as to their origin; both Indians and Esquimaux were undoubtedly buried in large numbers on this very island, if we can believe the records.

On the northeast of Bonne Esperance is Caribou island. This is another large island, thus making Bonne Esperance the third in size of the small group here situated. If we count Old Fort island, which also is larger, we find Bonne Esperance, the fourth and next largest of all the islands within a radius of some twelve miles that contain perhaps fifty islands large and small, and as many rocky knobs or crests rising above the water, arranged in a most singular manner to form broken and winding channels which are navigable with the greatest of caution, and then only by those who have gradually become accustomed to their intricacies. There are two ways of reaching Bonne Esperance by vessel: one is to take the channel inside the islands, the other to reach the harbor from the outside; the latter is easy while the former is quite difficult. Very small islands lie about the harbors on this part of the coast in such profusion as well as confusion, that the channels formed present a most intricate network of passable and nonpassable openings. Right here, about Bonne Esperance, occur many such places. Clustered as the islands and shoals are one can hardly pass them in safety unless well acquainted with them. Many of these passages, apparently safe to the sight, contain sunken ledges or single rocks that render them unsafe for large vessels; while many places, whose narrowness and dark looking waters would repel one, are the very passages chosen from their depth, with fair wind, through which to glide. Strange as it may appear, a wide and fair opening of water between these islets is an almost invariable sign of shallow water. Vessels can enter Bonne harbor by keeping close to the mainland following carefully the evident channel, keeping to the right between two small islands and following the narrow passage between them, and bearing directly to the left again running straight for the stage houses then in sight; but the safer way is to enter from outside, as it is called, that is,— if sailing in sight of the islands, but at a distance out to sea,—continue until the white beacon of Whale island comes in sight, steer for this and when it is directly northwest (all these points are magnetic points, which here differ by $36°\ 45'$ west of apparent points; that is, apparent north on the chart is $36°\ 45'$ east of true north), sailing in a north or north by west direction, until the fish houses are seen between the two small islands at either hand, when the pilot can steer directly for them. The harbor of Bonne Esperance is a neat sort of natural bay situated between the shores of the opposing islands. Either shore retreats in a semicircle, so that the inclosure forms an oblong semicircle of water; the outlet to this natural bay is a narrow strait in which the water is only nine feet deep at high tide. Of necessity, only small crafts, such as the numerous fishing vessels here abundant from Newfoundland, United States, and other localities, can pass this opening. On the other side is a similar bay, formed by the retreating sides of the other part of each island, from which it is easy to gain the open water again.

In this harbor it is no uncommon sight to see a hundred vessels of all kinds and descriptions at anchor. Of these the majority are from different harbors in Newfoundland, while of the others many are from the Magdalen islands, and some from Nova Scotia; numerous French crafts and a few American are also occasionally seen.

It is a pretty sight, I assure you, to see this out-of-the-world region so thoroughly alive and stirring, as it is in the summer, with all these small vessels from different parts of the world congregated here, often by hundreds, filling the bay from head to entrance; while others remain outside flitting about from place to place as occasion may require, all engaged in the same pursuit of fishing. The following partial list of the localities with the number of vessels sent out from each in 1878 will give you a glimpse of the business of the season. Halifax, 8; Quebec, 4; Newburyport, 2; Britain (Ang.), 2; Gaspé, 1; Boston, 1; Nova Scotia, 21; Newfoundland, 13; total, 52. These are but a small part of the number that were actually seen in Bonne Esperance harbor during the summer of 1878; but these were registered as dealing more or less directly in fish, and most of them remaining more or less of the season in or near that locality. Bonne Esperance and Salmon Bay, the latter being an establishment owned by Newfoundland parties, and situated about two miles away, are the largest fisheries this side of Blanc Sablon on the northeast, or Natashquan on the west; the former locality is only about twenty miles away while the latter is some three hundred. It is a great sight for the simple inhabitants dwelling near these fisheries when the vessels come in the spring and begin their work. The long winter is past, the bays at last open, and the vessels soon begin to arrive. Most of the inhabitants are very quick of observation. Let them see a vessel once and know her name, they will, unless great alterations have been made, tell her again under almost any circumstances.

As the vessels anchor one by one in Bonne harbor, the people assemble from the neighborhood around and the island becomes a scene of gayety and life. Of course it is gayety in a sort of primitive sense; but then the people think much of it, especially as it affords them so much enjoyment the coming winter in rehearsing at their firesides what they have seen and heard.

I will not now mention the religious character of the people, or the service as conducted in the little chapel on the top of the hill; but will only say that it is a most pleasing opportunity to visit one of these native, evening church services; to see forty or fifty of the native people gathered together, and with them the transient strangers from France, England, the United States, and all the places from which vessels sent out to the fisheries have come, from the various crafts in the harbor; to hear all join in song; and listen to English, French, and American as they lead in their hearty, heartfelt prayer. It is a good work that is done by the little mission there established and God bless them in their work.

Below the chapel, under the hill, lies the "Mission House," as it is called. Here reside several missionary ladies or gentlemen, sometimes both, who have given themselves to the work of attending to the spiritual wants of these poor people. It is here that the Rev. Samuel R. Butler, of Northampton, Mass., and before him several others, spent so much of their time while on the coast. Here, in summer, the children attended regular day school, but to which, owing to the distance at which everybody lives, few come; here also they come to Sunday school, which is usually well attended, since the people are free to go and come as they choose from their business on that day and they do so in preference to remaining at home. Not far from the Mission is the residence of Mr. W. H. Whiteley, who, as I have said, is the Magistrate for

Canada for this part of the coast. Mr. Whiteley's house is really a fine one for this section of the country. It is a good sized, two-storied affair, much longer than broad, as is the custom with arctic and sub-arctic houses, and very warmly built. Its white paint attracts one from the outside, while a cosey fire and a cup of hot tea are always handy within. Mrs. Whiteley is quite ready to welcome a "new comer," and the hearty, rosy children are as delighted to find a stranger to take notice of them as can be imagined. The sitting and dining room are combined; a large, square, or rather oblong, stove heats the room, and there are plenty of chairs, stools, benches, and an easy lounge ready for occupancy at any time. I shall not soon forget the cosey times I have had in that same room with the assembled family; and the games and plays with which long winter evenings have been whiled away. The many pleasant faces almost recall me there as I write, and the hope of some day meeting them again is present with me.

Outside of the house the contour of the island is rather peculiar; though if not strange to an inhabitant it is at least so to a visitor. The whole island is one mass of granite rock overlaid here and there with scanty vegetation. There are two principal crests of about sixty-five, and eighty feet in height above the sea-level; their rocky summits are crowned, as is usual with nearly all such elevations about the coast, with a pile of stones several feet in height which serve as landmarks: they are called Nescopies: the sailors call them the "American Men."

The other buildings upon the island are a small store and shop; here are kept a variety of articles of hardware, groceries, and dry goods, as well as a general assortment of articles of clothing, boots and shoes, hats, caps, and oilskin suits—the latter of which are so much used among the men. The assortment of nicknacks of one kind or another is always more or less limited, and confined to a few of the many useful articles of dress and use rather than of the kind to tempt the coppers of the mamma and papa, as is so customary in the United States and other parts of the world. It is rather a store of necessity than one of choice and amusement.

The room is a small one, and the various articles are piled in heaps in corners, and about the sides and middle of the room, for want of space. This is the regular trading port for the region around. If any article of commerce is wanted it is obtained here if anywhere on the coast: a barrel of flour or salt pork; a box or bag of biscuit as they are called, or more properly hardtack or hard crackers,—and as a rule they merit their name since the majority of them require long soaking in water before they are soft enough for use, to be fried, broiled, or eaten at all, and I have often seen them so tough that the repeated blows of a hatchet-back would barely suffice to break them; meal, of which varieties that commonly called oatmeal, is much used, while Indian meal is regarded by the majority as only fit to give the dogs, to whom it is fed scalded, though the poorer class are frequently obliged to mix it with their flour if not use it altogether pure; butter, salted down in tubs or firkins, and lard, both of an inferior quality; sugar and molasses, the latter of which is the chief source of the sweetenings used on the coast. A strange custom prevailing here is that of sweetening, with molasses the tea or coffee, though very little of the latter is ever used so far northeast, tea being a popular and more healthy drink, and the true, native Labradorians invariably take the molasses pot, even where the sugar is equally as easy of access, and use its contents where we should use the sugar. Besides provisions, nails, hatchets, axes, and tools of various descriptions—usually confined to planes, saws, chisels, and screw-drivers—are always on hand; large cross-cut saws can be purchased of the traders, as can other articles wanted if known and ordered beforehand. A few yards of any of the cheap patterns of dress wear, trimmings, gloves, stockings, underwear, coarse materials for overalls, and in fact a little of anything that long experience has shown to be in constant use, will usually be found somewhere in the promiscuous heap of materials stored in this room; while it would consume a chapter in itself to enumerate the variety of articles here accumulated. It is a great day when several of the inhabitants living say ten or fifteen miles up or down the coast come to the store to purchase their monthly supply of necessities. It takes a long while for them to settle upon what they want, and they pick out the articles they wish with the eagerness and apparent pleasure of a small child. Nearly every article has to be handed over a number of times before the one desired can be settled upon, and when it is very likely it will be exchanged for something more pleasing to the eye. Finally, the exchange is arranged and the parties start for home with their purchases. The general medium of exchange all through this region is trade. Money is seldom used, and its value still less seldom known. Both the English and the Canadian, as well as some United States money find their way into the Labrador markets. The Provinces have each a money of their own, and nearly every piece has a discount upon its real value. The general mode of reckoning is in English pence, shillings, and pounds. A pound being twenty shillings or four dollars (as it is in the majority if not all the Canadian provinces), the shilling is twenty cents or twelve pence; the English sovereign is taken for four dollars and eighty-four or eighty-six cents, and consists of twenty-four shillings twopence, or threepence half-penny; it is only in the Newfoundland province, northeast of Blanc Sablon, or Labrador proper, that the English gold brings its full value of twenty-five shillings. To complicate matters still more both the English shilling of twenty-five cents, and the Canadian twenty cent piece are freely used and equally abundant. Newfoundland silver is used as are all the other provincial pieces for their full value. American silver is occasional, and usually heavily discounted, while American gold is, I believe, the only gold taken for full face value and without discount. In American money the Canadian fifty cent piece is worth forty-eight cents, the twenty-five cent piece twenty-four cents, the twenty cent nineteen cents, the ten cent nine cents, and the five cent four cents; on the other hand a half-pence (pronounced hāpence) is generally two-thirds of a cent or one cent, a two-pence (pronounced tuppence) three cents, a three-pence (thrippence) five cents, a (four-pence (fōpence) seven cents, six-pence ten cents, nine-pence fifteen cents, twelve-pence the same as a shilling of twenty cents, and fifteen and eighteen-pence twenty-five and thirty pence: thus our quarter is in Labrador fifteen pence (not counting the discount which is usually five cents), our twenty cent piece nine-pence (with a discount also of five cents), our ten cents six-pence (discount of only one cent); our five cent pieces are often taken for their full value. The three cent piece is not used or recognized, and the fifty cent piece has a discount of from five to ten cents according to location. The Newfoundland Bank note of one pound, or four dollars, is always looked at twice before it is taken, sometimes with and sometimes without discount. It takes six large coppers to be worth a five cent piece.

In trading, it is customary to employ the usual productions of the country as a medium of exchange. Although it would be as impossible to make out a table of exchange as a full table of money equivalents for the coast, a few of the more important may be stated. Codfish at thirteen to eighteen shillings a quintal, herring seven six-pence to ten shillings a barrel, cod oil two to two and six-pence a gallon; seal skins dressed seven and six-pence to fifteen shillings according to the species of seal, undressed five to seven and six-pence, rarely ten shillings apiece; seal oil two shillings a gallon. Besides this, people living near rivers sell wood for twenty-five cents a load of ten long sticks, about forty feet long and eight inches through at the butts. Old iron picked up from wrecks is worth half a cent a pound, and everything useful has its price. Nearly all the trading on the coast is done on the credit system, and it is usually expected beforehand that half the people would not pay their bills if they could, and many of them never intend to, while still another portion are dependent entirely upon the catch of the next season, having, by former delinquencies, overrun their accounts, so that they are obliged to get credit in advance of the season upon that season's catch. No wonder the majority are poor, and kept so not by the power of the richer class, but rather by their own indolence in not profiting when an opportunity offers to make a little money. Most of them consider it best to let well enough alone, and having earned sufficient to support them through the winter, the rest looks after itself, while the time is then passed in "chatting" and smoking.

A curious story is told which shows how some are really incapable of keeping a perfectly understood account of their own money. A certain trader offered for a piece of valuable fur forty-five dollars in American money; the native thought the exchange over for some time and finally shook his head and said that he could not sell for less than ten pounds cash. Now ten pounds you remember is forty dollars, or five dollars less than the original offer. The wily trader in turn shook his head as if in hesitancy, but finally said that he would accept the offer, while the native went off chuckling, if I may use the word, that he had made the trader come up to his price.

CHAPTER VI.

Raspberries — Weather — Hudsonian Chickadee and other birds — Black-fly — Topography of country — Old Fort bay, physical features and surroundings — Superstitions concerning the raven.

SUNDAY, Oct. 3. To-day some of the people in the house brought in a few raspberries picked near the house, but whether they were of the species known as the dwarf raspberry (*Rubus triflorus*), or the wild red raspberry (*R. strigosus*), I could not quite tell as I did not analyze them; the berries were quite dry and unfit to eat. Neither of the species is rare along the coast anywhere, and it might have been either or both of these. A quiet walk about the island, which is about a mile and a half in diameter and four in circumference, occupied us a good portion of the morning, while in the afternoon the cool breezes found us enjoying ourselves outside the house in the shade on the lawn.

Monday the 4th. After a stormy, windy night, the weather continued rough and rainy all day. The wind increasing raised great billows upon the surface of the water, these increasing in height and fury dashed with incredible force against the rocky heights so numerous in the outer waters about the island. Huge waves would hurl themselves against the rocky exposures, and flooding them, pour down the opposite sides in broad sheets of water; or again they would break into showers of spray that would spread themselves in crowns, wreaths, and haloes of magnificence that would rival the most elegant artificial production, and put to shame the most wonderful of ancient or modern fountain work. Looking from the right from our door, a long line of low reefy islands stretched across our view, ending in a rising knoll at the left; over this I saw a continued display of hydraulic pyrotechnics that would have delighted the most fastidious with its magnificence of display. The waves dashing upon the upright side of the cliff sent spray high in the air over the hilly part of the island, while long lines of billows broke into foam all along the narrow stretch of beach. Several displays of lesser importance were seen in other directions, but none equalled this one. All through the day the sight continued, and only closed with the night.

With all this cold, wet rain, the thermometer has been averaging about 50°, varying from 46° in the morning to 54° in the evening. In spite of the weather some of the party went out and shot a couple of ducks. In hunting these birds, which were eiders, one has to proceed with the greatest caution. A good hunter will detect a single duck or a flock of ducks, even in rough water, at an immense distance. I have often been surprised at being told that there was a flock in a certain direction, when I could see nothing at all in that direction. Some five or eight minutes afterwards I would think that I had discovered a flock some ways yet in the distance, and upon giving notice to that effect would receive the reply, "why, have you just seen them? that's the flock we're after, the same I pointed out to you ten minutes ago." When people live so much by their eyesight, it is not hard to see how that sense can become so acutely developed as it is in so many of the people on the coast. I think I have mentioned before that men will recognize a vessel that they have once seen years after, and at an immense distance away. They will tell a boat, and the people who are in it, before one unaccustomed can distinguish that there are any people at all in it. This results, I think, partly from what one might almost call "reasoning from analogy," though no doubt *eyesight* has a great deal to do with it.

Wednesday the 6th. This is still another foggy day, and the sun made us but a short visit this morning. I shot a couple of sheldrakes, shellbirds as they call them: we had them for dinner and found them very tender and delicious. They were young birds, and of the smaller of the two species of *Mergus*, of which the females are so nearly alike, and the one known as *serrator*, the red breasted Merganser, so common in these parts; I found here the savanna sparrow (*Passerculus savanna*) abundant and breeding and also saw numbers of that familiar little hero of the north, the Hudsonian chickadee (*Parus hudsonicus*), so very abundant here. As this is a peculiarly characteristic bird of this region, a few words may be said of it. I found the Hudsonian titmouse residing all the year around both on the islands and on the mainland wherever I went during my stay on the coast, and their cheerful presence has dee-dee-dee'ed away the blues more than once. I first met them at Old Fort island in the summer, when they would frequently come and perch on the roof of the house, and occasionally fly in at the door and pick up crumbs from the floor. They were very tame, and would allow you even to catch them without much opposition on their part. The people of the coast are very fond of them, and will not allow a stranger to hurt one of them if they can possibly help it. While flying they will often dart about from place to place, or if it be in the air in one direction or another, with a quick, whirring sort of flight which reminded one more of the operation of quickly half opening one of our closed fans and immediately shutting it again. They fly only a short distance except when rather high in the air when their smallness soon aids them in escaping detection as they fly; at such times their flight is swift. When on the island their favorite resting place was the roof of the house, and we would often see several perched near each other on the ridge-pole, where they would remain a long time or until frightened away. Low, stunted fir growths about the island almost always contained several of these birds, who would play at a veritable hide and seek among the dense clumps of fir and spruce everywhere abundant. If any one pretended to watch them they would hide, and not even chirping remain for nearly half an hour quite still, or if stirring at all doing so so cautiously as not to attract the least attention, while often I would walk about quietly trying my best to get a sight at them and yet unable to do so. At other times the case would be exactly reversed, and I have found them in the bushes on the mainland near by, and spent much time in sitting down and quietly waiting while the little fellows, at first frightened by my presence, afterwards gained confidence and crowded around the bushes close to my feet, my hands, and my face; they did not, as a certain author once remarked of the black-capped chickadee, alight on the tip of my boots and peer at me, but they did peer at me from bushes within a few feet of my face, and certainly within reach of my hand had I grasped for them,— though I should undoubtedly have missed them had I attempted it. After remaining about for some time they would fly away, only to light on some bush near, or return again, to examine more fully the mysterious object which had attracted their attention; then they would chatter away to themselves as if comparing notes. If finally I raised my hand or my head they would dart off to some covert and disappear as if by magic. This chickadee is often the only bird that may be seen in the woody portion of the "lake regions," where in the heat of the day it is active and full of song, even in the summer. The darker the woods, or the more tangled the underbrush, the better these birds seem to like it. It is here the counterpart of our native black-capped titmouse (*Parus atricapillus*). That latter bird did not appear here during the year to my knowledge, although it is given by Reeks, in his list of Newfoundland birds, as common and breeding. The Hudsonian titmouse breeds all up and down the coast, but it usually prefers the interior and tangled undergrowth district, which is quite difficult of access. The ordinary note of this titmouse adds a very pretty and pleasing lisp to the dee, dee, dee notes which it so frequently utters, and which our bird usually delivers so plainly and clearly.

I also saw several white crowned sparrows (*Zonotrichia albicollis*), and though they were not remarkably tame I afterwards found them in large numbers breeding in the low evergreen shrubbery about the island. They have a pretty song, and are otherwise attractive companions, but I will say more of them farther on.

Thursday the 7th. Most of the day was spent in rambling about with my gun, and several species of birds rewarded my search which will be spoken of in their place, but my attention was especially drawn to the small flocks of the ruddy plover or sanderling (*Calidris arenaria*), which were occasionally seen alone or with large flocks of other shore birds. I saw numbers of them during my stay on the island, but seldom many at a time. They are very wild and hard to approach, and keep quite close together in small flocks of from ten to thirty; their flight is wilder and their call different from that of the other birds with which they associated. I found them very plump and fat, and they make very nice eating.

Friday the 8th. I saw to-day several very interesting species of birds, and while we are on the subject I will give you a brief account of the savanna sparrow (*Passerculus savanna*), and the white rumped sandpiper (*Tringa bonapartei*). The savanna sparrow is perhaps the most abundant of all the small land birds that inhabit these regions. It is a tame and familiar little fellow, and feeds without fear about the doorsteps, and in the dooryard, building its nest, laying its eggs, and rearing its young often in grassy clumps not two rods from the door. They are common all over the islands and on the mainland, and their song is a well known attraction to a native of the place. I shot a good many and found them to present an unusually decided shade of plumage, with the dark and white colors plainly marked. There was very little yellow about the head and eye, and of some twenty specimens none at all on the wing shoulders. I shot, one day, four of these birds, none of which had a particle of yellow upon them anywhere that I could distinguish; a small tuft of white feathers at the base of the primary coverts of the shoulder gave the appearance of a white edging in the place of the usual yellow. The birds were all remarkably full in coloration, and decided in plumage; the white very clear; the dark inverted arrowpoints quite distinct, as were also the grayish and buff edgings everywhere. One specimen alone had the buffy suffusion covering the breast. I cannot say that the rule holds good constantly, but in some thirty specimens the ♂ had the yellow on the wing shoulder, while the ♀ and young of the year of either sex had white in that place. It is everywhere abundant, and breeds on the ground.

Of the white-rumped sandpiper I saw several immense flocks on the flats near the house; they were quite tame, and I shot a great many of them. Some had the chestnut edgings of the wings very broad and deep, while several of them had either the head or neck, and one had both, quite ashy; the greater part of them had very little chestnut, that color being replaced by ashy; the chestnut edgings seemed to be on birds that were passing from the last stage of young of the year to adult birds, but I may mistake; both varieties were in the same flock—flocks were usually of from fifteen to one or two hundred in number. They would alight in the mud flats, and feed, running about in the black, slimy, clay-like mud or muck, running in the water nearly to the tibia and keeping quite close together meanwhile; they feed in the evening and at dusk chiefly among the kelp along shore, and I rarely saw even a single bird at high tide. They were very tame, and if I crouched and approached them on nearly their own level, I could get very close indeed. If discovered, single birds, as often small flocks, would remain perfectly quiet for some time. It was very difficult to see them as long as they remained still, since their color corresponded so closely to that of the mud or kelp where they happened to be. I have often at dusk had them fly from within a yard of my feet when after careful examination I had not supposed there were any near me. I saw these birds associate only with *Calidris arenaria;* the birds did not mix, but each kept in its own separate flock. An occasional *Ereunetes pusillus* was seen, but they were rare. Sometimes a single bird would be seen flying high and swiftly in the air, but generally their flight was low and irregular, their note uttered as two or three faint, shrill whistles, the same as when running about in search of food; they take wing on the approach of danger. Large flocks are made up of the union of a large number of single families. Most of the specimens obtained at this season of the year had a worn and faded look, and were not nearly as plump or as well plumaged as specimens that I shot later, with bright chestnut edgings to nearly all the upper feathers. One of these specimens had the head and neck nearly clear ash, of a very minute pattern. I often found specimens where the tail feathers were half black, and the other half white. I suspect that *Tringa bairdii*, that rare sandpiper, bears a stronger relation to certain forms perhaps of adult worn breeding plumage of *T. bonapartei* than is generally credited.

We were much gratified, this evening, by a fine double rainbow, of most beautiful color; both bows were well defined against a clear bank of cloud in the east.

Sunday the 10th. I saw what was either a large white hawk or owl perched on a stone near the top of a small hill by the house, but he soon flew away. We passed a delightful day out of doors. The weather was fine, and the lateness of the season protected us against the fury of that most pestiferous creature of these northern regions, the much dreaded black-fly. This insect, the *Simulium molestum* of the entomologist, is one of those *rara avis* that the naturalist lights upon occasionally much to his own personal inconvenience. It is an abundant native of all these northern regions, more especially inland, during the summer months; and of its development little is known. They fill the air during the months of July, August, and September, especially inland, making the country almost uninhabitable. They swarm on a still day in millions, and nothing but a breeze of wind will rid the air of their presence. They light on any part of the face that is incautiously exposed, and bite it most terribly until the blood runs. Their favorite places of attack are behind the ear and on the neck. This fly attacks the children even more savagely than it does the grown people. I have seen a child's face all bitten and swollen, while the poor thing spent most of the time crying and rubbing the inflamed portions, which only served to make the case worse. With adults the bite soon disappears. The account given of this insect by Harris, in his "Insects Injurious to Vegetation" is not accurate, for this portion of the country at least. I have found it more or less common from the beginning to the end of summer. Prof. Packard says of it, "Its antennæ are eleven-jointed ; the palpi are four-jointed, with long, fine terminal joints, and the ocelli are wanting, while the posterior tibia and first joint of the hind tarsi are dilated. The body is short and thick. The labrum is free, sharp as a dagger ; and the proboscis is well developed and draws blood profusely." Harris says, "The wings are transparent ; and their legs are short, and have a broad whitish ring around them." I have verified these statements, but not the following, again quoting from Prof. Packard, who says it "lives during the larval stage in the water. The larva of a Labrador species which we found is about a quarter of an inch long, and with the appearance here indicated.[1] The pupa is also aquatic, having long respiratory filaments attached to each side of the front of the thorax. According to Westwood 'the posterior part of its body is enclosed in a semi-oval membranous cocoon, which is at first formed by the larva, the anterior part of which is eaten away before changing to the pupa, so as to be open in front. The imago is produced beneath the surface of the water, its fine silky covering serving to repel the action of the water.'" Although they are undoubtedly blown by the wind to great distances, the fact of their being reared in fresh water — by fresh I mean not salt sea water, yet I imagine they prefer stagnant pools — accounts, perhaps, for such large numbers being found on the mainland, and so few on the islands outside, where the continued breezes from the sea carry them away as fast as they appear. If it were not for these tormenting little insects, exploration into the interior would be a comparatively easy thing. As it is, veils of mosquito netting do no good, for the fly is scarcely one-eighth of an inch long and would pass through the meshes at once ; handkerchiefs are used with little better success, for they will creep into the smallest openings and beneath the loose folds. A mixture is now made and sold, consisting largely of dilute carbolic acid and sweet oil, which, when applied to the face and hands, keeps these insects at a distance, for a time at least. The best and only sure remedy is to keep wholly away from them.

---

[1] See fig. 69, Packard's "Our Common Insects," p. 73.

Monday the 11th. This morning I shot several specimens of the horned lark (*Eremophila alpestris*), and noted the extent of the pinkish color on the wing coverts, rump, and neck usual in spring specimens in the high eastern regions. My long stay upon the coast made me quite familiar with this beautiful songster, and characteristic bird of the region, which is abundant all along the north shores of the St. Lawrence from Quebec northward. At Green Island in the river St. Lawrence, I found the lark quite common; at that time it was rather tame, and could be seen on the low flats of the island hopping about and feeding in close company with the sandpipers; they were all single birds and not flocks. I saw them all the fall at Old Fort island, both alone and in large flocks, and always more or less wild. I would often see them flying very high in the air, and uttering their peculiar querulous whistling notes; sometimes flying quite low and somewhat irregularly, but uttering their notes at all times while on the wing. Though common everywhere, they seemed to lead a sort of wild, solitary life that comported well with the wild, solitary region in which they dwelt; they preferred the plains, fields, and rocky knolls away from houses where they would hop about in twos or threes, or small flocks, picking up their food; occasionally they would perch on the tops of knolls as if to reconnoitre, then retire and go to feeding again as if satisfied that no enemy was near; they are very quick and active in their movements, and always wild rather than tame. I saw them often on the shore, and feeding on the kelp in company with the white rumped sandpiper, but never mingling with them as far as I could see. As their brown color corresponds so well with the color of the ground, it was often hard to detect them until a few shrill whistles and a hurried flight announced their flushing a short distance ahead. Several that I shot were remarkable for the amount of pink upon them. At times large flocks fly over the island high up in the air, while one of these flocks once alighted upon the island: their extreme wildness was something remarkable. One can hardly say enough of this most charming little fellow and beautiful songster. It breeds here abundantly, and the only time I saw it tame was at, and immediately following, the breeding season. The nest is placed on the ground, and the eggs, usually four in number, white peppered with ashy in a close pattern. It enlivens the long days with a fresh, and what we would call really remarkable "clean cut" song that, heard at early morning or in the evening, would induce one to believe the bird almost inspired.

Often on a clear, crisp morning I have seen the lark ascend by a series of spirals to an immense height: then, remaining on almost stationary wing, carol forth such a thrilling warble that it seemed more like the chant of a spirit than the song of a bird.

In the afternoon I shot perhaps the most cunning bird known about these regions where it is probably never common, the ruby crowned wren (*Regulus calendulus*). It was flitting about in a small clump of bushes when I first saw it and it me. I was then obliged to wait around for over half an hour before I could again catch sight of and shoot it. It will cunningly crawl or flit from place to place, and it is a mere question of who will continue this game of hide-and-seek the longest, as to whether the bird escapes or is finally obtained.

One cannot but enjoy these rambles about a "new region;" at least a region about which so little is known as this. There is a charm of novelty of situation, and to one busy hunting the delightful natural objects with which he is surrounded, the charm is heightened. I was often reminded, especially on the water, of the enthusiasm and joy with which Audubon must have viewed these abodes of the water-fowl when entering this new field of ornithology for the first time. How a botanist would have revelled in the new plants that would greet his eye! and there remain many yet that have not been identified; while I often think of the field for some enthusiastic collector of lichens, fungi, and mosses. The insect fauna of the region likewise needs studying up, and an expedition into the interior, like one through Newfoundland, would develop most interesting results.

Tuesday the 12th. We took a trip inland this afternoon, and I could not help admiring the beautiful bay which bears the name of the island at its mouth, and which receives that name from being the supposed seat of the old French and Indian wars traditional to this locality. Old Fort bay is really a most beautiful piece of nature's fancy work. Just outside its mouth a large expanse of water is surrounded on all sides by islands, between which narrow channels, in many cases too small and shallow for the passage of vessels, connect with the sea. Old Fort island, the largest here, except Esquimaux island, as it is the largest on the coast for miles around, is in a line with the mouth of the bay. The open water I have mentioned is relieved by a single rock prominent at high tide even; all about is deep and safe water in which vessels may anchor.

As you enter the bay, the hilly character, at least of this part of the coast, attracts your attention at once. The hills between three and five hundred feet high at the left send their wooded or precipitous slopes down to the sea, while the highland extends far back in series of crests. At the extreme end of this left hand promontory, and midway between the front face of the hill, stands the dark mouth of a sort of cave or natural hollow among the rocks, within which tradition stores treasures inestimable, guarded by apparitions most hideous and terrible; below it a grassy slope extends slanting towards the sea; above it on the right, the crest of one of the hills forms a good outlook to the whole surrounding region.

It is here that many affirm was the last standing place of a fort or battery which the settlers inside the bay (and the ruins of whose houses at a late date, though nothing now remains, were plainly seen,) were credited as having erected for the better defence of their abodes. The theory that the battery would be raised in such a place is very probable, and it would be quite likely that a battery would be placed outside the harbor rather than within it. I mention this as there are some persons who believe the fort to have been within the bay on the top of a long glacial ridge, which if it were not known to be of nature's own formation, would strike a stranger, especially one not examining the height personally, as being the most likely place for such a fort.

Inside, on the right hand, the elevations are low, seldom over one hundred feet in height. The country here extends back, like that of the other side in a series of elevations. The basin of the bay is like that of a fiord valley, and extends directly inward for a short distance, then bends in an almost easterly direction. From east to south the land is low, while from north to west and south the hills are often six hundred feet high, and a more or less level piece of country extends back in a west direction for a considerable distance. Towards the north the country is broken, as it is all along, though not to so great an extent as in this direction, into ponds and even in one instance a large lake. Labrador is known to be a region of lakes in its interior. Perhaps it is more so than many imagine. In some cases large lakes cover quite an area of country. They appear in such cases to be the resultant drainage of an innumerable number of ponds, large and small. Thus these ponds are ranged in areas of equal height, the highest ones being the smallest, while next will come an extent of country that contains several larger ones, and so on, each draining into the larger below and all finally into one lake. The general idea is that of a huge natural amphitheatre wherein the seats are tablelands extending back for several miles, so that the top layer or seat consists of several isolated and high peaks whose connecting medium is a marshy bog with small puddles of rain and occasionally springs of water; about fifty feet lower an area of country extends inward, towards the central pit of the amphitheatre, which contains several medium sized ponds with a drainage from the pools above, and with innumerable tiny rills flowing into them, and receiving more or less drainage from within its own districts. Below this still another series of ponds, much larger, receive drainage from the waters above, and empty themselves below either into another series or, uniting in some large pond, receive all this drainage and flow onward and forward, through valleys and rocky gorges, with precipices and rocky cliffs on either side, miles into the country. After some distance this again will unite with another large pond which receives a similar drainage from some other direction; thus, the whole country presents an appearance most unusually grand and wild, fit region only for the Indian and trapper, where the otter, beaver, and martin form the staple productions, and the flesh of deer and bear the staple consumption.

About two hundred miles from the sea the "Height of Land," as it is called, presents itself as a series of high hills, and really a part of that great chain of mountains which one strikes directly north from Quebec and which follow the country across the Labrador peninsula to above Cape Charles on the eastern part of the coast.

As this series of hills runs along the country at varying distances of from two to five hundred miles from the coast, the intervening region consists of a descending series of elevations, until directly on the coast line itself it assumes a height of from three to seven hundred feet. The "Height of Land," often contains hills from 1000 to 2000 feet in height, and while few are over that, Mt. Bache was found by the U. S. Coast Survey to be some 2160 feet high. According to Packard, "Its watershed" (that of Labrador) "is said by Kohlmeister and Knoch, to be a chain of high mountains which terminate in the lofty peaks of syenite at Aulezavic island and Cape Chudleigh, which are the highest mountains in Labrador, and rise probably over 3000 feet in height."

The river system of the peninsula is restricted to one or two principal rivers; while the stream system is ample, nearly every small bay having for its head a body of running water—and the numerous streamlets all along the coast fully support the view that there is an abundance of water inland. Let us return, now, to our description of Old Fort bay, and having chosen this, of the many similar places along the coast, see what beauties it possesses and what natural attractions it yields.

The outline of Old Fort bay, is, as I have said, a row of hills three to five hundred feet in height on the left, and another and smaller series of elevations scarce one hundred feet upon the right of the entrance of the bay. Directly across the ridge to the right, which is in fact a much twisted, contorted, and irregularly cut up peninsula, lies the western arm of Esquimaux river, whose mouth you remember is so nearly occupied at this point with Esquimaux island, that the passage between it and the mainland on the east is barely large enough for small boats. The bay extends directly inward about a mile, then takes a sudden turn to the right for about the same distance, giving to the whole the shape of a bent arm. Strange to say, no stream of any size enters this large bay. A small brook only, made up of the drainage of the neighboring hills, flows into it. To give you an idea of the extent to which the country is cut up by ponds, let me say that the distance between the end of the bay and the Mission station, situated several miles up the river, near the contraction in the stream just below the first rapids, is only five miles; yet there are three ways of going between the two places, and each time a line of three distinct ponds is traversed, and with the exception of one pond which is the first and same crossed on two of the routes, no pond is traversed twice; between all of these are elevations varying often from two to three hundred feet in height, though generally less than one hundred. The whole country is similarly cut up into elevations and depressions whose basins contain a pond, the accumulation of the drainage surrounding it.

A single stream enters the bay from the centre of the left hand side of the entrance; it comes from a line of ponds extending backward into the country, and I am informed that one of them is an excellent trout pond. The most interesting point in all the bay, the elbow as we will call it, remains to be spoken of. If we describe it as having the appearance of two semicircles placed side by side ⌒⌒ and with an island just off the joint, we shall present a very ▪ fair picture of the location. The larger of these curved pieces is the elbow proper. The left hand (the larger) is a sandy strip of beach with high cliffs about it, and a sloping ridge whose summit is a straight line of nearly a quarter of a mile in length above it. This elevation slopes gradually to the sea. Above, it presents the appearance of an artificial fortification lying between two high peaks, one at the left and the other at the right. The top of this ridge, nearly level for some thirty or forty rods, falls gently to a pond beyond. The pond lies about 225 feet above the sea level, while the top of the ridge is about 275 feet, thus making a difference of level between the two of fifty feet. The slope of the bank in front is some thirty degrees. It is evident that an immense glacier, receiving arms it may be from several quarters of the country in the interior, made its stand here, and thence crept down into the sea polishing off this ridge, and scooping out the basin of this part of the bay. It is along the bank of the eastern part of this cove that the old colonists chose their abode, and fixed their huts. At a late day foundations of these were still standing, and I have been informed that there are those now living who have dug up old copper coins, and relics of various other kinds about this same place. No signs of either relics or foundations are now to be found, although the most careful search has been made all about these regions. The second circular division of this beach presents a totally different aspect from that just described. Its central point is a mass of rocks, and rocks continue in greater or less profusion all along to the end of the bay, though especially abundant right in this particular place. There is a raised bank or platform, about one-quarter of a mile long, and thirty or forty rods deep, through which flows a small stream which has evidently eaten its way to and gradually sunk within a few feet above high tide, while the bank itself is scarcely twenty feet above the sea. Back of this are the hills, from three to four hundred feet high. Close on the rocky shore the kind people, who so cordially entertained us at Old Fort island, have their "winter quarters," while another family occupies the other side of the point. The little island opposite the house is one huge mass of rock, covered with scanty vegetation.

A remarkable formation exists just east of the house. You can pass by the large rock at the left of the building only at low tide, when you come to a sand cove and sand bar, the latter bare at high tide, that connects with another rocky mass, which, extending towards the sea, corresponds in its nature to the island above mentioned; all around is rock and mud, yet this little strip of sand is prominent and peculiar in its situation. The sea washes close up to it upon either side but does not cover it. A little way back is seen the slope of the embankment terrace and between the two the remains of a most curious structure. Here is represented the last remaining traces of the old colony, in the shape probably, of a concealed dock for boats and small vessels. It is an artificial pond, and, covered from all observation until this part of the bay is reached, its presence would never be expected unless looked for. A slight sand bank in that corner of the bay had so shut off this inlet that at low tide a natural basin of water was separated by this same sand bank from the water of the bay. This basin shows signs of being enlarged, deepened, and has an embankment around it the walls of which are kept in place by huge stones; these one can plainly see have been worked and built up around it. The stones are carefully arranged so that the bases are downward and the pointed or smallest end uppermost, while the interspaces are filled up with smaller stones and earth: the whole top is earthed over and covered around with a layer of large flat stones. This appears to preclude the possibility of the whole affair being a production of nature. Sheltered as it is, it would make an excellent hiding place or repairing place for small boats, which could easily make way over the bar at high water. Another peculiarity, however, presents itself; there is, at low tide, a drainage from the small basin into the sea through this sand bank.

Were there now no inlet to this small pond, as in fact there is, it would be drained twice a day while the tide was low, since it is very shallow at best. Advantage has been taken of this fact, apparently. A short passage has been made from the northeast side so that the brook, which I mentioned before as flowing in a channel through the embankment beyond, is somewhat slightly diverted so as to run into the basin. Now the fresh waters of this brook, running in at all times with a stream of several times the volume as the outflow at low tide, are continually freshening the waters in the basin, until before low tide is reached you have an artificial pond of clear, fresh water with sandy bottom and suitable for the cattle who come to its banks regularly to drink, and even the family supply is easily obtained quite pure enough for family purposes. The pond would therefore supply a large number both of cattle and of families. Though I have seen no evidence either for or against the theory that the early colonists had cattle with them, it seems to me at least very probable that such were, as I have suggested, the intentions of the people in making this peculiar structure. I will not now speak at length of the curious superstition of some of the people whom I have seen, that this structure in some way conceals large pots of gold left by the French, but will leave this and other superstitions of a like nature for some other time and place, if indeed they are worth mentioning at all.

Though there is little or no beach, properly speaking, the land slopes down quite close to the sea in one or two places; these have been chosen for building spots and houses erected accordingly. Back of the houses all is a dense mass of low, tangled spruce and fir, extending on and over the hills some distance into the interior.

I must here yield to a natural desire and describe to you two new species of birds which were procured here. The first, the Canada or tree sparrow (*Spizella monticola*) which is rare except in its migrations, apparently; the second, the long tailed duck (*Harelda glacialis*). The latter bird is called the *"coc-cau-wee,"* from the sound made by the males which resembles the pronunciation of these words. Another name for the birds is that of "hounds." The female resembles the female of another bird called the dipper or buffle head, sometimes the butter ball and spirit duck, but which is here called "sleepy diver," from the slowness of its movements in the water. The marked difference between the two is the absence of white on the wing of the long tailed duck; whether the young birds of the two species are distinguishable or not I could not ascertain. The people here cannot tell you which is the sleepy diver, as they call it, and which the female of the long tailed duck, or even distinguish the young, but call them all indiscriminately sleepy divers. It will never do for a stranger to tell them they are wrong; they think that you are the one wrong in all cases, and you cannot possibly convince them that a stranger can learn any more of any object connected with the region than the people of that region.

Wednesday the 13th. I shot a bird to-day that has a most peculiar name in the vocabulary of the natives; it is called by them the *Nan-cary*, pronounced as if spelt *nan-sary;* it is in fact the greater yellow legs (*Totanus melanoleucus*), and is more or less common in the late fall either singly or in small flocks along the beach with the small sandpipers and plovers.

Thursday the 14th. It seems as if I did little else but describe birds; but as there are more of these than of any other animals in the place, and as I have attempted to follow the outlines of my journal, I hope that in doing so I shall not render tedious a subject delightful in itself, but for which others may not care so much, while the omission of which would disarrange what I regard as the natural order of a series of articles of this kind. I will then tell you of still another new and somewhat rare species of bird, captured to-day, called the Lapland longspur (*Plectrophanes lapponicus*). The development of the hind claw of this bird is something remarkable, often reaching three-fourths of an inch or over. It is found either alone or in company with the immense flocks of snow buntings so common at the approach and departure of winter. The bird was feeding at dusk near the kelp on the shore and with several others probably of the same kind,—their flight and notes were like those of the shore lark so common here. It was rather wild, and was either a female or young bird. Though having seen the bird several times to my certain knowledge, I only succeeded in shooting a single specimen.

The wind has blown pretty hard all day. It seems no unusual thing for a wind storm to set in and last several days here, while often the wind blows with such force that it is dangerous to attempt any sort of navigation. Strange to say an Indian canoe ("cranky" as it is generally regarded) will "ride" with apparent safety where any other boat would be swamped in an instant.

Though the wind was not really severe, this afternoon, we had hard work to manage the boat to and from Old Fort bay, where we went to take a load of articles to be transferred to "winter quarters." The cold weather is rapidly coming on, and we must be prepared for it by moving into our winter home before very long. It is a desolate looking region, I assure you, but we will try and make things as comfortable as we can for all that. We have had several ravens hovering about the fish stage to-day; the people seem to regard them as birds of ill omen, and say that they are in league with the devil. You can rarely get any of the natives to shoot at one of these birds no matter how near they come, and they seem positively afraid of the results of so doing, fearing that it will bring them misfortune for the remainder of the year. The bird is really a very difficult one to shoot. I have often lain in wait for it with my gun, firing at it when both at rest and on the wing, at a very short distance off, and had it raise its huge black wings and fly slowly off with a harsh and hollow croak as much as if to defy both me and my gun. I have wasted more extra large ducking charges at the raven than almost any other bird, and have seen the least results. The bird itself is very common everywhere, summer and winter; breeding on the high cliffs and hill tops, and remaining about wherever there was any putrid flesh. It apparently loves to walk or fly about on the tops of the hilly crests on the mainland, and on the trees near the frozen bays in winter. It frequents the seacoast, and is common about the inland ponds and lakes. It replaces the crow, which rarely though occasionally is found in these regions. The scientific name for the raven is *Corvus corax*.

Friday the 15th. I became quite well acquainted to-day with the pigeon, as it is here called, otherwise known as the black guillemot (*Uria grylle*). This little bird is one of the most abundant of the waterfowl next to the eider ducks and Murres, that we have upon the coast. Near St. Augustine we saw this bird for the first time though it is found all along the Atlantic coast, as far south as New Jersey, growing more and more rare as it approaches the latter place where it was found in winter. I have seen them everywhere in the waters in and about the islands, though never very far from land, from the opening of the bay in the spring until the ice closes the last open waters early in December. I have found several stages of plumage (referable to the ages) of this bird which takes three years to mature. A very extraordinary form marks the second year's growth. The whole plumage is inky black both below and above, and with white blotches imperfectly rounded, the size of an ordinary thimble head, scattered irregularly all over it above and below; the bill is blackish carmine, the legs and feet dusky carmine. The wings with a pure white patch as usual. I think the white tail coverts were present, but am not sure on this point. I cannot learn that this plumage appears at any other time than in the fall of the year; they are rare here, and apparently pass this stage in some wild place or region where they are not easily detected. The hunters about the coast told me that they were rare.

In the early fall the pigeon is quite tame, but grows wilder as the cold weather advances. When pursuing them from a boat they are at times easy to approach while at others difficult and very wild without any apparent reason. It will usually dive "at the flash," but often when feeding it allows you to come quite near. In feeding, the bird bends its neck forward and dips its beak into the water; at this time, when the head is turned forward and a little away from the hunter, he is generally sure of hitting his game. Often the pigeon takes wing nearly as soon as it perceives a boat approaching, and it is then impossible to get anywhere within shooting distance of it; the flight is then rapid but easy, generally low and straight. When tame it usually escapes by diving "at the flash" and swimming a great distance under water, easily and in any direction. When wounded, they often dive, and, I think after the manner of many ducks, swim to the bottom and clinging to the seaweed die there. I have often watched them dive thus, but have not seen them arise. They stay around near the land feeding, on still warm days, often many together. In flying low over the water, if fired at I have often seen them suddenly drop down and dive, disappearing almost instantly. The flesh, especially of the young birds, is excellent eating and they are shot in great numbers; it is called the hardest bird to kill, next to a loon, that inhabits the waters of the coast.

The pigeon breeds in large numbers on several of the small islands along the coast. On one small island colonies of this bird breed exclusively. They lay usually three eggs in some exposed situation or in the cleft of some rock, making no nest, and let the sun do the greatest share of the hatching; they are oblong and ovoid in shape, tapering suddenly, the ground color being from greenish to pure white, and the varied streaks and blotches or spots scattered more or less thickly all over their surface, especially so in a ring around the top of the egg, are of black, or various shades of brown. Nearly all the birds of this family have what are apparently purplish spots, but these are black primarily and appear purple only from a slight covering of the white lime of the shell itself.

The weather had now become so moderated that the next few days were employed in "moving in," that is, in transferring the household goods and utensils together with the people and live stock into their abode for the long, coming winter. The house was much like the one we were about to leave, but rather more compact and a great deal warmer.

With the exception of a species of short-eared owl, peculiar to the region, no particularly new birds had been obtained. Though owls are generally regarded as rare in this region, I believe them more common than usually supposed, several of the brown colored species having been observed. In regard to the one mentioned, it was shot by one of the men who said that about dusk the bird attacked him and he could not drive it away until he had put the whole charge of shot through its body, and so badly blown it to pieces that I was unable to do anything with it but save a few feathers by which to determine the species. It appears to be an extraordinarily dark variety of our common short-eared owl (*Brachyotus palustris*).

CHAPTER VII.

Indian tents — New fields for research — Visit to the Indians — Seals' flesh — Dogskin boots — Cattle food in hard winters — *Coptis trifolia* — Spruce Partridge — Inland — Hypothesis of Aurora — Little Auk — Signs of wreck — Ascent of the western arm of the bay — Wreck of the Edward Cardwell — Picking up lumber — First snowstorm of the winter.

WE had hardly entered the bay before we saw in the distance the *mishwaps* of the Indians, who had chosen this for their camping place. The Indian *mishwap*, or tent, is a peculiarly arranged structure, and suited only to the wants of the people who occupy it; being the usual, movable dwelling place of this nomadic and roving people. It is generally called by the name of *wigwam*, and is the same, very nearly, as the tent-like structures that go by that name in western North America. It is composed of long, thin, rounded sticks that have been hardened by charring in the fire, and which are set about in a circle whose ground diameter is some ten feet; the tops loosely put together overlap each other a foot or eighteen inches. Around this are layers of birch bark, and over the bark more sticks are placed so as to fall each one between the other two all around the outside. All holes are then patched and covered; while the top remains loosely open to allow the smoke and bad odors to escape. A small opening in front permits the inhabitants to enter or leave by stooping very low indeed. The peculiarity about these abodes, and the feature that characterizes them even when seen at a distance, is the plume-like appearance of the top, as it is thus constituted. I know of no mere piling together of sticks that will produce this peculiar arrangement. By it, these tents can be distinguished as far as they can be seen. That the structure may not be visible a great distance, it is generally placed behind some protecting ledge or rise of rocks, though not always.

From the entrance of the bay then, as I have said, we caught a view of the Indian mishwaps, backed by the verdure of slopes, hills, ravines, ridges, and the various contour of a most uneven background in the profile of the evergreen spruce tops,—which low shrub is everywhere abundant outside as is the large tree inland.

On either hand a succession of hilly crests marked the boundary of the bay, whose inner arm or bend extended far to the right. Passing beyond the little island just off the central point, we came in full view of the house, with its line of rocky and sandy beach running around on either side; here we were soon seated by a roaring and crackling fire of good spruce wood.

Old Fort bay has much the general shape and direction of so many of the bays in this vicinity, so often termed "fiord valleys." They are long, narrow, for the most part shallow passages, between the rocks running a little north of east, and evidently of glacial origin. These little bays are quite abundant all up and down the coast, and undoubtedly would, at least to one well versed in such readings, describe a long and ancient story of glacial phenomena and local disturbances. The whole glacial question will finally, without doubt, obtain abundance of fresh, new, and useful evidence by a careful study of this region, and it is a wonder that no one has examined with a greater degree of care the whole Labrador peninsula. Here is a vast, and untried field for exploration. The North Pole is undoubtedly the ultimate end of research in this direction, but I venture to affirm that no one will be successful in that end until they have made a careful land exploration of this keystone to polar investigation, the Labrador Peninsula—from seacoast inward to the "height of land," and thence followed its great streams and leading trends of northward highlands. The greatest wonder is that as yet we have no definite knowledge of this new and unexplored field. But to return :—

After a good supper we went to visit the Indians and Joe Mark, the sub-chief of this division of the tribe. We found him, to speak plainly, in a state of beastly intoxication. He had come out to sell his furs, and having received sufficient to supply his demands for food he had used the surplus for drink, and that a little too freely, judging from the effects wrought upon his mind and body. He was lying down when we entered, but he managed to place himself in a half sitting and half lying attitude and carry on a conversation with a great deal of "talk-um" on our part and considerable muttering on his. We saw how matters stood, and soon came away and returned home; not, however, until we had obtained part of a young seal, that some one of the Indians had recently killed, and which we broiled on a spider for our breakfast the next morning. Let me say here, that the flesh of a young seal, when well cooked, resembles cow's liver so nearly that one can hardly tell the difference; and I believe that if I could place a dish of each before a stranger in Labrador who had tasted neither for a long series of months he would be unable to tell accurately which was which, so nearly do they resemble each other. We also obtained some dried deer's meat, which is soaked and fried, or eaten dry, and is very good.

Monday the 25th. I put on, to-day, my first pair of Indian, dogskin boots. They are made like long legged moccasins, the foot part being made of sealskin (the top only of dogskin), and the sole being soft and pliable, and as sensitive as a glove upon the hand. The foot is therefore free to move in most any direction, and thus useful especially in climbing, where one is obliged to grasp and cling by the clinch of the toes. It is quite trying however, to walk for the first few times on stony or pebbly ground, as the little corners injure the feet most terribly until they become hardened and accustomed to the peculiar feeling of having the bottom of the boot soft and flexible instead of hard and stiff; but one soon gets used to the change and then enjoys the freedom of *feeling* with the foot.

Wednesday the 27th. I attempted a sort of exploration of the country back of the hills, close behind the house, but found nothing but ponds and high hills, so that with a great deal of climbing and going around to get a very short distance only, I was obliged to return at dark having accomplished very little.

I made a curious discovery this evening. On returning home from one of these short daily trips I noticed a large pile of heavy brush lying over against the side of the stable door (why I had not seen it before I cannot tell), and upon inquiry found that it was the remains of the birch and alder tops with which the cattle had been fed the previous spring. It seems that, at this time of the year, when fodder is scarce, the cattle are fed with the slender, tender tops of these trees, and they are eaten with avidity and apparent relish.

About this time I discovered the plant *Coptis trifolia*, or golden thread, from the little, slender golden thread of a root which it possesses. It grows in abundance in these regions and farther west, and is plucked and sent to market in large quantities. It is a mild tonic and treated with hot water is taken with impunity.

One day, early this week, one of the men brought in a spruce partridge (*Tetrao Canadensis*), which he had killed in the woods. These birds are usually very tame. They fly from cover and alight in some bush, seemingly stupefied from being flushed, while I have often known the young fellows to knock them over with sticks or the ends of their gun barrels, without even taking the trouble to waste powder and shot upon them. One day towards the close of the week we amused ourselves by digging a species of clam (questionably *Mya arenaria*), which is found in the mud at low tide just here, in abundance. They were excellent eating, and made a very good soup. Strange to say, though they appear to be abundant here, the people seem to care very little for them, and seldom dig them.

Friday, November the 2d. Although this morning I climbed the ridge back of the house, and over and about the place that many of the people suppose to have been the location of the old times fortification and fort, but which appears upon examination to present few facts to confirm such an opinion; and though I also went over all the nearer peaks on this side of the first pond which is just over the ridge, I am in as much of a maze, apparently, as I was before, as to their exact position and extent. From the top of the successive elevations I could see pond after pond, and ridges and gullies after ridges and gullies, stretching onward and outward in every direction. A fair description of the country around here would be a series of ridges composed of crests of unequal height divided both lengthwise and crosswise by gullies, with basins of water filling the intervening spaces or valleys. The whole region is one grand network of ponds and hills. I had no instruments with me for the purpose, and if I had possessed them, am no map drawer. As has been before stated, a comparison of several readings of the barometer gives the height of the external ridge as 275 feet above the level of the sea to which it slopes easily and naturally. The pond beyond this ridge presents a lowering of fifty feet, while beyond this other ponds are situated correspondingly lower, the large pond or lake being lower yet. The hills on the left are most of them on a nearly average height—the two highest being each 600 feet above the sea level, and all the other prominent ones nearly an even 500.

If I mistake not, evidences of glacial and water action are locally very abundant, while loose bowlders and stones are scattered sparingly all along the top crests even, and small pools of water are abundant here and there on the highland levels four to five hundred feet above the sea. Here the soil is a black muck or mud, and reminds one greatly of some mucky patch of salt marsh along our eastern United States, exposed a few feet only at highest tide, and transported to some shallow basin between two or three surrounding peaks of similar height. In one instance, I found a large pond only one hundred feet from the top of the highest peaks which surrounded it. The gulches were frequent and full of streams, in some of which, especially in deep, shady gullies, were remarkably sweet and cold waters. All these places are overgrown with low, dwarf spruce and fir, or birch and alder. In one place a small stream started from near the top of a high peak. There was no chance for mere surface drainage, and there must either have been some secret spring or sort of artesian well pressure, forcing the water thus to appear on the very top of a rocky crest. The rock around seemed to be a coarse granite, with occasionally a place where several feet had been apparently scraped off and ground to a fine powder of sand and small pieces of rock, of feldspar principally, scattered all along over the surface of the underlying rock. Occasionally, veins of feldspar or quartz appear; the latter mineral is rarely found in a pure state on this coast. All the exposed rock appeared thus more or less scraped about here, while occasionally the patch extended down the slope of the hill one-third or even one-half the way to the bottom. There are also many small rounded cones or knolls, whose top is one mass of rough sand, with the rock only a few inches beneath. Another curious fact is that the beaches of most of the ponds have a portion at least of their extent of this same material, the rocks in place lying a little way from the edge only; the rest of the beach is often of a fine pulverized quartz and feldspar sand, totally different from material of the neighboring rocks. Fine beds of clear, nearly straw colored sand are not uncommon.

Wednesday, the 3d. We were fortunate in observing a most beautiful aurora this evening. The barometer indicated 29.00, and the thermometer 30° Fahrenheit. The sky was perfectly free from clouds, and the air crisp. It first appeared in the east, then in the north. The primary appearance was, as is frequent in such cases, a semicircular band of light. In this case small pencils of light floated about in the air. Very soon a thick, heavy band of several longitudinal scroll-like narrower bands appeared; the whole, resembling very much a long ribbon, extended itself across the horizon from these points, and apparently very low down in the atmosphere. The whole band was in rapid undulating motion from the north towards the east, and resembled the progressive onward motion of a huge serpent. The appearance was quite striking and very pretty. The band was extraordinarily dense, and very bright. At first its edges were very clean cut and well-defined; gradually the light extended itself to the northeast, while the eastern end enlarging and travelling faster than the northern, the mass soon presented a singular and nearly circular appearance in the northeast; ten minutes after this massing together of the light the whole disappeared, and the sky was entirely overcast with a light, thin, luminous curtain of this mysterious, electrical, vaporous substance. I saw many very pretty auroras while here, but none surpassed the one just described. I found some of the inhabitants of this region singularly superstitious regarding this aurora, in that they fully believed that it danced to the sound of any musical instrument. It was solemnly declared to me that if I should blow the flute, or play upon the violin, the cloud would descend and dance in the air just above me and out of reach. On the subject of this curious phenomenon, Mr. Richard A. Proctor says:—

"One of the most mysterious and beautiful of Nature's manifestations promises soon to disclose its secret. The brilliant streamers of colored light which wave at certain seasons over the heavens have long since been recognized as among the most singular and impressive of all the phenomena which the skies present to our view. There is something surpassingly beautiful in the appearance of the thin "Auroral curtain." Fringed with colored streamers it waves to and fro as though shaken by some unseen hand. Then from end to end there passes a succession of undulations, the folds of the curtain interwrapping and forming a series of graceful curves. Suddenly, and as by magic, there succeeds a perfect stillness, as though the unseen power which had been displaying the varied beauties of the auroral curtain were resting for a moment. But even while the motion of the curtain is stilled we see its light mysteriously waxing and waning. Then as we gaze, fresh waves of disturbance traverse the magic canopy. Startling coruscations add splendor to the scene, while the nobler span of the auroral arch from which the waving curtain seems to depend gives a grandeur to the spectacle which no words can adequately describe. Gradually, however, the celestial fires which have illuminated the gorgeous arch seem to die out. The luminous zone breaks up. The scene of the display becomes covered with scattered streaks and patches of ashen-gray light, which hang like clouds over the northern heavens. Then these in turn disappear, and nothing remains of the brilliant spectacle but a dark smoke-like segment on the horizon.

"Hitherto the nature of the aurora has been a mystery to men of science. Let it be premised, then, that physicists had long since recognized in the aurora a phenomenon of more than local, of more even than terrestrial significance. They had learned to associate it with relations which affect the whole planetary scheme.

"Arago was engaged in watching from day to day, and from year to year, the vibrations of the magnetic needle in the Paris Observatory. In Jan., 1819, he published a statement to the effect that the sudden changes of the magnetic needle are often associated with the occurrence of an aurora." The statements are then given in his own words, and from them the following deduction is made: *"From all this it appears incontestably that there is an intimate connection between the causes of auroras and those of terrestrial magnetism."*

This strange hypothesis, was, at first, much opposed by scientific men, but gradually it was found that physicists had mistaken the character of the auroral display. It appeared that the magnetic needle not only swayed responsively to auroras observable in the immediate neighborhood, but to auroras in progress hundreds, or even thousands of miles away. It has been found that a much closer bond of sympathy exists between the magnetized needle and the auroral streamers than even Arago had supposed. It is not merely the case that while an auroral display is in progress, the needle is subject to unusual disturbance, but the movements of the needle are actually synchronous with the waving movements of the mysterious streamers.

"I may notice in passing that two very interesting conclusions follow from this peculiarity: First, every magnetic needle over the whole earth must be simultaneously disturbed; and, secondly, the auroral streamers which wave across the skies of one country must move synchronously with those which are visible in the skies of another country, even though thousands of miles may separate the two regions.

"Could we only associate auroras with terrestrial magnetism, we should still have done much to enhance the interest which the beautiful phenomena are calculated to excite. But when once this association has been established, others of even greater interest are brought into recognition; for"— I take the liberty of italicizing for emphasis this portion which is printed in Roman in the text—"*terrestrial magnetism has been clearly shown to be influenced directly by the action of the sun.*"

"We already begin to see, then, that auroras are associated in some mysterious way with the action of the solar rays. The phenomena which have been looked upon for so many ages as a mere spectacle, caused perhaps by some process in the upper regions of the air, of a simply local character, have been brought into the range of planetary phenomena.

"Most of my readers have doubtless heard of the zodiacal light, and many of them have perhaps seen that mysterious radiance, pointing obliquely upward from the western horizon, soon after sunset in the spring months, or in autumn shortly before sunrise, above the eastern horizon. The light, as its name indeed implies, lies upon that region of the heavens along which the planets travel. Accordingly, astronomers have associated it with the planetary orbits, and have come to look on it as formed by the light reflected from a multitude of minute bodies travelling around the sun within the orbit of our earth." After a short account of the spectroscope and its use in analyzing substances especially those reflecting light or luminous in themselves, he says: "Recently, however, zodiacal light has been analyzed by Angström, with a result altogether unexpected, and at present almost unintelligible. *Its spectrum exhibits a bright line, and this bright line is the same that is seen in the spectrum of the aurora borealis!*"

Furthermore: "Of all the phenomena presented to the contemplation of astronomers, the tails of comets are undoubtedly the most perplexing. Now there is one feature of comets' tails that has long since attracted attention, and will remind the reader of the peculiarities common to the zodiacal and the auroral light. We refer to the sudden changes of brilliancy, and the instantaneous lengthening and shortening of these appendages. And the eminent mathematician Euler was led by the observation of similar appearances to put forward the theory ' *That there is a great affinity between these tails, the zodiacal light, and the aurora borealis.*' .. It is far from being unlikely that these long vexed questions—the nature of the aurora, that of the zodiacal light, and that of comets' tails—will receive their solution simultaneously;" and he further adds: "I had scarcely completed the above pages when news was brought from America that the spectrum of the sun's corona, as seen during the recent total solar eclipse, exhibited the same bright lines as the aurora. Lastly, it has been found that the peculiar phosphorescent light, sometimes visible all over the sky at night, gives the same spectrum (very faint of course) as the aurora and the zodiacal light. What we learn certainly, therefore, from the facts above stated, is this—that substances of the same sort emit the light of the aurora, of the zodiacal gleam, the tails of comets, of the sun's corona, and of the phosphorescence which illuminates at times the nocturnal skies. But when once we have reason—as in the case of the aurora we undoubtedly have—to associate electricity with any particular form of luminosity, we seem clearly justified in extending the explanation to the same form of luminosity wherever it may appear."

Although I have already taxed your patience with long quotations of such a strictly scientific character, I cannot conclude them without giving Prof. Proctor's own deductions from this series of arranged facts. He says:—

"I believe that the key to the whole series of phenomena dealt with above lies in the existence of myriads of meteoric bodies travelling separately or in systems around the sun. They are consumed in thousands daily by our own atmosphere. They probably pour in countless millions upon the solar atmosphere, and from what we know of their numbers in our own neighborhood, and of the probability of their being infinitely more numerous in the neighborhood of the sun, we have excellent reasons for believing that to them, principally, is due the appearance of the zodiacal light and the solar corona."

I have occupied much more time in the discussion of this most interesting and highly instructive theme than I had intended, but, as you can see, the phenomena dealt with could not have been explained with less. We will now pass on to some of the less scientifically important, but still, we will trust, interesting portions of our diary.

Just here a short account of one of the characteristic birds of this region may be of interest. I refer to the little auk, or sea dove (*Mergulus alle*), so common some years in the waters about the islands and harbors all along the coast. From Oct. 15th until the ice set in, I found these little fellows common everywhere in the waters of the bays and harbors, and they were generally quite tame. The people here regard their arrival as a sign of cold weather, but it certainly did not prove to be the case this year, since the birds were unusually abundant and the year an unusually mild one. The popular and local name is *Bonne homme* (the French for good fellow) and is pronounced as if spelled *Bunnum*. It associates with the black guillemot, and possesses with it many habits in common. It dives at the flash of the gun, swims long distances under the water, but is generally very tame and quite easy to approach though quick in its movements. I have seen them killed with an oar after a long chase in a boat. When first taking flight they half fly and half push themselves along the surface of the water, since their small wings make it very difficult for them to fly freely. I have seen one pursued in a boat by a number of men who amused themselves by throwing the oars and pieces of wood, together with the ballast of the boat at it, not a single missile hitting its mark, since the bird was able to dodge each article thrown at it by diving and appearing in a most contrary direction from that looked for; to the surprise of all the bird at last escaped without so much as a single wound. I have noticed nearly all the changes of plumage in this bird that I have seen in the pigeon during the first year, though the head, so far as I have seen, is always black. It is a familiar little fellow, and seldom killed, unless scarcity of food demands it.

Thursday the 4th. Some of the men started off early this morning hunting for logs or pieces of wood from what appears to be a wreck. The lookout in these regions for wrecks is at all times sharp and continued. It not unfrequently happens that a barque or brig, and in one or two cases a steamer, going from Quebec or Montreal to Newfoundland or Liverpool, is lost or led astray by the fog and wrecked on some of the many treacherous rocks on this part of the coast. Only yesterday one of the men returned with a large piece of the bulwarks of some ship that had been evidently cast away. It looked quite fresh, and hearing in addition that one of the owners of a large establishment here had sent in a hurry for several men to help him do some work the nature of which he was shrewd enough to withhold, we fairly concluded that there must be a wreck somewhere near. While they were away investigating the matter I took my gun and started off, proposing to climb the ridge on the western arm of the bay and see what results might be obtained in that quarter.

I first ascended the hill at the foot of the bay. The path was an old Indian foot path, and most of the way ascended almost perpendicularly. I reached a level after much trouble, and found that the needle of my barometer registered three hundred feet above the sea's level. I then went carefully all over the top of the height, and was much interested in finding the singular features presented. The elevation seemed to be a plateau three to five hundred feet high, with several crests arising from seventy-five to one hundred feet higher, but with a general level at the distance given above. There were several small ponds, much mucky ground, and several patches of what we should call, on the seashore, mud flats. Deep ravines were plentiful, and several times I found myself suddenly and without premonition within a few feet of a perpendicular wall of rock,—in fact once a regular precipice reaching several hundred feet below and nearly to the sea level. The whole ridge is divided by a deep gully through which a large stream flows from a chain of ponds, the first of which could be barely seen in the distance, and which is full of trout, the inhabitants tell me. Between the shore and the southwest side of this stream the ridges continue but they are cut up with more gorges than the northeastern portion. I found no less than three deep clefts, starting from near a common centre and running in contrary directions down to the sea. Beyond is a deep cliff, and several small gullies, running into a large open place that must have reached nearly to the sea level, which presented an almost impassable barrier to the coast line. After a long detour I at length reached the beach, or rather the place where there might have been a beach, and found nothing but rock close to the edge of the water, with no sign of a footing anywhere. I clambered over the rocks for about three-quarters of a mile and found a perpendicular face of rock that must be climbed or return must be made as I had come. Determined not to return I with difficulty climbed over one hundred feet of this precipice, when I am confident that a single false step would have sent me to the rocks at the bottom, and thence around the edge of the face of the rock. I had but about two miles to go to reach home, but three times I was obliged to climb steep heights from near the sea level to about two hundred and fifty feet above (where often the undergrowth of thick and tangled spruce alone would have made the ascent quite difficult) and three times descend again. It was half tide and I could not walk around as it is possible to do at dead low tide. The top level of the hills above was protected by overhanging ledges so that I could not ascend them; thus I was obliged to pursue a winding course over the outstanding ridges of the rocks to the eastern face of the cliff. It took full five hours for me to accomplish the distance home, short as it was.

Friday the 5th. This morning I saw the tracks of a small herd of deer that had passed during the night. They were plainly visible for a long distance on the thick, spongy moss which everywhere carpets the ridge just back of the house. Towards evening the men returned bringing the looked-for news—not that we wished a vessel to be wrecked for our special benefit, but should there be one we desired to know of it and see it if possible,—there had been a large brig wrecked on her passage from Montreal to England laden with lumber. The men reported the harbors and coves everywhere along the shores as full of logs and deal boards. The crew, it appears, were saved, but the vessel was a total wreck. As a short account of this wreck may be of interest I append the facts as, being present, I was able to obtain them.

It was on the evening of November 30, that the boat and men returned from a short sail up the bay, where they had been to visit some traps that had been set there, bringing with them news that a large piece of the bulwark of a vessel was lying above high tide on one of the islands, and that to all appearances there had been a vessel wrecked during the preceding stormy weather. I think that it was later in the same day we heard that a gang of men had been sent for in a great hurry by one of the chief men on the coast, for the ostensible purpose of doing some work on the framework of a building that he had for some time proposed constructing; putting together these two circumstances it seemed safe to conclude that something unusual had occurred, and it also seemed equally safe to suppose that that something was a shipwreck.

In such a locality as this, remote from habitation, the struggle for life is by no means easy; and at such a season as this, when time hangs heavy, it is not to be wondered at that the news and this probable interpretation of it spread like fire, and everybody was awake to be off and see what was to be seen, or find what was to be found. The people about could hardly wait until the next morning before starting off in their boats, and it was yet early, in fact before daylight, that a party from the house, with a small sack of provisions, in case they should be obliged to stay away over night, started in search of the supposed wreck. Those of us who remained at home of course did our best at speculating as to the results of the search, but it was not until the next day that we learned the truth. Meanwhile, several parties, also much excited over the news, called upon us in the evening, they also eager to be off. We fed and housed them for the night, and with them indulged in all kinds of speculations as to the probabilities and possibilities of the case. As yet none of us knew the real state of affairs outside, but that there must have been a shipwreck, no one seemed to deny. Then came the questions: Where was it? How was it? When was it?

As each of these questions was discussed separately by all parties present, it was some time before they were disposed of; when they were, we varied the conversation with queries as to the size of the ship and nature of her cargo. Of course all united in the hope that she might be a large vessel, and laden with provisions, as that is the thing most needed here; but we could hardly hope that the reality would equal our hopes and expectations, and it was finally agreed that should the cargo of the supposed ship, that we felt sure had been wrecked, prove to be lumber, we should be equally satisfied.

The party that had just gone from the house proposed staying over night at a neighboring island, and to proceed along the coast of the various islands and mainland the next morning hoping to make discoveries; the party that had just arrived, too late to accompany the first, seemed unsettled as to what to do. In fact they were so wrought with excitement that they seemed ready for almost anything. Although it was already night when they arrived, some proposed rowing at once to the island, where the first party had gone, a distance of four miles, at least, and with them, starting off the next morning. We easily dissuaded them, from such an attempt, however, and talking over the outlook of the case we passed away the time until slumber called us all to its embrace. The next morning we waited patiently for our party to return (as our friends of last night had left early) and relieve our suspense, for we too shared a feeling of anxiety as to the result; but it was afternoon before the boat returned, and not until then that our desires were at least partially gratified. The relics brought home in the boat gave us no longer any room to doubt that there had been a tolerably good sized wreck somewhere. There were iron and copper bolts, hinges, bits of rope, a bed sacking, a box of books, a long pipe, a blacking brush, and any amount of small material that had been picked up around the shores of the islands, but what presented the most substantial evidence of the disaster was a genuine barrel of flour, superfine extra. The men were full of news. The islands swarmed with deal boards and logs everywhere. Oak and pine lay about in confusion. Here was then at least an answer to one of our questions. There had been a shipwreck to the westward; how far as yet we did not know, and the lumber, of which the cargo must have been largely if not wholly composed, lay around us, and could be had not for the asking, but for the picking up.

The boat soon unloaded, and the men provided with their dinners; we then began to look about us, and prepare for another cruise, to find out, if possible, where the wreck was. We were soon ready, and getting into the boat started on our expedition. Knowing that the wreck was to the west, as the drift of the logs and deal was from that direction, we made up our minds to stop that night (as it was nearly night when we started off) at the house of a neighbor, about four miles up the coast. It was now nearly dark, the wind had gone down, and, much against our wills, we were compelled to take down sail and row. Three stout fellows at the oars, however much the swell might take the boat, were more than a match for the waves, and she spun along at least seemingly fast, until we had rounded the corner of the bay, and come into still rougher waters.

We passed one or two boats, and thought little of it at the time; we afterwards found that they were on the same errand as ourselves. After a couple of hours of hard struggling at the oars, we came in sight of a glimmer of light down the bay or deep cove past the headland that had just been rounded; soon it became brighter, and we passed into the more quiet waters within the bay, and rapidly approached the beacon and its well known shelter. It was quite dark when we moored our boat alongside of the rocks. We saw to our surprise, in the same shelter, and within a stone's throw from us, the boats of nearly all the people on the coast, for a dozen miles eastward. It seemed that other people had come in search of the wreck as well as ourselves, and showed us strangers the rapidity with which news travels even on this coast, where the houses are four, six, or ten miles apart. Surprised as we were, we finished mooring, and started towards the house. The scene that burst upon us reminded one strongly of some fanciful legend of pirates or sea-robbers. Here the dark outline of the house, back of which tall cliffs frowned out a gloomy reception, was lighted up by a fire on the rocks to the right of the doorway, around which was assembled a group of men who went and came in and out of the darkness beyond the flames. A crane hung over the fire and kettles were suspended a little above the flames containing the tea of the several parties who formed the group; to the left of the house a wide expanse of darkness wrapped the cliffs, the water, and the ground in one sea of dusk. Approaching the house, the scene presented a livelier aspect and we were better able to see about us. The house of our friend had been literally taken possession of. Later in the evening when more boats had arrived, we counted twenty-four persons who had thus invaded this retreat, and established themselves until morning.

You may imagine the confusion of twenty good voices in loud conversation (loud talking seems to be the rule with the people on the coast) over the prospects; add to this the excitement which prevailed on every hand, and the bustle over the dishes, as party after party (each of whom, by the way, brought their own provisions) sat down or rose up from table, and you have the scene complete,— no, not complete, for the room was none too warm, it being a cold night out and the atmosphere breathed and felt of tobacco smoke so forcibly, that one could "cut it," as the expression is.

After a great deal of talking and listening at the time, with what was learned afterwards, I have prepared with a great deal of care the following story of the wreck:—

WRECK OF THE EDWARD CARDWELL.

The Edward Cardwell, a full rigged barquentine, bound from Quebec, P. Q., to Liverpool, England, after several days out (how many we did not learn), encountered dense fogs off the banks, and for about three days had been sailing in this uncertainty, feeling her way slowly along, the officers not knowing where they were going, but supposing themselves somewhere near the Newfoundland shores. At one time the fog lifted for a few moments, and then the white beacon of Whale island met their view, but the immediate shutting down of a still denser fog left them again in the uncertain condition in which they had been before. Steering as near as possible in the direction of the beacon, it was not until rocks suddenly loomed up near by that the pilot found himself at the entrance of a narrow pass near a rocky shoal with the mainland some half a mile on the left. The ship was under too much headway, though it was moving but slowly at best, to stop or back out of her perilous position. The pilot headed her straight for the opening, and called to all hands to prepare themselves for the shock. One young man sprang to the cabin door and called to the captain, who not having time even to take up his watch, which was lost, rushed on deck only just in time to secure a place in the boat, which the frantic men had lowered, and were about severing from its fastenings to the ship. The ship struck and went to pieces in a few hours afterwards; the crew, nineteen men, were just saved, but having lost all. The men rowed to the neighboring shore, and finding the empty summer house of a Mr. Belvin, one of the inhabitants of the coast, they broke in the door and made a fire, remaining there that night. In the morning they took one of Mr. Belvin's boats, as their own had been destroyed, and rowed along the coast and islands until they reached the abode of Mr. W. H. Whiteley, about fifteen miles from the wreck, where they tarried until they were soon after carried to Greeley island lighthouse, from which place they were taken to the Newfoundland coast, and thus reached some port from which they took passage home. Mr. Whiteley, the Magistrate of the coast, agrees substantially with my statement. The ship went to pieces soon after it struck, and the next morning (Tuesday) logs, deals, and rubbish of all sorts were to be found everywhere on the mainland and islands to the eastward. The vessel contained few provisions, but these were mostly lost in deep water. The rocks where she struck are called on the chart the Porpoise rocks, and the water about the shoal varies from nine to thirteen, and even thirty fathoms; the distance to the mainland is about a mile, and from the opposite coast of Newfoundland some thirty miles.

Let us now return to the cottage and see what is going on there. The evening wears slowly away, the men enjoy themselves and pass their time in smoking and talking. Some are jovial and hearty in their manner, while others, quite the reverse, are gloomy and morose. It is easy to see who are friendly and who avoid each other, for the men cluster together and engage in low or loud conversation as the subject of which they talk be private or public, while others sit in the corners, on the floor, or in chairs resting their heads upon their hands, or, leaning against the wall, are far in the land of slumbers. One man stands warming himself with his hands behind him, and his face away from the stove facing the crowd, while another perhaps will be talking loudly and boisterously, gesturing violently at the same time as if to impress the group more with a sense of his own importance than to give a statement of the real condition of some important issue; perhaps this same person will soon change his position to a slight bend of the head and body as, with one finger held up very near to his eye, he makes an outward and downward gesture, as he delivers himself of some whispered secret opinion, at the same time that, having delivered his opinion, he straightens himself up with the air of one who has relieved himself of a, to him, tremendous thought.

In one way or another the time flies. One by one the men stretch themselves on the boxes and benches in the corners; tipped up in the chairs, and on the floor besides the fire, they doze off to catch a poor apology for sleep in these uncomfortable positions. We can only get intervals of rest as somebody is constantly opening and shutting the door in passing in and out; this occasions so much noise and cold air that soon even the air from the stove grows chilled and we with it.

At length, after a number of twistings and vain attempts to sleep the earliest of this adventuresome party arouse the rest by their preparations for early starting in the shape of making a fire, boiling the kettle, and preparing and eating an early breakfast. Between three and four o'clock the first party leave, and are followed by the others at intervals of different length, but near enough to each other to prevent our going to sleep again, until at daylight we are about the last to leave the house with a good warm breakfast in place of a good night's sleep.

As most of the other boats are engaged in a similar expedition as ourselves, to follow us will be to follow them. The wind is against us and the waves are high, but we start off without much trouble and row, head to the wind and waves, out into the passage and towards the nearest island. The shore is plainly visible as we row along, and a sharp lookout soon discovers a log lying on the beach and a deal close by; we row to them and have soon carried the deal above high water mark while we note the place for future use; beyond are several more deals, and further on others; soon we come to a cove full of strewn rubbish composed of bits of wood and hay and straw, with many sticks and broken boards while several large oak and pine logs lie, as they have been tossed by the waves, wedged in between the stone and rocks. These logs are, as are most of those found, from eighteen inches to two feet in width and thickness, and from thirty to fifty feet in length; while the deal are about two inches thick, from ten to eighteen inches wide and about twelve feet long. Each is of three qualities and stamped with the Quebec market initials of "A. F. A. K." or with the word "Montmorenci." With considerable difficulty the big logs are pried over and over until they reach the water when an iron bolt is fastened to them and a rope attached drags them out into the water where the tide, which is on the flood, rises sufficiently to float them.

In this way a raft or rather tow is soon made of four fine, pine logs and, elated with our success as wreckers on a small scale, we start off for home. In a day or two the deals were found floating about by hundreds, and the work of collecting them as also of marking and tying the logs to identify them, continued all the fall and even into the winter. This is the first wreck that has occurred on the coast, near here at least, for over thirty years, I think, if my information is correct; and though we certainly wish no harm to anybody, we can but rejoice that the misfortune of the ship will be so fortunate for the people of the coast.

Wednesday, Nov. 10th. The men have spent a greater part of the day cutting wood. Those who can obtain wood near by without the necessity of going into the interior up the river, and rafting it down, as many of them do, content themselves with a smaller article, and continue to make clearings in the low spruce and fir about their own place. The majority of this wood varies from four to six and even seven inches in diameter, while the trees are rarely over fifteen feet in height. The tree is cut, the branches trimmed, and the limbs thrown in a pile upon the ground; the trunks are then piled on the sledge and drawn by the dogs to the house. In winter the men are often obliged to go chopping wood after a heavy fall of snow. It is then a matter of no pleasure to walk half a mile or a mile through the deep snow to some chosen locality, and there remain cutting for many hours, while the snow from the branches falls down your neck, as you stoop over to chop, and the wet often finds a hole, be it ever so small, in your boots; while, to endure the cold, the thick clothing one is obliged to wear renders such violent exercise anything but comfortable. When the wood choppers return at night there is always a hot supper waiting for them, and the roaring and crackling fire sends out a genial heat that dries the wet garments while it comforts the spirits of the men.

Friday, the 12th. The first snowstorm of winter came upon us to-day. It began in the morning and snowed most furiously all day; by evening the ground was covered to the depth of nearly if not quite a foot. The snow here differs from that of New England and other parts of the United States, in that it is dry and not damp. It packs heavily, and when walked on generally gives out that crisp sort of echo so often observed in walking anywhere over lightly packed drifts. In this climate, after our first snowstorm, winter is upon us, and we can safely conclude that we are shut in from sunlight and society until the next summer. A thin coating of ice has already formed, and we can probably soon be able to traverse the bays in our sledges. We have fully started upon our six months of ice and snow.

Before I go any further, let me here stop for a few moments and review a little. I have not fully described to you our quarters either here, in our snug inland retreat, or those from which we so lately removed on the outside island; I will therefore try to give you a little idea of how we live, and in what we live; and, as most of the families possess similar establishments, we will try to give you the general idea of a Labrador home.

CHAPTER VIII.

A Labrador home — Houses — Where erected — Stage — Shop — Stable — The house — Papering — Family — Occupation of its members — Out-of-door life.

IN describing a Labrador home, I shall be doing justice to nearly all by describing one, since all are modelled and furnished on about the same plan.

There are, of course, a number of houses modelled after the fashion of those "in the States," as the expression is here; but they are the exception rather than the rule. The best house, perhaps, is owned and occupied by Mr. W. H. Whiteley, the magistrate of this section of the coast, and situated at Bonne Esperance, a little island at the mouth of the Esquimaux, or, as it is rightly named, St. Paul's river. This is a comfortable mansion-like affair, and is built like many of the so-called house taverns so common in country places in New England and other states. Its white exterior shows for a long distance up and down the coast, on a clear day, especially if the sun be shining and serves as a beacon to the inhabitant and voyager in these parts.

While Mr. Whiteley's is a palace beside the other houses, there are those that are hovels beside what I am about to describe as characteristic of the larger and better class of abodes. These hovels, or rather huts, for huts they are in the true sense of the word, are of the rudest kind. The logs, posts, and most of the boards are hewed out by hand from trees growing a little way in the interior, and brought down on rafts by the nearest river; on the border of which the hewing and trimming, which render them fit for the purpose for which they are intended, are generally though not always done and in the fall of the year.

The localities chosen for the erection of house or hut are generally two, one for a summer house in some open situation, and the other for what is called "winter quarters;" and as winter embraces the greater part of the year, it is important that this latter shall be, as it invariably is, in some sheltered cove on the mainland where, if possible, high cliffs protect it on all sides, except from the sea; if such a place is not found, as sheltered a place as possible is chosen. When the house is a summer house there are usually cliffs on the north side, or if not cliffs high rocks, and the exposure to the sea easterly or southerly.

A hut is of the rudest make. The sides are of logs, the bottom and floor of single boards, the roof of rough rafters, and the top of thin deal or clapboards; but a house is of different construction.

I shall not stop here to describe Old Fort island, as I shall do so further on. I will simply say that it is the largest of the neighboring islands,—except the one called Esquimaux island, —and is about four miles from the mainland. The owners, or rather the dwellers thereon, regard this as simply their summer abode, while the winter house, is located on the mainland. The name Old Fort is historical; it being so called in memory of old times in connection with the French and Indian wars.

The relation between the mainland and the island, as is seen by their names, is very close; and this little family of settlers have taken possession of both places, which they have held for many years, and set up their abodes thereon; the winter house being at the elbow of the bend in Old Fort bay.

The house on the island is placed about forty rods from the water on the east, on a small bank of rising ground about ten or twelve feet above the sea level at high tide. The whole island is low anywhere, yet the plain here happens to be smooth and well

DESCRIPTION OF THE STAGE.

covered with grass and vegetation. On the southern side the land slopes down regularly to the sea, and an elliptical shaped beach of rock and sand, visible only at low tide, separates the land from the water, in this direction. On the west is a series of low, rocky elevations; in the north, another series of much higher knolls is terminated abruptly by the water. In the centre of this little plot of ground, comprising about one one-hundredth of the whole island, the house is situated.

I say the house is situated, but it would be better to say the houses are situated; for there are generally several buildings connected with a well conducted fishing post, or summer residence. I will give a brief description of them:—

The stage consists of a platform some sixty or seventy feet long (according to the necessary distance), and built from the beach into the sea — generally so that the farther end will always be some feet above the water even at the highest tide — and about sixteen feet wide. It is built on posts or poles which raise it some six or eight feet above the ground, and covered with boards. The regular fishing boats are generally moored only a short distance from the wharf or stage in deep water, while several small boats are fastened to the stage by means of which the men get from the wharf to their boats and back. The inner half of the stage is called the house, and is covered over with a sloping roof and board sides. It encloses bins for salt and fish, barrels for either or both, and the general necessary things contained in such places. This house has usually a loft for the storage of nets, or anything not needed for immediate use but which are too good to be thrown away. A simple board walk leads to the front door, while the back partition, generally open to the stage beyond, completes the fishing house and stage, where cod are split and cured, salmon and trout salted, mackerel cured, and where all kinds of fish are prepared and preserved. One curious fact may be mentioned: that the primitive way of fastening doors exists here almost everywhere in spite of the cheapness of door fastenings as purchased of the traders; the whole contrivance is made of wood, and the door is opened or shut from the outside by a cord which passes through it by means of a small hole, the inside end being fastened to the latch, and the other to the door by another hole and a knot in the string. This makes a loop upon the inside which answers for the handle. The doors of all the houses, barns, stages, and shops are similarly fastened.

Next to "the stage" comes "the shop." This is another small house with single room and a high loft, and is situated not far from the house and the stage. It is built low, the foundation resting either on or near the ground. Its size is between that of the stage and the house proper. In it are kept the extra stores ; the flour, potatoes, turnips, salt pork or beef, butter, tea chest, and other articles not in ordinary use in the house. In one corner is a tool bench, on a shelf above are numerous cans with remnants of paint for painting boats and perhaps the kitchen floor ; above this, on a series of nails, hang saws, shaves, planes, old iron hoops, and all sorts of articles usable and unusable that can hang up, while the bench beneath is cluttered up with a little of anything and everything that you can imagine. In the opposite corner the scythe and hoe lean against the wall, while a little way from them a very small, coarse grindstone, mounted on a carriage that threatens to fall to pieces every time that it is touched, leans rather than stands. On the wall, over against the stone, a small window frame is nailed on the inside of a square opening ; it often contains but three whole panes and a broken fourth, the hole filled with an old felt hat. By this, aided by the additional light of the open door, barely light enough enters to enable one to see where to get or put away anything, which is generally anywhere. This shop door looks as if a part of the partition had been cut off, at the farther end and on the same side as the window, and a couple of cleats nailed crosswise, one above the other, to hold the boards together ; the whole affair having very poor, jagged hinges on one side, so that the door opens and shuts very hard and squeaks proportionally, and a latch on the other.

On the floor, just between the door and window, lies the komatik or dog sledge ; just above hang the dog harnesses ; and next to them the rackets, or snow shoes, by means of which the men, and sometimes the women and children, with a little practice, walk easily and quickly over the light and often very deep new fallen snow. In the only remaining corner stands a heap of rubbish which extends underneath the bench nearly to the other side of the room. It is composed of every namable thing that you can imagine : scraps of leather, old shoes and boots ; pieces of wood, long and short, thick and thin, picked out for special purposes ; old iron bolts, hinges, spikes, and rings ; old pans and paint dishes ; pieces of rope of various sizes and thicknesses, cork bobs for fish nets and wooden blocks for the same purpose, with an occasional "snatch-block," as the sailors call it,—being an oval piece of wood hollowed out with a wheel inside such as is used for hoisting articles by rope,—and in fact a large assortment of general rubbish beside.

At a short distance from the shop stands the stable, if the family keep a cow, a goat, or any other animal requiring a building of this kind. This is the simplest sort of a shed or barn,—with a top hay loft, and a few plain partitions which serve the animals as stalls,—while even a manger is wanting, and the food is given to them upon the floor of the upper end of the stall. Many families do not keep such animals, not being able to afford them ; then the stable is of course useless and unnecessary.

Passing now directly to the house—only noticing several boats lying upon the sand or on the bank above the beach, at the right of the stage, and the ever present pile of wood, partly cut and partly in long rugged pieces, with the fish flakes, which will be spoken of in connection with the fishing business—we will try to describe it.

The house is, of course, a primitive affair, and perhaps little better than the abodes which our forefathers were accustomed, after a while, to erect upon "the rude and rugged shores" of some seacoast town of our own New England or Atlantic states. It generally faces the south,—that is, the door and longest side do, and is about one-third longer than wide. It is built with one full story downstairs, and an attic beneath the sloping roof; a partition running from floor to roof divides both stories into two rooms each, the largest of which is about square, and the smallest one half the size of the large one. Windows are few and far between; the upper story usually with one at each end or with none at all as the case may be,—which case is usually governed by the money or time at the disposal of the builder at the time of building—and are always with the smallest kind of glasses and sashes possible to admit any light; the lower story usually has from two to four on its sides, rarely any on its ends. The doors are usually three in number, one upstairs and one downstairs in the partitions (these are more often doorless openings), and the outside one of all; they all resemble that of the store house before mentioned, at least in one sure respect if in no other, namely, that they press with difficulty upon the hinges and squeak horribly when the process of opening and shutting, which happens so many times in the course of twenty-four hours, occurs. The upper story is reached from below by a narrow pair of stairs, or a ladder, leading through an opening in one corner of the room, it is safe to say three feet square or even less, and it requires a good deal of practice to perfect one's self in the art of ascending and descending safely. In the construction of the house the building materials used everywhere are rude or good as the tenant can afford; the outside is clapboarded or shingled, and there is no cellar, except a rough hole scooped out underground and lined with hay and coarse grass, and boughs perhaps; with a cover cut from the bottom of the floor. The furniture consists of a large and ample stove (two storied like the house) with a baking oven running its entire length above, the stovepipe ascending straight upward, forming its own chimney outside of the roof; the height of the stove being some four feet above its legs which raise it some eight inches from the bottom of the floor. It is placed between the two partitions and nearly in the centre of the room; for its accommodation a large piece of the partition is cut wholly away so that the warmth will heat both rooms equally.

Besides these the tables are all home made, and of proper

sizes to suit their different uses, being of plain deal boards varnished or painted as there is no table-cloth laid at the meals on top. The chairs are also home made, plain, high in the back, and with seats of woven strips of deerskin or sealskin with or without a cushion of patchwork or white cloth filled with ducks' feathers,— withal quite comfortable. A rocking chair made after this fashion, as it often is, is a comfortable affair, if not quite a luxury. In the smaller of the two rooms is, as the expression goes, "a poor apology" for a book-case containing a few catechisms and books on the Bible, with perhaps the old times Fox's "Book of Martyrs," a dilapidated Pilgrim's Progress, one or two Bibles, a number of indescribable volumes many of which are in French, besides a volume of "The Leisure Hour," a London magazine of good reading for the household in general, and perhaps one or two torn books for children. The shelves are loose or crooked, and the books present the appearance of having been caught in the act of tumbling.

The small room down stairs is a bedroom; it contains a bureau, and, as do the two rooms up stairs, a bed each, either boarded or corded to hold it together, in which is of course a tick filled with feathers from ducks and other birds, as are the pillows also; the bedding is of the coarsest kind suitable for cold winters of from 20° to 40° below zero with fierce winds of unknown velocity per hour. A simple mention of the angular pantry, built in the corner of the house down stairs, with the lower part cupboarded and the upper part shelved and open, holding the plates, cups, and saucers, a platter, a bowl, and one or two pitchers (of a small, brown, glazed stone pattern) with the knives and forks, will do for this table furniture. Placed in the opposite corner is a small table with a washbowl and dish of soap, below which is a pail of water with a small pail inside for a dipper, above which, at the side, hangs a towel, and in front of which is a quadrangular piece of glass, with or without a frame, with mercury parcelled behind it promiscuously,—the whole called a looking-glass; with these one or two carpenters' chests for tools containing clothing or other articles, and a bench to sit on, and you will have before you a pretty fair picture of the house and furniture. Three more subjects remain to be spoken of.

First, the papering. Any one might reasonably be surprised at the idea of papering such a house as above described, for two reasons: that there should be the means for such a luxury here, and at the way in which it is done. Roof, boards, rafters, the sides of the house up and down stairs, the doors, and the cupboard are all papered — the articles used being anything in the shape of book, pamphlet, or newspaper. I have spent more dull, gloomy mornings than a few, reading the titles, looking at the pictures, or reading the stories, pasted at the head and sides of my bed, and you will be surprised at the following list of literature which actually occurs on the walls of our palatial mansion on this out-of-the-way Labrador coast. I give you the list directly as I took it myself from the papers whose titles they represent: The Montreal Witness, Sunday School Times, Advance, Child's World, Christian World, Child at Home, Protestant, Apples of Gold, Well Spring, Herald of Mercy, American Messenger, Juvenile Presbyterian, Young Reapers, Christian Messenger, British Messenger, Home Missionary, Christian Family Almanac, Nation, Youth's Temperance Banner, A German paper, Sabbath School Messenger, Boston Journal, Springfield Republican, Christian Soldier and Christian Guest, Child's Paper, National Quarterly Review, Youth's Companion, Cottager and Artisan, Northern Messenger, Harper's Weekly, Every Saturday, Our Little Ones, Life Boat, Foreign Missionary, Young Missionary, Sabbath School Visitor, Colporteur and Dominion Monthly,—all these I saw, and there might have been others that escaped me. Although it may surprise you to see a list of thirty-nine papers, most of whose names are household words at home, the way in which the people get them is also curious; it being, I am informed, a regular custom with the Mission to send, at Christmas time, a bundle of old papers — of which they are always receiving a large number — to each family living near. About two weeks after the receipt of these, and usually just after the holidays which here embrace the twelve days from Christmas to old Christmas day, the 6th of January, the ladies of the house begin. They patch up the old places, repaper the dirty ones, and spend their time pasting on the new papers in every spot that needs them until the pile is exhausted and there are no more; then the ladies scold terribly because there were not half enough papers, and say that they better not have put on any, unless they could have papered the whole house over anew. When the papering is completed it presents á very curious appearance. As I am now writing there appears on the partition beside me, a copy of the Montreal Witness Extra, for May, 1870, in the centre of which is a large portrait of each Mr. Moody and Mr. Sankey, and a sermon in full of the former; in another paper next to it, whose title is torn off, is another portrait—of Mr. Henry Varley, and also an account of his last service in the Hippodrome; above this is the fancy label of a box of Loring Brothers Malaga Raisins with a portrait of that gentleman in the centre, a vine of luscious grapes hanging on either side of him, and a lot of vessels and water below the left hand, and a steam factory on the right, the whole done in colored ink; a copy of the Child's Paper is above, and the Sabbath School Messenger, at the side of this, has a picture of the lyre bird on one leaf, and a full sized illustration entitled "The Frozen Regions" on the other, which represents a vast number of curiously formed icebergs along its sides, a sea beneath in which several large blocks of ice float carrying a soldierly row of solemn looking penguins and several seal, and a mass of dark clouds overhead. Quite near me an old Boston Journal relieves occasional monotony by an editorial on Disræli, and a sketch of the "War on the Danube," with several other things. Near the head of my bed is a picture of a lady holding a little child on her lap, a small girl talking to a squirrel which is seen as a small black speck away up in the dense foliage of the neighboring trees, a fox-hunting party, and a picture of two small boys of which the story beneath says that the one because he got angry pitched the other into a pig pen,— from which he was rescued by a kind old gentleman, who also appears in the picture; the paper is called "Apples of Gold." It is supposed to be a moral lesson paper for children; but I will not stop longer to describe these things, but pass on to the family, which comes next in order.

Here also we come to a difficulty: that of describing a Labrador family. It would be unkind to describe the family where I stopped while on the coast, also any one particular family might feel justly indignant should I describe *their* family, and yet to do justice to the subject a description should be given. Still we shall not be out of the way should we suppose a family composed of a middle aged man and his wife; either an old gentleman or an aged grandmother; perhaps a daughter or a son (from 15 to 20 years of age) or both; two or three small children and a baby; and, to aid in times of general confusion, when such times come, which happens more often than the opposite extreme, several large, fierce, full-grown dogs and one or two puppies that are always in the way, and in a continual state of warfare with themselves, the people in the house,—who are always scolding them—and everybody and everything in general. When the houses have porches, as nearly all the winter houses do, the dogs and children live in the porch together nearly all the time, —in fact it is often difficult to tell which make the most noise, and in the general confusion that continually prevails, to pick out or distinguish the one from the other. Of course the utmost simplicity of dress prevails among both men and women, as the richest here are poor at best; the goods worn are coarse and thick, but rough as they are, they are better for the harsh treatment they receive than if they were of a much nicer quality. There is, of course, a certain atmosphere of home even here, but it is often hard to distinguish it, or tell when it is present, as the prevailing confusion which such small quarters necessitate is rarely lulled; and when it is, peaceful sleep usually reigns. I do not wish to convey the impression that somebody is always quarrelling with something, but there is a constant chatter going on most all of the time, and when quarrelling is not in order, as it frequently is, the loud talking of different parties between themselves takes its place. It seems to be the usual way of putting one down, as we say, to see which can talk the loudest. If one has something to say, and anybody appears to differ from the opinion expressed, the one who can talk the other down always comes out ahead.

The occupation of the different members of the family can be very briefly stated as that of earning a living in the summer, and living in the winter. It is hardly necessary for me to say that this means that what is earned during the summer in fishing and in other ways is consumed, and more besides, in provisions, and clothing the family for the year; and though I make no allusions to any special family, there is hardly an exception to the rule that there is scarcely a person on the coast but owes for one, two, or even three years back provisions; this is due to several causes, of which laziness forms the chief.

In former years those persons upon the coast who kept little shops of provisions and the necessities of life, as also the traders, were obliged to trust out large amounts of goods on the credit of the following year's fishing. This was well enough as long as the fishing was tolerably good and the people were not forced by hunger to give untrue reports of the work done, since a falling off of the supply of fish and a little prevarication brought them provisions, etc., without much overwork; but one or two years of scarcity of fish soon left the people no means of paying their old debts, and making promises which they could not perform, the traders began to refuse them credit, and now there are few families on the coast who hold their own and prosper.

In the summer the men fish; in the fall they cut wood and do little odd jobs necessary to the preparation for winter; in the winter they keep things about their place in order and prepare for spring and summer, which come almost together as the ice does not go away till late in May, by mending their nets, boats, and dog sledges or komatiks; this is usually finished by the opening of the season when fishing begins again. In summer two or three days are taken to collect eggs of sea-birds which abound on all the islands,— enough for family use only. The down of the sea-birds is kept for beds and pillows and the flesh proves a pleasing variety from the usual diet of fish, otherwise so universal and abundant. The women stay at home mostly and keep things in order there; cooking the meals which usually consists of the most simple fare: bread with or without butter (some use lard for butter), rarely a piece of pork, and tea of the usual kind called black or breakfast. The main stand-by is either codfish or herring with an occasional mackerel; while the red berry and baked apple form excellent preserves. The grandmother or the grandfather, of course, does little but exist, so to speak, though the former keeps the family supplied with good warm knit stockings, and makes and mends boots. This may seem a queer statement, but one has only to consider that the boots here are very different articles from what are obtained in the "States," as the people here say, and that they are made after the Esquimaux pattern, of sealskin, and with soft tops and bottoms, to be convinced of the fact.

The children are, as I have said before, a constant source of disturbance, and they with the dogs are always under foot; if it is not one, it is the other, and more often it is both. They grow up together and fight together; all at once the child becomes large enough to be of use, and then he or she is up for himself or herself, and is either ordered about by the women inside to attend to such duties as they are able, or by the men outside to help them. The dogs are a mongrel half breed. They fight all the time, and eat anything that they can get hold of, from leather, or rather sealskin, which is used in the place of leather, to meat in its most putrid condition.

The out-of-door life and surroundings of the people are neither varied nor peculiar, and they live here much as such a class of people do in other climates, dressing to suit the season, and paying very little attention to their appearance, except during holidays or Sundays which are scrupulously regarded; the latter, by simply keeping the day — for in winter it is usually impossible to get to church, and in summer it depends upon the wind, unless they live too far away, as to whether they can get there at all — on holidays by dressing in their best, and having a good time, a dance, or a shooting match;

the men usually, if not almost invariably, ending up with *a drunk*. The utmost hospitality is extended to strangers, and, as the various houses are often at a distance of eight or ten miles apart, it is frequently the case that a person, travelling from one place to another, is of necessity compelled to seek food and a night's lodging; when such is the case personal quarrels are invariably forgotten, as it is considered the height of meanness, though I use the word only for want of a better, to let personality interfere with, you might say, the necessities of travel. The men are scrupulously a prayerful race; and, with the great number with whom I was often obliged to "rough it," I know of hardly a case where the men did not each regularly kneel in the morning and at evening before retiring, and say their prayers without the least hesitation, no matter how many were around.

CHAPTER IX.

Dinner off fresh meat — Credit and shiftlessness — A Labrador snowstorm — Wind — Preparing for storm — Storming hard — Firewood — Storm increases — Sleepless night — Another day of it — A grand sight — Violence of wind and wave — Destruction of stage — Calmer weather — Beautiful ice scene — End of storm — Thanksgiving Day — Komatiks and rackets.

SATURDAY, NOVEMBER 13. We went to Bonne Esperance partly with the intention of staying and visiting, and partly to mail our letters which of course we found were too late, and consequently obliged to remain over until next spring. Encouraging prospect! We had for dinner a piece of fresh pork which the shipwrecked crew of the Edward Cardwell had presented to Mr. Whiteley. It tasted very nice, especially as we had been living on salt pork in a log cabin for a month past. Pork is with me at no time a favorite dish, and it is only a luxury when nothing better has been afforded for a month or two previous. The following Sunday was spent in doors, in reading and in pleasant conversation with this most agreeable family.

Monday it came off clear and cold. I had a chance to observe the island quite closely. Mr. Whiteley has greatly improved it since my visit in 1875. He now has a little shop or store, and sells a great many things to the people. Of course he only attempts to keep in stock those things absolutely needed by the people for food and clothing. One is obliged to give so much credit here that it hardly pays to keep anything, much less an assortment of useless articles to please the fancy of some wordly-minded maid or fellow. A very few send to Quebec every year and purchase a few articles of gorgeous colors, and display a dress disproportionate to their manner of living; but the majority are well contented with more simple yet durable attire, and toil on, winter and summer, with no greater ambition, apparently, than to become the wife of some lazy young man who can barely support himself, and who generally succeeds finally in supporting neither himself nor her; but the people are not all of this shiftless class, though so many of them incline that way.

This afternoon I gave away, with much reluctance, my thermometer, with a promise exacted in return that an accurate series of readings should be kept up four times a day throughout the winter. The parties of course failed to keep their agreement. It is cold to-day and freezing, with the wind northwest.

Yesterday, and to-day (Thursday) the wind has continued northwest. One of the boats at work on the wreck returned this morning with its mizzen-mast, a huge, iron-bound affair about seventy feet in length, and together the men hauled it ashore, out of reach of the water. It has been cold, cloudy, and threatening weather all day.

Friday it snowed hard all day, and the wind began to blow very fiercely, increasing in strength towards night, while the temperature continued to fall. A snowstorm here is somewhat different from one in the States. The snow begins to fall very moderate, while the clouds gradually grow heavier and heavier, and the flakes fall thicker and faster until the sight becomes so blinded that, dazzled and bewildered, one can with difficulty distinguish objects a few rods away only. It comes with a fierceness scarcely credible, and a suddenness hardly less so; while it will often clear up as quickly as it came on.

Saturday was a quiet day, but cold, with the storm and wind still heavy, the latter freshening towards night.

Sunday, Nov. the 21st. Last night about midnight the wind began to blow and the elements to war fiercely. This morning the wind increased in violence, and spring tides rose to a greater height than they had been seen before for a long time, and nearly carried away the woodpile in front of the house: this is a large, conical shaped pile of fir and larch sticks, each ten to thirty feet high, and about eight inches in diameter at the base, stacked with their small ends upward of course, thus making the whole affair look like an immense Indian wigwam. It is placed in front of the house and on a slightly descending slope, about ten rods from the sea at low tide. The temperature throughout the day scarcely varied from 18°. Frequent snow squalls, a wind direct east, and a sudden and tremendous fall of the barometer, told that we might expect a "spell of weather," as the people say, or even worse, with the possibility of a hurricane. As a means of preparation, although it was Sunday, the old adage of "a work of necessity," though it was hardly of "mercy," seemed to justify us in mustering all hands and preparing for the worst. The worst appeared then to be the hauling of the big logs,—as many of them as we were able—which had been towed ashore from the wreck as far up on the beach as our limited force of four men and ten children would permit. This was not far, however, as solid oak logs some eighteen or twenty inches square, and thirty to fifty feet in length, are anything but easy handling. We then hauled all the boats, those at least that seemed at all exposed to the fury of the wind or water, as far up on the rocks as we were able. They were very heavy, and to haul them we were obliged to use a "tackle." This is an oblong block, with two wheels inside, separated by a narrow partition, over which the ropes run easily, while the block is fastened to the boat by a large iron hook. The end rope is fastened to a ring in the top of the block, while the rope passes over the wheels and through a single wheeled block some distance back, this latter block being fastened to a large immovable anchor. In this way a small force will literally run away with the log or boat attached, which a large force may exert its utmost to move with the hands. After working hard all the morning, it seemed as if we really had everything prepared for the storm, should it break in fury upon us.

About noon the thermometer rose to 36°, and the sky showed signs of clearing; but it was only a sign, for soon the wind started up again, and blew a perfect gale from the southwest, and the darkened clouds, that everywhere enveloped the sky shutting out the faintest shadow of blue, began to send down rain in torrents. We now began to realize that a Labrador hurricane was fairly upon us. Soon the rain gave place to hail, then the hail to rain again, and even fierce flurries of snow scattered huge flakes in every direction. The wind blew harder than ever, and it soon became dangerous to go outside the door. About two o'clock in the afternoon the tide reached so great a height as again to threaten the woodpile in front of the house, and though this was placed higher up on the beach than last year even, and very near the house, the waves reached the foot of the pile, and gradually began to lap against its butts as if to undermine it; there was real danger that if we did not lash it with ropes the whole pile would be carried away with the tide.

In this cold region, wood is by no means as abundant as it is in most countries. Here the coast produces little save stunted growths of fir, spruce, and birch; the latter only is really fit for firewood. Generally each man is obliged to go up some of the rivers near his abode, and cut his own wood from the larger growths ten, fifteen, or even twenty miles inland. There the trees are from twenty to thirty or forty feet high, and six to ten inches in diameter at their bases. These trees are trimmed, then formed into rafts and towed down to the stage-head of the dwelling for which they are intended. As all this requires labor, the wood becomes correspondingly valuable. It is generally kept by being piled with the butt ends resting upon the ground, and the smaller ends resting upon each other in the air, like the ends of the poles of an Indian *mishwap*. At Bonne Esperance the wood is nearly all so piled; it would thus be easily undermined, and probably all lost if carried away by the tide. Hurricanes are no respecters of woodpiles, and we expected each moment that it would be necessary to brave the tempest and rush out and lash the pile lest the waves should carry it bodily away.

About four o'clock the tide turned, but the wind had increased rather than diminished; and blow it did; hard and strong, fierce and cold; the clouds were as thick and dark as ever. An occasional flurry of snow came down, and the scattering raindrops began to freeze as they fell; it was hard to find standing places where the ground was not frozen and treacherous. The wind had also drifted the snow, into ridges and drifts of uncomfortable depth, though, thank fortune, the cold had hardened the crust so that one could readily walk upon it, could he once gain a foothold; thus with ice, glare, and drifts it was nearly impossible to face the wind that whistled and blew so terribly. The temperature by this time went rapidly downward, until about dusk it reached 18° above zero,—not very cold for this region, but just in the beginning of winter cold enough to freeze everything liquid that presented its surface to the air.

The wind continued to blow, fiercely and more fiercely, long after the dark heavy clouds had shut out what glimpses of daylight remained struggling faintly with the approaching night; and we could hear the howling and roaring of the tempest without, as the mingled sissing and whistling of the wind combined with the crashing and the thrashing of the waves against the shores, and the thug! thug! of the broadsides of water that fell upon the rocky beach. It was a fearful night. Any other than a strong, well built house would have with difficulty stood against the tempest; and, believe me, there was very little sleeping done that night.

Monday the 22d. The storm is not yet over. We awoke this morning and found the same war of elements to whose music we listened as we sank to sleep last night. I had the pleasure of witnessing this morning, and in fact throughout the day, a sight that I shall not probably see again soon. The sea in all its rage and power, lashed by the wind and augmented by the tide, vents its fury upon itself. Huge ridges of wave press forward like an army; suddenly each end concentrates its waters toward the centre of the ridge and with a grand onward, upward rush sends up a huge mass of spray and white foam which still shoots upward in smaller angry sprays and jets, while the mass of wave below sinks down into the water, or boldly crashes or tumbles over itself as it splashes on

SITUATION OF STAGE-HEAD.

the water in front of it,—an angry sea, lashing itself into foam-covered patches here and there, and everywhere, as far as the eye can reach.

It is next to impossible to do justice to a tempest on these Labrador shores. While on our own coast at home I have seen presented a truly magnificent sight, when a storm sent long ridges of foaming and sparkling waves, with their watery foam-bearing crests towering up ten, fifteen, or even twenty feet into the air, following each other with regular step, beating at length upon the sandy and often rocky shore with quick splashes, that sent the foaming and watery masses high up on a beach extending miles in uninterrupted distance in either direction, and felt that I could go home and tell of a storm at sea, and of its fierceness, grandeur, and magnificence.—yet the memory of such a scene is of little account in comparison to that which I shall now describe, and which I not only saw and felt, but that those around me who have witnessed the terrors of a tempest upon these shores not only saw but felt, and which you will soon see they have cause to remember.

Bonne Esperance island, where we are at present, is a small island not more than two miles in circumference. It contains two small elevations, one or two small ponds of water, and is separated on the north and northwest by a narrow band of water from the mainland. On the western side of the island are the stage, and the several buildings connected with the fishery department which reach to the water's edge, extending from this backward towards the path. A board walk extends up the embankment to the level above where the fish flakes are spread; back of these are sheds and outhouses, while a descending slope brings you, a little to the left, to the house which is nearly on a level with high tide mark in front, and which looks directly out upon the waters of this little bay-like inclosure, thence to the waters of the open ocean. On a perfectly clear day the highlands of Newfoundland can be seen fifteen miles directly east. Close in-shore the island is one mass of rocks. Sometimes low, but broadly rounded tops of bowlders show themselves, while on the southeast a low, receding cliff receives the force of the waves in this direction. Just beyond the house is a small sandy depression called salt-water pond, since it is filled with salt water at high tide only. All these peculiarities of the locality are seen at a glance from the front doorstep, and the porch itself is only a few rods from highest tide marks. In this out-of-the-world region, this bleak, cold, desolate Labrador, over a thousand miles from home, I am spending the winter. On this morning, in this terrible weather, while still uncertain as to that which may follow, I stand and gaze upon a Labrador hurricane. On this little island I am far enough from land to get all the benefits of the raging ocean, to see its whirlpools and billows, and watch its majestic, towering columns of water as they rise and break in all possible shapes to the right, the left, and in front of me. It is, however, sufficient; I shall remember the sight for the rest of my life. While I cannot do justice to the scene I can only add my own feeble expressions of the terrific violence and the awful grandeur of this day's scene as it stands pictured on my mind. The whole sea in commotion, actually stirred to its very depths, and breaking into foaming masses, in places where in calm the depth was thirty and even forty feet; and you could even see the water black with mud from the clayey bottom, of frequent occurrence here. From a short distance seaward, a long line of undulating wave quickly forms, increasing till its crest is a sheet of foam, while the wave itself breaks up into smaller masses some of which sink into the waters below, and forming sort of pits or whirlpools are lost in a well-like abyss, while others raise themselves again high in the air and shower forth spray like the jets of a Parisian fountain. Each successive wave thus turns and twists itself into the utmost variety of forms and shapes, while wave succeeds wave with the greatest rapidity.

The narrow islets in the distance beyond are but playthings for the waves, and huge billows roll completely over the lower ones, while white spray tosses itself from one side to the other of the higher yet still low crests. It seemed as if the waves on either side of these heights delighted to show their mighty strength, while they vied with each other in throwing their spray over them and into the sea beyond. Now all the rocks and points of land, of which there are many jutting out into the sea on either side, are in turn covered with a mass of foam and white-capped spray, while the water rebounds high into the air fifty or a hundred feet at least; sometimes it breaks over the rocks with a report like thunder, sending long sheets of glistening spray vertically forwards. All these varied scenes we beheld in one moment, and almost at a single glance, and more beside. The wind, the rain, the blinding sleet or snow; the dark heavens, and still darker horizon; the foaming, seething, and hurrying, the turning and twisting masses of mad, white, frothy, granular (for I can think of no other word to express the peculiar effects of light spray upon a darker ground of water) watery crests that rise and fall, or cover the whole surface of the water as far as the eye can reach, are all seen in a moment. No pen can do justice to the terrific grandeur of the scene; no picture can give a real impression of its awfulness. My memory can scarcely retain the thoughts that the moment or moments (for the storm thus continued without respite all day) inspired. And yet I have not told all.

To have simply witnessed a storm of this description, and known that it could do damage to any of our property, would in itself have been a sight to have recalled continually in after life. Remembering the care and pains taken to save everything useful in this out-of-the-world region, the expense of transportation, and the real value of any little improvement when once made, you can go with me to another part of the island, not far distant, and look with renewed awe upon the destruction going on there. Struggling fiercely against the wind, just before the additional dusk of evening set in, we hurry down the little hill at the west to the stage-head and wharf, to see if all is safe there. Three weeks ago to-day the Edward Cardwell was wrecked, as I have before described, and the cargo of huge oak, pine, and other varieties of wood logs, beside deal boards, scattered far and wide along the coast. The gentleman with whom I tarried (Wm. W. H. Whiteley), finding that he could dispose of them to good advantage, sent out boats to pick up all that they could find, while he offered to purchase for cash, or trade from the little shop of provisions and dry goods, of all those who should bring him either logs or boards. In this way he gathered a large lot of lumber. The huge logs had been hauled above a supposable high water mark—for this heavy pine and oak timber requires a dozen men to remove a single log—and been allowed to accumulate on all sides about the stage-head, which was thus closely hemmed in with these solid timbers, many of which were eighteen inches in breadth and width, and forty to fifty-four feet in length. There they had lain, rising and falling lazily at the highest tide only, for the past two weeks. The stage head, of which I have spoken, is a sort of shed built out into the water upon logs that inclose huge masses of stones to weight the platform and hold it in place, while the main building is propped up with upright posts, buried some distance in the earth and mud below, supporting the flooring at a distance of some eight feet from the bottom at low tide.

At the stage-head the boats are fastened, and here the fish are cured and packed; here are a great majority of the other stores of the fishermen,—the boats are housed for the winter inside the building; while barrels of fish, flour, and hogsheads of cod oil, with all sorts of implements and utensils are stored also. There is often a second stage separated by a platform from the first, on which platform are stored boards and plank of various kinds, hogsheads empty or full of refuse cod liver, or blubber as it is termed, while the stage house itself stands farther back, the platform with its railing being nearest the sea. While all this hurricane is raging, and while it is almost impossible to walk ahead a dozen steps, it seems proper to "take a look at the stage" to see that all is right there; and what do we see? In this little sort of natural harbor the waves are stirred with almost the force that they are in the open sea, while the water breaks to the bottom in huge billows which, lifting themselves in their fury, rush forward and hurl themselves on the jam of logs that I have mentioned as lying all around the stage; the logs are gradually breaking loose and drifting about at the mercy of the billows. It is spring tide, the water is at its height, and we are powerless but to stand and watch the scene, while ten or fifteen huge logs are dancing about as if they were playthings. Now the water breaks over both stage-heads, making it impossible for one to rescue the provision and other material there stored. The foam flies in blinding sheets over boards, barrels, and hogsheads (or puncheons as they are here styled) alike; it dashes against the sides of the stage house, and freezes in heavy masses wherever it touches. The wind whistles, or rather hurries past us for it flies too swiftly to whistle, and still we can only watch the scene.

Soon the logs are nearly all loose from their moorings; we watch the waves as they catch them and hurl them with terrific violence against the slender underpinning of the stage house,—which but for this gale would have been sufficiently tight to have stood all ordinary weather during the winter—and crush down the foundation posts as if they were small sticks. Crash follows swiftly after crash. A dull *thug*, and the farther part of the stage house falls, roof and sides, upon the precious stores contained within, while the inner edge of the platform, thus loosened of its foundation posts, sinks several feet. The topmost crests of the waves sweep over the whole, though not with sufficient force to carry anything away. Over this slippery mass it is impossible for one to think of walking for an instant. We rush for the inside of the stage, after opening the large outer doors at the end, and are appalled to find half the flooring already swept away and the large new boats balancing on the edge of a slender support that threatens to give way and engulf them instantly. There were four of these boats, each one worth at least one hundred dollars, and had they been carried away, it would have been a great loss and one not easily replaced. As it is we are in time to save them, and do so at great risk.

While doing this another crash comes—for the logs are still being hurled against the underpinning of the stage house, though their number and clustered weight now hinder what otherwise one or two logs might have easily accomplished, in the destruction of this with also perhaps that of the other stage entirely—and another part of the stage and platform, thus undermined, falls. We rush outside and are just in time to see the water lift it with its waves; to see the platform bend lower and lower until, with a final crack, it parts, and hurls barrels and boards upon the rising crests of the billows surging upward to receive them. Powerless to hinder it we see several barrels of fish, and five barrels of flour of another man—who could ill afford the loss—go towing about with the logs on the watery billows, mingled with boards and debris of hay, chips, and all sorts of material swept clean off the stage. Presently two logs catch one of the barrels of flour between them; opening for a moment they come together again with a crash, the barrel is burst in an instant, and a cloud of flour flies in all directions, while cakes of dough go floating off on the waves. Three barrels of flour and several of fish are speedily disposed of; one apparently sinks bodily as it disappears and is not seen afterwards, while but one is saved whole and another in part. But unless the storm increases the remaining damage will be slight, and we return to the house. During this gale, to-day, the barometer went down to the lowest that some twenty years of readings have given it upon this part of the coast, reaching 27.32; the thermometer 19°, and the wind still southwest varying to north. At length night comes, and we go to sleep again listening to the roar of the tempest, which, however, shows signs of abating; still we are anxious for the morrow.

Tuesday the 23d. Our hopes have not deceived us, and this morning we awake to find the tempest moderated to such an extent that we can calmly view the extent of last night's disaster. The waters are comparatively calm, though they still toss about the logs, boards, and miscellaneous pieces of wood that have gathered upon its surface; chips and debris are floating about on all sides matting the surface of the water like a carpet which undulates with the motion of the waves beneath. The further end of the stage house has fallen in a mass upon the stage-head, which has lost the greater part of its underpinning and part of its platform; while the right hand

AN ICE SCENE—STORM ENDS.   143

floor, inside the building, has fallen out entirely,—it is a wonder what has kept the whole building from going. Great masses of ice cover the ruins; the sides of the stage house that still remain standing are covered with sheets of heavy frozen matter, while huge blocks of icicles hang from the edge of the roof. The railings of the stage beyond hang with icy masses that fall in solid sheets nearly to the ground. Everything seems covered with this dull, opaque, heavy saltwater ice. We see before us a sea of frozen, wooden matter. We spend all the day in cleaning and clearing away, and in trying to find the extent of the damage done; in relaying the broken foundations, strengthening the beams, raising the broken and bending, though not yet fallen, portions of the platform, and in general repairs. Night finds us more cheery, and sanguine that one or two more days' work will right matters again.

Wednesday the 24th. To-day the storm is fully over, and the men have labored hard at clearing away the rubbish, and once more righting things. The wind has been mostly from the north. The water has calmed down once more, its surface stirred only by the low, long lines of wave that occasionally advance and break upon the shoreline everywhere around the island; the whole water is still colored a dark clay green, an evidence that at this point the sea had been stirred to its very depths. The magistrate says that he has never seen it of so intense a color during the twenty years he has resided on the coast. Everywhere upon the shore are clams and mussels, shells of many different varieties, starfish, echini, and holothurians of many kinds, besides innumerable other species of sea dwelling animals. The beaches were everywhere literally covered with these treasures of the deep, while the children brought them home by the armful. Beautifully colored starfish, some of them immense fellows a foot or more from end to end of arms, and brown, red, and gray, both light colored and dark, all told of an unusual commotion in the elements of both air and sea. By this time the sky had regained its usual and natural hue of hazy blue, with scarce a cloud save in the far horizon where a dull, heavy shadow of the hurricane hung like a ghost or ghoul that seemed slowly to sink lower and lower, while it grew fainter and fainter, soon disappearing entirely in the distance and leaving us once more a fresh, free sort of feeling that, perfectly natural to the region, seems to defy *ennui*.

Thursday the 25th. Alas! that I should be obliged to spend such a day in such a place. I shall hardly dare to suggest to you that it is Thanksgiving Day, but here I am in an English province, beyond the American frontier, where Americans seldom go, to say nothing of carrying their holidays with them; in a land, the people of which are too poor to celebrate to any great extent should they ever feel inclined, while living too far away to pass the time in complimentary calls; in families, whose chief diet throughout the year consists of bread, without any butter, and tea, without any sugar,—excepting what game may fortunately be captured; where breakfast, dinner, and supper are the same; in such a locality, though with the better class of residents, I pass my Thanksgiving. That I may not think myself worse off even than I really am, I cut a slice of cold roast pork, and imagine it the best of turkey; another slice answers for chicken; while a third stands equally well for mince pie. I then start for the woodpile where I work off the effects of so hearty an exercise, as the eating of all these delicacies, by sawing wood for the remainder of the afternoon. Thus ends a Labrador, New England Thanksgiving.

During the remaining days of the month nothing particular has happened save that the goodman of the house where I am stopping has been in bed sick. The first of the month, however, finds him much improved.

Wednesday, December 1. Although it is very cold the bay shows no signs of freezing yet. These winter evenings the children amuse themselves with games. Many of our New England and other games find favor, though dominoes seems to take precedence of all others. Checkers are played quite frequently. Of course cards are the prevailing game along the coast, and the old "stand-bys" seem to be "high low Jack" and "forty-five," the latter being apparently a characteristic Newfoundland game, as Newfoundlanders indulge in it at all times of the night or day, and are apparently never too tired to play when they can "form a hand," and

> "When once agoing,
> With pipes aglowing,
> They sit it out till morning."

Thursday the 2d. The boys and young fellows harnessed the dogs for the first time to-night, but did not use them much. As I have a few hours to spare I will try to describe here the komatik or dog sledge and its use, as also the racket or snow shoe of this region.

In winter the greater part of the travelling is done in one of two ways: either on sledges called "komatiks," drawn by dogs, or on large pads that are called "racquets," and which are worn upon the feet. As each of these requires a special description, I will try to give one.

The komatik, as has been said, is a sort of sledge or sled, and looks very much like a magnified specimen of one of those latter articles. Its dimensions vary from nine to thirteen feet in length, from two to three feet in width, and it stands about eight inches from the ground. The wood is wholly pine, and the side bars are cut out of thin deal-board, planed down to about one or rarely two inches in thickness, with the front ends turned up like the front runner of a sled; the sides are often bevelled so that the bottom is one-fourth or one-half an inch wider than the top. The upper part of the sled is made of a number of thin pieces of wood (usually thirty-two) of equal length and about four inches in width, with the ends rounded, and then notched—for a purpose that will appear hereafter. The top and bottom pieces are similar, but of double the width, while the thickness of all is about the same, generally one-half an inch, though the end pieces are perhaps a little the thicker. Each piece has two pair of holes bored through it on either end, the distance between each pair being that of the width of the top of the side bar, and the distance between each hole of each pair about half an inch; between each pair it is then gouged out crosswise about one-fourth of an inch deep, while the inner

HOW THE KOMATIK IS MADE.

pair is recrossed at right angles by another gouge, the purpose of which will soon be seen. A curious fact is that all these holes are bored out with a red hot iron to make them smooth and even. On the side bars, at a regular and previously measured distance apart, are bored holes to the exact number of the crossbars. The holes are bored, one a little above, and the next a little below the preceding one, so that when done the whole presents two unequal rows as here shown, . ˙ . ˙ . ˙ . ˙ . ˙ . hence the liability of thus splitting the soft pine in the sewing process is lessened.

The next work is sewing the parts together: for this a coarse salmon net twine is threaded into a needle used for the purpose, and each crossbar is sewed into the corresponding hole in the side bar, in and out of the holes on either side of the bar itself, and drawn as tight as possible; the needle then slips under the twine through the groove across the inner pair of holes, and a loop and a stout pull fasten it; thus each bar is sewed on till all are tight,—but we have not yet finished. The forward end of each side bar must be strengthened by a long, thin iron placed lengthwise along the inner side of each bar (this is the usual and best way of strengthening the ends), and screwed tight to the boards. Then come the shoes.

Every komatik has shoes or runners as do our sleds, but unlike them they are of whalebone. Whales are so often found dead on different parts of the coast and towed to some harbor where the flesh is cut up for the dogs, and the bones saved for various purposes, that the large rib-bones have become a regular article of commerce among the people; the bones are some eight or ten feet long and nearly or quite a foot wide, with perhaps two inches of thickness. These bones are obtained, then strips the full length and an inch and a half wide are sawed off, and being trimmed they answer perfectly for runners. With a gimlet, holes are bored through them about six inches apart, and they are fastened to the bar, which is also bored into, to correspond, by small pointed wooden pegs driven tightly down; the knobs of the pegs are then sawed off, and the sides of the runners, if they overlap, are pared and the bottoms planed smooth. From the forward end of the bone a small portion of each runner is trimmed down thin almost to the board, and to this a piece of hoop iron is fastened which is brought around over the point of the bar and cut off close to the first crossbar; it is then pegged, through holes, or screwed down. This part of the bar never touches the ground, being curved slightly upward; then with a hole through each side bar at the end, like our sleds, through which to pass a rope if needed, and with a plentiful supply of paint, our komatik is complete.

A komatik is drawn by harnessed dogs, and it is a strange sight to see one of these hobgoblin, arctic turnouts travelling at a smart pace over the ice and snow of the frozen bays from place to place, and watch the eight, seven, to even three or two dogs, attached to the sled by a long thin thong only, trotting or galloping along many rods in front. You would hardly believe, at first sight, that the two belonged together, but rather that some fairy means of conveyance had suddenly dropped from above, or appeared from an unseen corner below, and was travelling off on some mysterious Arabian Night's adventure; and truly, the snow-capped hills, the icy and snowy plain of frozen sea, add to this not unpleasant romantic delusion. A close inspection will show that each dog is encased with a thin, narrow band harness that simply goes around the body at the belly, with another piece going around the neck and around and between the legs, which is fastened to the former beneath; on the top of each a long band reaching to the length of several rods follows on behind with a loop at the very end. Each dog is thus harnessed. The komatik also has a band fastened near the front crossbar by holes in the runner, and buttoned together with a loop and an angular button. The loop on the end of each long dog band is passed over the button of this komatik band, the button fastened in the slit, and the team is ready. One dog is always fastened some distance in front of the others and is styled the leader; the others are fastened at various distances apart, but always many rods in advance of the sled. The team is guided usually by the voice, with or without a whip of the Esquimaux make or pattern, many yards in length on a short handle; with a circle of thick rope to throw over the runners and impede the progress of the sled in case of accident or sudden desire to stop, and which is called a drag; and a long stick with which to pound and sound the surface of the ice to see if it be safe to cross in doubtful places, the team is ready to start.

One would think that such narrow bands as these of which the harnesses are made would be easily broken; but though the width is seldom three-eighths of an inch, the sealskin, of which they are made, is so tough, stout, and unyielding, that they will wear rather than break apart. A trace, as it is called, is often seventy or more feet long; and when you consider that a large muscular dog is either dashing forward in short, quiet leaps, or straining his utmost to draw a komatik on which a load of eight hundred pounds and over is often fastened (three barrels of flour and other things being often taken at a load), you can judge somewhat of the strength of these thongs. If the going is bad the strain is in all probability more than doubled. I have said before that the thong wears rather than breaks, and when it does give way it is more often by the weakness of some closely thinned place or the rotting of some portion of the trace than by any other means. Sealskin thong is used everywhere for rope, when it can be procured, for tying or binding. No wonder that the old legends, which till now I had regarded as such in reality, were more than true, when Indians bound their captives to trees quickly with deerskin bands (for deerskin is nearly as tough as sealskin, though it perhaps gives more easily), which it was impossible for them to break. The quickest and easiest to make, yet surest tie is called a double half-hitch; the rope is doubled over itself in two loops with both ends projecting from the inner side of the loop. It is made in about three seconds, and the more one tries to stretch it the tighter it becomes, especially if the cut ends are fastened to some object behind or even to themselves. But the dogs (these wretched half-breed of Esquimaux and wolf perhaps, that spend the greater part of their time in fighting eachother, to whom play is fight and fight death, and I do not exaggerate these brutal furies) have started, and the footmen follow.

The foot, as I have said, is encased with a pad called a "racquet." It is a bent bow of wood with two crossbars, the intervening spaces being thickly woven of deerskin thong, except a small opening where the toe goes, and which is below the middle of the upper bar. There are great varieties of form, called usually from some fancied resemblance to the tail of an animal. The beaver, the otter, the porcupine, and the bobtailed rackets are used perhaps more frequently than any others about this coast, though the long racket is used throughout many of the Canadian provinces.

In walking one takes the usual step, though perhaps a longer one than otherwise, having the feet much farther apart, and in the walking position the convex portion of the top part of the racket of the hind foot fits almost exactly into the concave portion of the bottom part of the racket of the front foot. In stepping, the wide part of each pad passes over that of the other; you will thus easily see that in hurried walking, if each step does not at first clear the racket of the other foot, it is impossible to take a step with that foot which thus sustains the whole weight of the body, and the impetus given to the body invariably plunges one down into the snow. With the swinging motion necessitated by the unusual space between the feet, a little practice soon accustoms one to walking easily over the lightest and deepest snow if it be dry, as it usually is here, and not wet and sloppy.

A short time since the dogs were ready to start off on a journey or trip with their master or driver; and now several strong men without stooping, and with a motion peculiar to habit from long practice, drop their rackets upon the ground and adjust their feet in them,—now both start together for the trip. The going is not very good for the sledge, and the runners cut deep ruts in the snow, already upon the ground to the depth of over a foot on a level, as it is slowly passed over. The dogs travel with difficulty, and need constant urging from their driver who keeps up a continual shouting and crying out at them.

A string of a dozen or more rapidly repeated words which sound more like a series of *hi, hi, hi, hi,* etc., or *ki, i, i, i, i,* etc., sends the troop off at a quick pace, while the leader is easily turned to the left by a series of sounds, of which either *rudder, rudder, rudder,* or *da, da, da, da, da,* or *udder, udder, udder, udder,* seems to be the only interpretation (I have found no one yet that can tell me the exact word used); and to the right, by another sound like *oŭk, oŭk, oŭk,* or *owk, owk, owk,* repeated in a hollow, guttural tone. These are the regular sounds for guiding the leader, while a continual shouting or clapping of hands and a variety of any small words are poured forth till one would easily imagine the driver to have seriously shouted himself hoarse. If any object appears in the distance, this too is a theme for the urging forward of the dogs, who seem to go well enough without all this noise. A crow flying close along the ground, and a komatik in the distance share alike the *o-look', o-look* (which is grunted rather than spoken out), *crow, crow,* or *caw, caw, caw,* or *komatik, komatik, komatik,* to which is often appended a single shrill *hi.* Whether the dogs need this constant urging, or whether it be a custom that seems to have been handed down or not, I cannot conceive. Meanwhile the men who are walking have nearly or quite kept up with the sled. The long strides enable one easily to double the ordinary walk of a person, so those behind have kept quite near. On they both go — the dogs at a smart trot which occasionally breaks into a gallop, and the men who present a truly comical appearance as they press forward swinging their legs with their huge appendages and their arms, occasionally their whole bodies, with the violence of the exercise. The wind, which blows the light snow on the top of the thick crust of the late storm in whirls and clouds all about them, sings around their ears and faces, making the one tingle, though encased in a warm covering, and the other ruddy with the glow of health. It is foolishness for one to venture off in such weather, as is here of every-day occurrence, without a sufficient amount of good thick and warm clothing; and even the dogs seem to be provided by nature with an unusually thick coat of long flowing hair as their best protection from the severe cold liable to occur here at almost any time with a few hours' notice.

A journey of six to ten miles brings them to their destination, and then a halt is made. The trip may be simply to a neighbor for some visit, or to borrow or return some loaned article, or it may be to the provision depot for a supply of goods or articles for the use of the family. The molasses keg needs refilling or the tea chest is empty, perhaps the butter is all gone, or soap, matches, or broken dishes need replacing with new supplies. Often the men are out of tobacco which, to them at least, is a necessary article, when the greater portion of the time is occupied in filling the room with volumes of deep blue smoke while assembled around a (almost literally) blazing hot stove telling stories or silently enjoying the smoke and passing time away. It may be that the housewife needs a new dress, or the children extra clothing, while often warm shirts and mittens of swanskin are to be procured for both. At any rate the articles are obtained, often, I am sorry (for the families' sake) to say, on credit of next year's "ketch" of fish, and the little party turns toward home again, which is soon reached, as are also the warm fire, the hot supper, and bed.

CHAPTER X.

Trip up the River to the Mission — Ice pictures — Bad walking — On the Old Fort — New scenes and bad walking — Pleasant Sunday — The return — Journal — A komatik ride — Christmas gathering — Wood cutting — Work for the evenings — Making sealskin boots, mittens, and other needful and fancy work.

Saturday the 4th. With one of the men I started to-day on a tramp up the river to the Mission station, about seven miles distant. It seemed good to be on the move once again, although we got much more of it than we had expected before the day was ended. The river was frozen but a part of the distance, so we were obliged to go by boat to the land at its mouth. It did not take long, however, to get the boat ready, and we were soon on our way. At first we rowed through the soft masses of ice that coated the water everywhere around the north side of the island, but finding this passage closed with ice too thick for our boat to break, we retraced our way, and, fortunately, found the passage on the other side clear all the distance to the land on the opposite side of the bay. The ice that seriously impedes passage at this season of the year is called here *slob*. It is a thick, consistent mass of frozen salt-water that lies in huge patches all over the surface of the water from land to land. While in this soft condition it is easily rowed through; but the danger is, that, as the cold strengthens at any time of the day or night, it is liable to congeal suddenly, even at a few moments' warning, when it grows harder and thicker every hour. If a boat is within it, the congealed mass has at times been known to surround it so as to prevent escape. The mass is thus too hard to allow the men to rescue their heavy boat, and too soft to walk upon. The whole sheet, meanwhile, cracked from the edge on either side, slowly but surely moves with the current until it is gradually taken out to sea to be lost in the gulf or ocean. Judge then the fate of those unfortunate beings who have remained in the boat, thus inclosed, moving only when it moves, halting only when it halts.

The passage on the west side of the island, as I have said, was fortunately clear, so that we gained the opposite side of the bay without accident or delay. This left us half-way to our place of destination, the remainder to be tramped over the hills, with snow knee-deep to opposite the houses, to which we must get by shouting for a boat to come and take us over should the water between be open, as we had reason to fear. Having called at a house of one of the inhabitants near by to deliver some messages, we returned and began our walk, or rather tramp, over the partially frozen ice of the river at this point and towards the hills beyond, over which we were obliged to travel.

I have read, in books of arctic travel, of snow-capped hills and of snow-filled valleys; of rivers and bays frozen over with dark, semi-transparent salt-water ice, but never before had I experienced the pleasure of beholding its reality. Now I saw them in all the half-frozen splendor of a semi-arctic latitude. I could also tramp over their treacherous surfaces with a feeling of perfect safety knowing that the distance to the houses up the river was not far.

The walking was by no means easy. We first crossed the river on the ice which at this point was sufficiently strong to bear us. The ice was not very solid, and big holes and huge cracks were to be seen everywhere about us, so that it required a great deal of manœuvring to find secure footing and a safe passage between them. We would walk along safely enough for some distance, and then the dark colored patches of water, seen on the surface of the snow, would show us where the dangerous places were; then again the ice contained large cracks, and we were obliged to prove its solidity with a stick before trusting our feet to step upon it. Sometimes the ice would be as large floating cakes when we were compelled to jump swiftly to get safe from one to another, each step sending the cake deep into the water beneath, so that the person behind would be obliged to wait until it had regained its position once again before attempting a similar passage.

Along the edges of the river the ice had formed and cracked again, leaving the walking very dangerous as well as difficult; this often necessitated the climbing of long, steep, icy slopes before gaining a secure footing. Then again the ice had formed over beds of sharp rocks, often at high tide, and the water retreating had undermined the support, when suddenly, while walking over these, they would give way and we would fall often several feet on the rocks below, making most treacherous as also dangerous travelling. Again long open stretches of water would compel us to go by the land, either around some inland pond or *lac salé* (salt lake, as the people call these inlets of the sea, and of which there are so many all along the coastline), or over some low and narrow, or high strip of land to the river again. Sometimes we would crawl along the edge of some high and sloping, or steep and rocky crest, often coming suddenly to the brink of a precipitous height of twenty to thirty feet, where a single false step would have sent us to the rocks or sharp ice below; or perhaps we would suddenly sink to our armpits into some concealed, snow-covered spruce thicket, from which we would extricate ourselves only with great difficulty.

From some high hilltop we could see lofty crests sloping to some narrow or often perpendicular cut, through which the river, now frozen and now with open glistening waters, ran towards the sea, a distant maze on our south. A mile or so ahead we could see the buildings, and the white church with its steeple, of the little Mission station. Here are about a dozen buildings where many of the families that live upon the islands outside in the summer, together with the foreigners who conduct the school and Sunday church services, pass their winter quite cosily and more or less merrily in teaching and being taught.

It was a difficult tramp, but a delightful one. At length we reached a position on the hills directly opposite the houses on the other bank. After a great deal of hallooing and shooting blank discharges of powder from our guns, a boat started out from the other side, and slowly approached us; soon we were on the opposite side and close beside a nice warm fire, drying our wet clothes and partaking of the hospitality of a kind-hearted inhabitant of this little settlement.

Here I found two young men who were destined for the same point that I hoped to reach that night, so I decided to avail myself of the opportunity and accompany them.

We first called on some of the inhabitants of the place, and found them cordial and genial people, well meaning and hospitable to strangers. I found myself invited to partake of bread and tea at each place, and at last was obliged to refuse absolutely even the tea which was thus generously pressed upon me, and which is the beverage so abundantly partaken of all along this coast. At last we had finished all our calls, for the present at least, and so we all started for Old Fort Bay, seven miles distant across the river, the hills, and several ponds. Since our journey presents a continuation of the one I had just taken, except inland instead of along the direct coast line, I will try to give you some idea of it.

The scenery here is very similar to that we had just witnessed, with the same features of frozen river and lakes, and journeyings over hills and snowy slopes; but there was enough variety to make the trip new and pleasant, rather than full of tedious monotony.

We started on our journey by rounding the bend of the river which had this year been frozen over earlier than usual, when we came at once upon a long stretch of open ice. In this part of the river, as in fact in any of these salt-water lake basins, the water usually freezes several times before it finally becomes caught on either side. Each time it freezes, the soft ice loosens and goes floating down the river; thus several days of alternate freezing and open water occur usually before the ice finally catches for the winter. Strange to say, this year the ice caught and held the first time, and so, as we were yet quite early in the season, we walked over a freshly frozen yet perfectly solid surface in the direction in which we were going.

We had hardly rounded the turn before one of the fellows, whose eyes had in this case been sharpened by expectancy, espied the fresh tracts of the ptarmigan in the snow of the left bank of the river; but of course the birds had long since gone. Undoubtedly they were not far off, though we had no time to hunt them up. We continued our walk, therefore, enjoying the clear, cool, and healthy air while drinking in the unusual sights, at least to me, of hummocks and hillocks rising in the distance, one above another, and stretching one beyond another, with varying gorges, and again solid walls of granite, into the distance beyond. After travelling an hour with such views constantly presented to us on either hand, we passed a little ridge of ground and came to another so-called *lac salé*, a bend in the river almost converted into a lake by the stricture at its mouth. Passing over the frozen surface of the lake we came to another ridge which, passed, brought us again to water—this time a pond. A succession of two or three of these ponds crossed by low, narrow ridges of rising ground brought us to the head of the eastern arm of Old Fort Bay, which we found barely frozen, and for the most part a terrible mixture of broken ice, rocks, and water. We had great difficulty in getting from the ice to the shore, as the cracks were large, and very wide; but we succeeded in doing so at last, when we found ourselves at the foot of a large, heavy ridge of hills which extended for the remainder of the distance between us and our destination, varying from four to five hundred feet in height, and by no means easy to ascend. Had it been high tide our way would have certainly led over these hills, as their perpendicular faces towards the water would have rendered walking in that direction entirely out of the question; while the way would have been picked out only with the greatest of care in the dusk of evening, in which we would walk among spruce thickets, over stones, and down steep declivities, quite dangerous indeed in the daytime,

We had no boat by which we could row the short distance now separating us from the house to which we were going. The tide was dead low. On we went, the stones and corners of the rocks hurting our feet—for we wore the dogskin boots of the Esquimaux,—while the huge cakes of broken ice often caused us to stumble in quite a hopeless manner. Again, in spite of the low tide, the cliffs came almost down to the water, and we were frequently obliged to wade in the water up to our knees and much above the top of our boots, or climb over most dangerous places at the risk of slipping down into the water beneath. To add to the disagreeableness of our situation the darkness now became so dense that we could scarcely see a couple of rods ahead; and this was what we termed luck being on our side against walking over the tops of the high hills before mentioned; but we stood it manfully, and at last reached the little basin just before the bend that would bring us to the shore. Here the ice was quite fresh, being formed from a little brook that runs into this natural or perhaps artificial hollow. It was here so slippery that we could hardly stand upon it, while the broken cakes made the walking almost impossible. We stumbled and fell, then tried to climb up the slippery inclines only to fall quite back again. I think that that little distance of scarce a mile and a half, from the head of the bay to the house to which we were going, cost me more severe travelling and labor to attain, than any other similar trip that I ever remember of taking in my life; but we reached it at last.

It seems to me almost as if I could recollect each individual step of the way, and sitting in a cosey chair by a large snapping fire, I wondered how I had the strength to go through with it after the twelve steady miles that I had already tramped since morning,—and of such tramping! To give an idea of how little these strong, robust fellows think of such travelling, one of the two men who had just come with us insisted upon returning after tea with a young fellow whom we met here and who was going that way. Seven o'clock at night and so dark that one could hardly see a rod ahead! over slippery ice on which one could scarcely stand much less walk, through water up to the knees, crawling over ridges of rocks to fall from which would have been indeed dangerous, then five miles more of steady tramping before reaching home. One may draw his own conclusions as to the endurance of these men, as this is a fair sample of what they will do every day for weeks at a time, while hunting, without any apparent ill effects.

One may well imagine that I did full justice to the nice, hot supper that was laid out before me, and was soon after snugly tucked beneath a double covering of heavy blankets to seek the rest so much needed.

Sunday, the next day, was most charming. The sun came out bright and warm and we all enjoyed the beautiful weather. We had some birds for dinner, the first we had had for several weeks. After the meal, although it was Sunday, since the men must get back to their work the next day, we all started for the river again. The water had become so open that we accomplished the worst part of the journey in a boat, and walked the remainder in comparative ease and with very little trouble, reaching the Mission station by evening.

I will not say much regarding the Mission here, leaving that for another place, as it is worthy of special consideration. I simply called upon the genial people there, and enjoyed a short but very pleasant interview.

I left a small stock of medicines at the Mission house, having brought some with me from home, and soon started off. I saw some poultry in one of the houses. They were barred up and carefully fed upon scraps from the table. The hens furnished a few eggs, and were apparently about the only specimens of this species of fowl on this part of the coast. Strange as it may be, on the lower part of the coast, some sixty miles below this place, I found hens so abundant—having been brought over from Newfoundland—that I purchased several dozen of eggs for the reasonable sum of a shilling, or twenty cents, a dozen.

At the house of one of the inhabitants where we stopped to

visit, we found four Indians who had come from several hundred miles in the interior, with their fall catch of fur to trade for provisions. As they were journeying in the same direction with us, we proceeded on together. We started about ten o'clock in the forenoon and, after a tedious tramp over the hills, reached the bend of the river, found the boat, and were soon rowing the remaining distance to Bonne Esperance where we arrived in time for supper.

Tuesday the 7th. The Indians, having finished their trading, returned home this afternoon.

Saturday the 11th. A small party went out in the boat to-day and shot four ducks and a pigeon, which gave us a taste of fresh meat once more.

Monday the 13th. The men spent a greater part of the day in mending their fish-nets.

Tuesday the 14th. A flock of ducks appeared just off the island, and we got a shot at them as they clustered, killing seven. In the evening the young folks amused themselves making molasses candy, while the elder people joined heartily with them in the disposal of it.

Friday the 17th. The cow was killed to-day, and we had the first taste of beef we had had for months.

Friday the 24th. Yesterday I again went "into the river," as it is here called ; that is, went to the settlement up the river, and to-day, the ice being regarded as safe, I had my first real ride on the Labrador dog sledge, or *komatik*, with a native driver as guide. Our team was a small one, only three dogs, but they drew the sled so fast that it might have been twice the number and I not have known it. Along the ice of the river and bays we glided, over low hills and across snow patches, and over grass and moss laid bare by the wind ; we went, literally, "over hill and dell," while we often passed rapidly places flooded with water, where the delay of an instant would have sunk the sledge. Now up some steep hill we helped to pull the sled, while down on the opposite side we went faster than the dogs could go at full gallop. On across the country we went, until, landing upon the very verge of a high precipice, we were obliged to come to a halt. Here we tied the dogs, turned the sled bottom upwards, and descended the slope by a narrow, circuitous path, which brought us to the house of one of the residents, where we dined. We found here a very pleasant family, two members of which had spent some time "in the States" in good society; after enjoying with them a very pleasant chat, we returned to the sled and continued our journey. I was amused to see the eagerness of the dogs to be " on the go " once more. They strained at their harnesses, and whined and barked while jumping, with the evident intention of either starting the sled or breaking their traces.

Our way to Old Fort Bay lay in much the same general direction as that in which we had walked a few days before; but the hills are so cut up with gorges that come nearly to their base, that nature has formed four different routes between the Mission and Old Fort Bay. The scenery was quite similar, but riding we had more of an opportunity to take in the arctic-like views everywhere presented. The day was fine, and the outline of the hills beyond was very decided upon a clear blue sky. We appeared to be rushing along through a narrow, winding valley road with receding heights on either hand. On a level with us, yet on either side near the base of the hills, the falling tide had caused the ice to break in cones, and blocks of all sorts of forms and sizes. Still on we went, the ice often bending beneath us, while the dogs reminded one of childhood's fairy tales. The sight was grand, while the weather was fine, cold, and with little wind. The inner bay was frozen over, and we rode to the doorway of the dwelling for which we had started.

Christmas evening there was a social gathering at one of the houses up the river. About fifty people were present and passed a very pleasant evening. In this case the old adage that "distance lends enchantment to the view" was well illustrated. Most of the inhabitants live at distances of five to ten miles from each other, which makes calling upon one another a circumstance of some importance. When once people do get out on such an occasion as an annual Christmas dance, they stay long enough to enjoy the visit thoroughly,—they did so on this occasion.

Wednesday the 29th. Early in the morning we started off with our dog-team for the bottom of the bay. Here we tied the dogs, and with our axes started up the snow-covered slope of the hills to where the spruces and firs were abundant. None of the wood was large. The snow was up to our knees; it covered the evergreen thickets with dense patches, so that when we started to cut a tree the shaking would dislodge the snow in large patches that covered us completely, while it slowly crept down our backs and up our sleeves. Still on we labored until we had loaded the sledge, when all started for home with appetites sharpened by the keen, subarctic air and the healthy exercise. It was quite fortunate that we procured our wood when we did, for Thursday was as warm as it had been the night before, and the ice, so much melted, began to break to such an extent as to render the travelling extremely hazardous, though it soon froze up again.

During the long winter months the women of the house spend their evenings, and for the most part their days also, in making boots, shoes, and nicknacks of various kinds. Of course they can do this, since their time is almost entirely at their own disposal, and, after the regular work of the family is done, the remainder of the day and evening falls heavily upon anyone of a naturally nervous or industrious disposition. The location of the dwelling forms another inducement to industry, since the long winter evenings must be spent entirely within doors, and work of some sort must be constantly provided.

It must be remembered that except in a few places, such as the Mission and several small collections of houses used as winter quarters and which have been built from a quarter to half a mile distant from each other, the houses are, for the most part, miles apart, and visiting in the evening is quite out of the question.

It is comparatively easy to point out the industrious portion of the female population of the coast; everyone knows them. To substitute fictitious names for real, Mrs. Goodey will make fine Esquimaux sealskin boots, and will do other similar work, though attention to her large family makes it impossible for her to spare much of her time for outside work. Grannie Roberts is also noted for her nice, careful sewing of boots, pouches, or sealskin bags to wear on the back, in which to carry provisions, game, or other articles that the hunters may require, while she takes in such work as filling pillow cases and bed ticks, making hunting and warm working jackets for winter, or mending socks, mittens, and other articles for general use or wear. She is a good old lady, and thought well of everywhere, while her work is always well and cheaply done, and her nearly fourscore years combined with her remarkable cheerfulness give her a good word from everybody on the coast. Further to the westward work from Aunt Jane's is known in all directions.

If I have described elsewhere a pair of native shoes, as they are often called, a brief description of them here again may not be out of place, since it is necessary to have a clear understanding of the process of making them. A good deal more than at first appears to a purchaser depends upon every little point in the operation. To begin,— suppose Grannie Roberts is to make a pair of sealskin boots for some buyer. From a lot of sealskins one is selected either from a harbor seal with the hair on, or a large harp from which the hair has all been scraped off; in either case the skin, to be the most serviceable, must be well scraped of fat on the inside and dried for two or three months on some frame on which it has been stretched to its fullest extent in the sun, exposed on the woodpile or roof of the house (after the hair has been taken off if a harp, and with the hair on if a harbor seal). These dry skins will not shrink, and for every purpose of wear are infinitely better than the shoes, sold in large numbers, made of quickly dried skins, sewed upon wooden forms, which shrink and tear, while they soon wear useless. Out of them the bootleg is cut, from a paper pattern of any kind the wearer may choose. All, or nearly all, *bottoms* are cut from like patterns to fit a foot of any shape, but invariably from the dried skin of the harp seal, the dryer and older the better, since they stand more wear the older they are. The pattern of the *sole* is an oblong oval, while the *tongue* or top piece is more or less lance-shaped. After soaking over night in water to soften it, the sole is taken and the whole edge for about an inch and a half is bent inward, then the toe is puckered in creases, as is also the heel, while the tongue fits the space left after the bootleg is temporarily fastened on, all the pieces overlapping enough to allow for sewing. These puckerings are made by simple creases of the needle at the time of sewing. All seams are made—if the sewing is done in a scientific manner, and not simply to "sell the boot," as the expression goes— by the simple overlapping of the two pieces and sewing each edge tightly to the part beneath, while the ridge thus made by the seam, if rubbed with a piece of wood shoemaker fashion, will be hard and shiny as well as very tight. In all sewing the skin is so thick that the needle can be run through it and out the same side without perforating the skin; thus a seam admits no water through the sewing, if the thread and overlapping pieces are drawn tight.

The upper edge of the bootleg has a doubled piece of cloth sewn around its edge, though sometimes sealskin replaces it, through which a piece of tape or braid of any color to suit the wearer, about a yard and a half long, is threaded, and the skin, being quite flexible when on the foot, is drawn tightly about the leg, the braid wound about twice and tied with the string end hanging outward; this secures the boot firmly and yet not painfully to the foot by the leg and, though the string often gets loose and the bootleg often slips down, it seldom gives much trouble to the wearer.

A curious operation that might escape one's attention, as well as a curious fact in connection with this operation, is that the puckerings of the heel are held together by running two, three, or four small threads at about equal distances from each other—the stitches being taken through the bend in the creases on the inside of the boot, from side to side, around the heel where they are drawn tight and fastened to the seam above; another fact is that the creases of the toe are not thus fastened. Why the former should be done and not the latter I cannot ascertain; it would be a curious fact to study into if one could spare the time. A proper sealskin for bootlegs will cut from two to five pairs, according to the size of the skin,— as the pattern for all adults is usually the same,— while a proper skin for bottoms will fit six to eight pairs of boots. The bottoms are not scraped, but the legs are scraped quite clear of the vellum from the inside of the skin. A skin that is dried in the house has a yellowish look while one dried out of doors in the sun is white as parchment on the inside. Should it happen that a person's feet are in the habit of sweating much, the whole inside of the boot is rubbed with a tan made of birch rind,— but I do not understand the exact philosophy of it. When one first purchases a pair of boots they are generally quite dry; they are then oiled carefully with the hand, with seal oil, until every part is fully lubricated, the inside is then rubbed on a stick with a polished and nearly sharp edge, as is often done by shoemakers, in a certain stage of their own bootmaking, to accomplish the same result,— the operation is nearly similar to the manner in which pegs are rubbed out of boots. After this operation they are hung in a warm place near the fire until the oil has soaked into the skin when they are ready to be worn, and if properly made will, with the roughest wear over stones and ice, unless cut or otherwise unusually injured, remain, with occasional reoilings, water-tight for at least two months. At the end of about that time, the bottom or the heel is worn through and the sole must be tapped,— this is done by simply cutting out a piece of skin, round and the size of the whole heel if for the heel, oblong and the size of the sole if for the sole, which is then sewn on with a tightly drawn single thread from the outside. Such a patched bottom will last a month or six weeks longer and then the whole bottom gives way and is usually replaced by a whole new piece from the ankle down.

All shoes are made substantially upon the same pattern; while for house wear the leg part is dispensed with and the bottom extended upwards far enough to bind as a slipper or tie around the ankle as a shoe. Such is Labrador and Esquimaux foot-gear as worn on the whole or nearly the whole coast. Their price varies from poorly made boots at $2.00 to the best at $2.50 to $3.00; while the scarcity of seals will sometimes render them even more expensive. A dried sealskin for making boot bottoms averages in price at $1.50. The bootleg is often made of dogskin similarly dressed to the sealskin, but the same general character prevails in all, however made. In winter the men usually wear moccasins on their feet. These are generally made of dressed deerskin or mooseskin, and worn by those on the coast who are fortunate enough to have procured the skins either by purchase or trade, by their own success in hunting, or, as is generally the case, directly from the Indians. The process by which the skins are tanned in the best manner seems to be kept a secret. A moccasin is generally made in much the same manner as a boot bottom, and in place of the leg is a simple binding of colored cloth doubled to allow a piece of braid to be inserted which, tied, holds the moccasin to the foot, while many are simply bound without strings. In some cases a wide piece is sewed on to the top that may reach around the ankle, while a loop on each side holds a strip of deerskin that ties around the ankle holding the moccasin fast to the leg.

Moccasins are of endless patterns and varieties: some are like slippers and very plainly made; others are more carefully prepared, by ornamenting the tongue with beads, colored cotton, or porcupine quills wrought into figures, flowers, and forms of many varieties. Very often the shoe is tanned and rendered quite brown by this process. Sometimes the toes are pointed, the side fringed, and many are the devices for varying the make and pattern so that the taste of the purchaser may be gratified in his selection of a pair. Deerskin moccasins are only worn on snow and in snowy weather; for being of a soft skin the slightest wet will at once shrink and spoil them. The snow here often falls in large, deep masses of a very dry nature, and only at this time these shoes are worn,—but they are never worn alone; the universal accompaniment is a pair of leggings made of thick swanskin, which is a sort of very thick, woolly, cotton-like cloth in common use here for all sorts of articles of warm wear. The legging answers the purpose of a bootleg, and since it is only worn with the moccasins in the snow serves remarkably well for that purpose. Leggings, made either with a sock or without one, pull on the legs over the pantaloons; a loop often passing from side to side, under the foot as in riding pants and patent hunting oilskin or rubber breeches. The moccasin is then put on over the bottom part of the legging, and the top secured by some bright braid as before mentioned in the case of the boot. A little matter of pride comes into notice here,—that is, the tasty bordering of the seam of the legging, on either side, since the seam is always worn outward and the braid tied with colored worsteds so that the ends hang jauntily outward also. The whole outfit forms a very pretty fancy piece, and reflects the good taste of the wearer.

Neither shoes, boots, nor moccasins, of a soft bottom, are ever worn except with several pair of thick stockings and one or two pair of swanskin *vamps*, as they are called; these are simply cloth-like slippers, and much resemble a stocking cut off just above the instep with the edges bound or sewed over and over with worsted, and a central flap an inch or two long from the middle of the front edge in which is made a loop and by which the pair are looped and fastened, the one to the other, when they are hung up to dry, as they usually are every night. One can easily see that, compelled as the people are to take long walks, the foot-gear must be, as it is, very warm and protecting to the feet; and yet, though at first sight those skin coverings would seem cold and productive of cold feet the reverse is so extraordinarily the case that one can stand in water all day and not wet the feet, unless the boot is poorly made, or stand on the ice in the coldest weather and seldom suffer from the cold penetrating to the soles of the feet. The main difficulty is the getting used to such "strange feeling shoes," and in walking over small, loose, angular pebbles which are everywhere abundant on the shore, large rocks giving little or no trouble at all. In summer generally the smallest amount possible is worn on the foot. Strange to say, sometimes sealskin bottoms are put on leather-topped boots. Often American and English boots and shoes, or rubbers, are used, but these seldom in winter except on Sundays or extraordinary occasions. In the house sealskin shoes, much like a moccasin, are worn by the members of the family large and small, almost without exception, while in warm weather the children go barefooted.

The next most important articles of wear that the women make are sealskin mittens. The sealskin mittens of the Esquimaux, and those which are worn all along the coast, are articles probably peculiar to this, as to other Arctic regions. The sealskin is the same as that used for most articles of wear here, and must be remembered as the harbor, not the Russian, Northwest, Alaskan hair seal. The skin is dressed as usual, and the mittens made with the fur outward. They are odd looking articles outside, while the inside is at first quite tough and rough with the natural wrinkles of the skin, caused by heat or dryness. These, like the boots, are worth more if made of well rather than imperfectly cured skins. The whole length of the mitten is from twelve to fourteen inches. The top is quite wide while the rest of the mit narrows to the hand which is made of a short, wide, rounded piece of skin sewed to the main part of the mitten. It is a simple affair, and yet, like the boots, when worn with ever so thin an extra covering inside, it is nearly impervious to the cold. As a further protection there is a border at the top consisting of a strip of muskrat, otter, or beaver skin, with the fur outward, and from one to two inches wide. Though somewhat clumsy, it is a rather pretty affair to look at, especially if the pattern of the sealskin, as it often does, varies from silky ash to almost black with roundish spots of ash black centred; sometimes a skin is nearly pure black (the hairs, silky at the tips only, reflecting a delicate velvet). The color of the skin and the curing seem to sell the mits better than anything else, and a prettily spotted pair is almost always chosen in preference to one plainly colored.

We have still to describe two articles of wear before our hunting apparel is completed. First, the sealskin hat or cap: this is made like an ordinary cap with a rather pointed crown (made of cornered pieces of skin running from top to bottom), with ear flaps and strings to tie beneath the chin. Secondly, a hunting or "*nunny bag,*" to sling over the shoulders and carry the provisions or any articles of use or luggage: this, too, is entirely of sealskin make. It is unnecessary to enter closely into the details of the work on these articles as the sewing is usually of the same type in each article as that on the seams of the bootlegs, while the style may vary according to the taste of the person for whom they are made. The nunny bag is a spacious bag, wider than high, with an immense lapel. It is carried on the back between the shoulders, and secured by bands which slip over the arms and rest on the shoulders.

As we have gone so far in the hunting or tramping dress of the Labradorians, a short account of their other principal articles of outside wear may not here be out of place. Of course the general clothing in the winter months, whatever it may be, is of the warmest possible kind; the heaviest flannels are always used, and sometimes several pair, while the cloth of which the coat and pantaloons are made is as stout and thick as can be obtained. The men wear cotton or perhaps a sort of duck overalls, and cossacks; the former need very little description being simply what I have named them, and, worn over the pantaloons, are with them, tucked into the boots. A cossack is a loose short jacket. It is made of swanskin, and the long sleeves reach to the hand while the robe or hood for the head is cornucopia-shaped, and fastened to the collar behind. The binding is of calico. It is secured around the waist by a scarf the ends of which hang to the left; or the belt holding the hunting knife (an article always worn, concealed or open) is simply strapped around the body.

A person attired in such an outfit as I have mentioned is warm and well provided for almost any sort of weather that may come. He is ready to meet the thermometer at 30° or even 40° below zero, while by leaving off some of the flannel underwear he can readily adapt himself to a warm day. Long tramps are thought nothing of; hospitality, as I have said before, is extended to him from every house upon the road; hardships seem nothing; while he who endures the most, and speaks the least about it, soon acquires the reputation which he has worked to earn, of a fellow who will stand almost anything. The great occupation in winter is visiting the traps and hunting. I might have placed these occupations in exactly the reverse order but that more is secured by trapping, hence the more important, than by hunting, which usually furnishes only a temporary supply of game for the table, such as partridges, rabbits, and in some cases deer. The partridges are the ptarmigan, the spruce partridge, and rarely the sharp-tailed grouse; the two former being very abundant, while the latter is rare. The various animals, except the porcupine, which is clubbed with a stick, since its gait is so slow that it cannot run away from one, though sometimes shot are more often trapped, and these will be spoken of in another place. The deer-hunting forms an occupation in itself. There are several cabins built near the well-known deer hunting grounds in the interior of the country some ten or twenty miles away, where parties, wishing to enjoy this sport, and secure some fresh meat for the table, make their headquarters; from here they take long tramps, and often shoot several deer to a man in the course of a season. The cabins are very small within, and some ten or twenty men will huddle together in this confined place in the evening (if the deer be unusually abundant during the day) and spend their time smoking and playing cards.

A dingy little cabin scarcely larger than an ordinary room sixteen by twenty feet in width, with a long bin-shaped bunk or berth on each side, capable of holding six or eight men each, as a sleeping apartment; a stove in the middle of the room; a room full of tobacco smoke; and the shouts and confused voices of so many men, are anything but pleasant to one whose nerves are at all delicately strung; yet, as I have before said, these men think nothing of hardships, being bred to them from childhood, and though they often go forty miles a day looking for game, over hills and down gorges of the most difficult walking, and have started off early in the morning sometimes before light, going all day with only a taste of food, returning late in the evening, they will then spend the greater part of the remainder of the night in revelling, with only a few hours of sleep between this and another day of the same sort. Nor do I exaggerate a particle, when I say that this life is continued sometimes a month at a time, through all sorts of weather. Such is the life of these hardy people in winter when they go out for a "good time;" and in summer, during the fishing season, it is fully as bad; but the people are, for the most part, pleasant and friendly, and a stranger has no cause to complain for want of being favored.

The fancy work in which the ladies indulge to a greater or less extent, especially in the winter evenings, may be known as pouches, pockets, "*hossacs,*" watch cases, and sometimes cushions and a variety of beadwork of all sorts and patterns,—the latter being mostly worked by Indian squaws, who, with the men, often live in tents near the coast in the spring and summer time when they sell all sorts of articles of their own manufacture and handiwork. While watches are rare on the coast, the various patterns for watch cases, of beadwork or cloth or on sealskin, are various and very pretty. As I am writing I have one now hung on the wall at my right. It is about six inches long, and three broad at the widest part; the shape is rather sharp ovoid. The main part is of harbor sealskin plainly but very neatly worked with colored beads on the upper part, while the outside of the pocket has three little knots of the same on either side of the round opening for the face of the watch, which opening, with the upper edge of the pocket, and the whole outer edge of the case has an edging of purple ribbon, on which a string of white beads is sewed in small scallops entirely around it; the inside pocket lining, as shown through the opening in front, is of red silk, and the back of the whole affair is of brown cotton cloth. It is really very ornamental, and quite useful; various patterns are made besides this; but, as a rule, the plainer and simpler the more attractive they are. Hossacks are long strips of cloth on which a series of three, four, or even more pockets, of a variety of depth and width to suit the maker, are sewed, the top of each pocket just reaching to the bottom of the other; and the whole making a strip some twelve or fourteen inches long by four or six wide. When the body of the piece and the lining of the pockets are of good cloth, the trimmings an edging of colored ribbons with bows at each corner of the top of each pocket and at the bottom of the last one, and the face of each pocket filled with sealskin, beadwork on sealskin, or colored cloth groundwork, or, as is more often the case, of the heads of ducks and other birds, the effect is most striking, and the ornament one which would grace the boudoir of the wealthy as well as the library of the student.

The head of a merganser or sheldrake, with its purple reflections, and long, linear, glossy, and most delicately curved feathers; that of the loon with its metallic gloss; of the king eider, or kingbird as it is called, with its delicate green on a white background,—are the most frequently used pieces; while the teal, widgeon, and various other birds are sometimes substituted and, placed in the most conspicuous places, add greatly to the attractiveness of the article. Pouches and pockets, especially for carrying tobacco, are usually made and sold in large numbers. They are manufactured of harbor sealskin—lined or not—bordered, fringed, worked with beads sometimes over nearly their entire surface, or plain according as the maker may see fit to work them. The rounded lapel is terminated by a long, thin strip of sealskin, to which is attached a piece of wood, bone, or the tooth of some animal, which ties and fastens the article when rolled up. If it is made to roll up tightly it is called a pouch, while if it retain its shape it is called a pocket. The market for all these articles is chiefly near home and their making a matter of pleasure rather than work.

CHAPTER XI.

New Year's Day — How to walk on Rackets — "Fish, dogs and seal," the general topics of conversation — Obtaining skeletons — Larch poultices — "Small Talk — Low temperature — Deer stories — Trapping — Indians — Up the river — At the Mission — Harnessing the puppies — A racket walk.

SATURDAY, January 1, 1881. New Year's day passed much like any other day here, and differed little from either the Christmas or Thanksgiving that had preceded it. The "old wife's" saying, that the twelve days after Christmas determine the weather for the twelve months in the year, is here strongly and strangely believed, especially by the elderly people. I am of the opinion that, generally, the people are rather inclined to superstitions. Sayings like the above, together with such as the month "comes in like a lion and goes out like a lamb," or the reverse, are frequently quoted; and though half in jest I fancy them to be more than half believed. One will find a very fair practical example of the use or belief in the value of Herschel's weather tables by the moon, here in the old wife's almanac. Such elderly ladies almost invariably inquire when the moon appeared before telling what weather may be expected. Strange as it may be, they seldom assert that the weather will be "so and so," but say "I have always noticed;" or "the last time" it was so and so, so and so happened—thus they predict the future from the past.

I made my first trial to-day of walking on rackets. Racket-walking is a feat very difficult for a stranger to acquire readily. The motion is different from anything I know of; the peculiar swing of the body much like that of a sailor walking the slippery or un-

balanced deck of a vessel. The impression upon the snow is about
) as shown in the figure. Place a number of these figures in a
(line, one before the other, and you have the impression; im-
) agine the foot as it swings the circle of the loop and you have
(the step. I walked with one of the neighbors into the river,
) as it is called, that is, to the Mission settlement, seven miles
away; my feet were sore for days afterwards, but I soon became
expert in the use of the rackets, and before many weeks was
using them as freely as if I had lived in Labrador all my life.

Wednesday evening a party of neighbors called from about fifteen miles to the westward, and amused us with the news, of which there was very little, and the gossip of which there was a great deal. They were very pleasant, and concerning their hobbies — fish, dogs, and seals — quite intelligent. Hunting is generally the chief topic of conversation in the winter, and though game appears scarce this year, I have the word of so many that I cannot doubt the assertion that last year ('79–'80), two young fellows shot and snared eight hundred rabbits and about three hundred ptarmigans; they sold part of them farther to the north for a shilling (twenty cents) a pair, while those remaining not eaten were salted down for future use.

Tuesday the 11th. We were nearly turned out of the house for the day and the rest of the week, by the owner using the only available room for a carpenter's shop, while he made him a new komatik; for some trifling reason, however, the sled was not a success, and was used but very little, the old one being preferred in its place.

I was very fortunate to-day in getting a large number of skeletons of mammalia, from a gentleman now in charge of the (this year's) unused habitation of the Hudson's Bay Company's post at St. Augustine,— I mean unused this year by the company. There were several skeletons of the beaver, the mountain cat, as it is here called, or Canada lynx (*Lynx Canadensis*), several specimens each of the common red, the cross, and the patch fox, together with one of the white or arctic fox (*Vulpes lagopus*), besides several of the weasel and mink, one martin (*Mustela Americana*), and a variety of the common red squirrel (*Sciurus Hudsonius*). It often amuses me to hear the reports, so frequently current, of the fabulous "wealth of the American gentleman who has lately come on the coast, buying everything that is of no use to anybody."

One fellow brought me a common porcupine and said that he heard that I was giving five dollars for porcupines, but wanted to know if I could not give him six! I gave him a dollar, and considered that he had made a pretty good bargain at that. He was contented, since he had been induced to ask the price by his father and others who undoubtedly thought that they could easily "make a good thing" out of the American who might not know the difference. With reference to one other animal whose skeleton I procured, I would say that the wolverine, or glutton (*Gulo luscus*), — called "*Carcajou*" by the Indians — is becoming either more and more rare about this locality, in fact all along the coast, or has retired far inland. It is seldom caught; its fur rarely appears in collections — that is in comparison to what it did ten years ago even — and is so poor, and the price so low, that it would hardly pay one to hunt it. The Indians have ceased to capture it, and out of a thousand dollar batch of fur you will not find more than ten dollars worth of its skins. The animal has undoubtedly gone farther into the interior, where it hunts the deer by pouncing upon it from some concealed spot in the trees above, when the animal passes, and tearing its throat sucks its blood.

Monday the 17th. While up the bay this morning there came on a tremendous snowstorm. The flakes were larger I think than any that I ever saw before or have seen since; it often appeared as if I saw them fully half as large as my hand.

For the last three or four days one of the men has been suffering intensely with a felon on his thumb; all manner of poultices and applications have been tried to cure it, but none have been so effectual as the soft, outer rind of the common larch (*Larix Americana*), boiled in hot water and then kneaded into a poultice. It healed the sore with wonderful rapidity. It reminds one how rare serious cases are in this region, where physicians are so "few and far between." The people are seldom sick, and when they are nature is its own nurse assisted by the experience of the "old women" of the coast.

Saturday all hands amused themselves making molasses candy, a great treat in this region; it tasted very good and homelike I assure you. A little luxury of this kind is highly appreciated in such a region, and especially since so little sweetening of any kind can be procured. This year provisions have been unusually high everywhere along the coast. Flour, which usually sells for from seven to eight dollars a barrel, has already reached twelve dollars, and is still going up; it is hard to be obtained even at this price. Many of the poorer families are feeding on corn meal, which is generally refused here until the last extremity, since the majority of the people regard it as hardly fit to feed the dogs with. I suppose, in this case, the climate has a great deal to do with the prejudice. Corn meal is evidently and eminently a southern dish, and suitable to the warm climates. Besides what I have mentioned, the saltfish has already given out in the majority of the families along the coast, and the preserved salmon, trout, herring, and mackerel, are being used up fast. Last year the game was so abundant that not half of it could be eaten; this year there are no indications of any, and the Indians, from two hundred miles in the interior, are telling the same story. Some of the old inhabitants say that they never knew such a dearth of game during thirty or forty years' residence on the coast.

Several cases have come to my knowledge where whole families have been obliged to separate and hire around in turn to their more fortunate neighbors for the winter for their board alone, to escape the poverty and destitution which would surely have overtaken some of them had they continued living together for any length of time during this excessively cold weather. Add to this the wrangling of families and often members of the same family (happening in several cases, over the cargo of the wrecked Edward

Cardwell), and it is not strange that this should be regarded as an unusual year on the coast of Labrador. Still another drawback exists, and one that would work in the exact opposite way in any other country: the weather has been mild instead of cold,—the bays hardly frozen over. Now if the bays do not freeze fast sledding between places becomes almost impossible, since the dogs must draw the sleds over steep and high hills, and can carry only a small load; while if the weather be cold, the bays freeze quickly and sleds draw immense loads with the greatest of ease.

It is an old saying that "you cannot load a well-made komatik." The sled balances so nicely and draws so evenly on the ice that you may pile on all that you can, yet once start the load and the dogs will draw it fast enough. This does not necessarily prove that the dogs are not powerful creatures, or that they do not exert great power in drawing the loads imposed upon them. I have seen three stout dogs draw over a thousand pounds of old iron (upon one of these sledges) over seven miles in about an hour and twenty-five minutes; while again I have seen these same dogs draw a load of twelve twelve-foot deal board plank, weighing not one-half as much, and when the sled became stuck in the slush, all their force could not move it. Though this would seem to prove that the sled is easily drawn after being once started, such is not always the case. It must be remembered that dogs must exert a tremendous effort to draw even the small weight of an empty komatik over the ice that is smooth as glass and presents no unevenness upon which they may rest the foot to keep it from slipping. I have seen several of these creatures harnessed in such a position where it was impossible to assist in the carrying, and even very little in the starting of the load; for instance, there were five large, smart dogs harnessed to a huge oak log, eighteen inches square and fifty feet long, embedded in the snow and ice. A few pries with the pick loosened but did not start the log. The dogs strained, often running backward, then rushing forward with a great jump that brought them to the end of the line, with a thug like the sound of a drum, while at other times they strained every nerve, before the log started; but, once started, was drawn without difficulty.

The lowest temperature that I observed occurred this week when, about seven o'clock one morning, the glass was at 27° below zero; it must at the very least have been 30° below during the night. This is generally the average winter temperature in this region, on cold winter nights and mornings, while it often goes down to 40° below and sometimes freezes the mercury. This winter the majority of readings for the thermometer have been hardly to zero, or barely below it—consequently the bays have not frozen over, travelling has been most difficult, and the people have suffered accordingly.

In the poorer communities I have been struck with the greed with which everything is saved or hoarded up against a time when it may be needed. Nails are often of as much value as if they were made of nickel; pieces of wood of peculiar shape are saved; the hoop, stave, or head of a barrel, if strong, is carefully laid away; while each little thing is saved or hoarded with the care bestowed upon some sacred Penates, that is kept to be looked upon rather than for use. Everything has its value while there is little that is apparently useless.

I suppose that to-day, Thursday, Feb. 10, one of the most exciting stories (since verified) came to us that we have heard for a long time. I have reference to a party of deer hunters who have just returned from the interior with report of a large herd of deer having appeared there, about a day's journey eastward from where we now live. Their success has been unusual. Large herds have been seen, and a great many deer killed by different parties along the coast. One man living in the little settlement up the river had the rare fortune to kill four in one day. It appears that the hunter alluded to started out alone from the cabin, one morning before breakfast, and, coming up with a herd, was fortunate enough to kill two deer with the same ball—both falling together. He returned to the cabin to breakfast, and said that he should want some one to go with him with a sledge and dogs to procure the deer and bring them to the cabin for him. While waiting for the men to harness the dogs, and get in readiness, he said to them that he would just take his rifle and have a turn over the hill beyond to see if there was anything in the shape of game to be seen, hardly expecting to find any so near the cabin. He returned in a short time saying that he had shot two more deer, as before, both with the same ball, taking two of them as they happened to be running abreast. Of course, those in the cabin were wild with excitement. During the hunting season several parties shot deer and some of them more than one, but no one approached the above record.

We now had fresh meat, and made good use of it, I assure you. It was quite palatable after a uniform diet of salt fish and pork for four months previous. Later on we obtained deer's meat of the Indians, smoked by them, and prepared as our dried beef; they cut it up into small pieces, and eat it from their tin dish much as we would bread and milk, without the milk, however. This dried deer's meat is, in fact, the Indians' bread for a large part of the year, while they are out on their hunting expeditions. The Indians conduct their hunts in a much more systematic manner than would at first appear. They start from the coast and travel about a hundred miles directly inland before pitching their tents, carrying everything with them, of course, by the water of the numerous inland ponds and lakes, or on their back over portages,— a portage being generally spoken of as a narrow passage over some embankment which separates the waters of one lake or pond from those of some other farther on—when they camp, and the men immediately start out on the look, first, before any hunting or trapping of other game is attended to, for deer. They travel by concentric circles gradually widening outward, and return in much the same way home. Thus it is impossible for them to miss the tracks, on the snow, of these animals, should they cross them in any direction. The tracks first found, the impressions are followed with accuracy and swiftness, day and night, until the herd is found, when, I believe, generally, part remain to hunt while the others return and fetch the tent and utensils to within a few miles of this new locality. As long as there are deer within thirty miles of the tent the Indians remain in a given place and proceed with their hunting. Several deer are killed, their flesh hung in strips over the fire and smoked—to be afterwards laid away for extreme use only; the bones are either made into a soup—as they are full of oil and marrow, or roasted, then cracked and eaten; while the hide is soaked in brine and the hair taken off by a scraper, much like our chopping knife—if indeed there be any difference—but by them called "*oodloo*," or, as pronounced, "hoodloo;" it is then washed, cleaned, dried, and white-tanned and preserved (dressed) with the brain of the animal, in which the skin is rubbed and kneaded with both hands and feet until rendered quite soft and flexible.

When the supply of food has been assured the hunters next turn their attention to the traps. They set deadfalls, principally, for all the variety of animals captured, and are usually more successful in capturing martins, than any other game, the number of these animals annually captured being simply enormous. The next most abundant species is the beaver; then come the otter and Canada lynx; perhaps the red fox should come in after the martin, at least after the beaver, in point of numbers at any rate. In this manner the encampment, consisting perhaps of four men, three women, and five or six children, will continue to work their way five or six hundred miles inland in winter, eventually coming out in the spring by the same road—though not always—that they went in on the preceding fall, with a load of valuable furs, and in a half famished condition. They then sell their furs, pay part of their debts—for every one gets large credit from the traders who often charge enough to make up for it—and live in plenty for a time following. It looks strange to see them, as I have, furnish their wigwam, or mishwap; they borrow a stove, let the chimney run out at the top of the tent, and try to semi-civilize themselves, while they buy large quantities of everything that is eatable from the particular trader of whom they procure their goods—generally each family getting their purchases of a different party—and do little for the next month but eat and sleep. They are, generally speaking, a peaceable set, and only savage when their apparent—to them at least—rights are infringed on. The whole number on the coast is about 1400; they do not exceed a well ordered regiment, and doubtless one-half of these only could be relied on to fight, even should any real difficulty arise, which is not likely to happen at any time in a country at once so cold and so remote from human habitation generally. They have enough sense to see that it is for their own interest to keep on good terms with their white neighbors,—for who would purchase their furs if they did not do so? Strangely enough, an Indian will purchase anything that, setting his eyes upon, he desires, provided it come within the reach of his means, or that his credit allows; it may be a shotgun worth a hundred dollars, a boat worth twice that amount, or a solid and expensive gold watch,—and cases of the latter kind have occurred frequently. I have in mind one where an Indian ordered and obtained a valuable gold watch and chain worth about $150.00; he used them for awhile, and then exchanged it about a month after for a $3.00 silver one that, at the time, equally pleased his fancy. Nor is this either an extravagant or an exceptional instance on record of like stupidity.

In the afternoon of the same day, Thursday the 10th, I took a guide and went several miles farther up the river. It was a most pleasant and delightful walk. We followed a winding path, or portage, over a series of hills and vales; the deep snow on which we walked nearly covering a small growth of firs and spruces, probably six to eight feet high—the path lying over these. On the distant left rocky knobs and crests, with rounded tops, were everywhere apparent, while, on the right, high cliffs bordered the river.

We were now in the valley of the narrow river. High hills were on either side; beyond and ahead, uprearing tier upon tier, dark blue and long, uneven ridges of crests had been upheaved by nature towards the light blue sky above. The river, bending to the left, seemed to lose itself in the distance among the bases of one or two bold cliffs which appeared to bar its passage. It was a grand scene: the passive river, bound in ice and crowned with snow. At this point the stream is nearly a mile and a half wide. About the same distance can be seen ahead before the cliffs shut the view in that direction. The scene is one of a vast inland lake, enclosed on all sides by cliffs and hills.

Returning home I had a full view of the ridge across which the portage here runs. Like many, which I saw in various other places about the region, it is without doubt of glacial origin, and was perhaps formerly of equal height with the surrounding elevations on either side, but was worn down by the abrasion of some local arms of the glacier entering the river — perhaps the course of the former main glacial stream — at this point.

In the evening I visited the Mission, and found a young folks party in progress. It pleased me to see the effectual way that the teachers had taken to reach the juvenile hearts, and promote, for a couple of weeks to come, scholarly attainments in the recitation room.

Sunday the 13th. It snowed hard all day. Monday was no better. It was St. Valentine's day, which is here rigidly kept like the majority of other Saints' days and holidays, as a "fête day;" no one did any work, and while the women "slicked up," the men got "set up" — if they could find anything to get set up with — and spent the most of their time in smoking and sleeping. It snowed steadily until Wednesday morning, when it stopped, for a short time only, as if to ascertain the results, to begin again with renewed force and violence. Sunday was about one of the most uncomfortable days I experienced during the winter. The wind was cold and piercing, strong and penetrating. The ground was covered deep with snow, and the mist in the air — if I remember right — heavy and wet. Monday the little puppies, now nearly two-thirds grown, were broken into the komatik; it was a most curious sight. The process, though it appears brutal, is the only one that seems effectual. The young dogs are taken and tied tightly into a harness, an extra thong is passed into the mouth and then tied above and around the whole muzzle as tightly as it can be drawn; this is done principally to prevent the animal from biting the thongs and freeing itself. The other end of the harness is then fastened to that of one of the large and fierce dogs already secured to the sled. Of course, then, as the large dogs go, the smaller ones are obliged to follow. If they trip and fall, as they frequently do, the big dog drags them along until they are jounced on to their feet again. Thus on they go, rolling over and over, bounding from side to side, and all the time uttering most dismal and horrible groans and cries. Gradually they become actually hardened and seem to enjoy being thus pulled about, and soon they are loosened and harnessed, several of them separately, under the lead of some old head dog. After this the best and most obedient of them is fastened to the head dog, in advance of the others, and taught to be urged forward, or to be turned to the left or right at the shout of the proper turning words from the master; they are then harnessed all alone with this trained head puppy as leader, and if they go all right, exercise and the whip alone are necessary to keep them in training and practice.

Tuesday, February 22. Washington's birthday! How happy I am that the dear old gentleman was not born here in this remote frozen region; he verily would have died of the blues without having handed down to America an event to celebrate. I fired several rounds in honor of the occasion,— much to the disgust of the people with whom I was staying, who, as Englishmen, of course cared little about celebrating any save their own fete-days — and concluded the day with a walk, upon those curious articles the rackets, which I will try to describe.

In describing a walk in rackets I hardly know how, at first, to begin. I might follow on foot any one of the many excursionists who are so constantly and continually going and coming to and from the interior, or the dwellings along the coast, but that, being unaccustomed to long tramps, I could not give a true account of such experience; or I might give fanciful accounts of dangers and occurrences that possibly might have happened to me or anyone else unacquainted with the ground to be gone over had such a journey been attempted. I do not like to mix the fanciful and the real unless circumstances so happen that there seems to be no escape, and yet I fear that the faint description of a really short, but to me long and tiresome walk, or rather tramp of this kind which shall be told, will be far from giving you a true idea of what a Labradorian day's march, over hill and bay, may be. Though the hills are high, their caps snowy, and their sides slippery; though strangers would soon be tired out by excessive fatigue in climbing and slipping over them; the people here think no more of it than if the tramp were one over a level plain that we would walk with ease and comfort. The whole coast for many miles inland is one vast extent of hills, from three to five hundred feet above the sea level; and yet the men go over them from place to place, visiting house after house, stopping simply for a few moments' rest or chat with some neighbor, or to eat a frugal meal at another's hospitality,— for hospitality is offered here even among those who are enemies in every other way, and it is counted a sin to refuse such when houses are often a day's march apart—while a day's march of twenty, thirty, and in rare instances forty miles, of such travelling is far from being unusual. One may wonder how such journeys are made, but it is impossible to account for them other than by the natural hardihood of the people here, who live and thrive on the coarsest of food. Not long since a man walked a distance of about seventy miles in two days; quite recently, parties have gone deer hunting, twenty miles into the interior, stalking deer all day, returning to their simple cabin at night, having travelled forty miles. Nor are such events uncommon; the people here think nothing of it, and, in fact, tell of the many miles that they have walked with considerable pleasure. It is of course pleasant to ramble over these snow-capped hills; to see the beauties of nature, expressed in the indescribable language of nature, from elevations and depressions, from ponds and gorges, and snow alternating with rock or discovered lichens, or chilled vegetation; but a stroll over a bay of frozen ice, with hills about and around one, and islands here and there, while you walk comfortably along and fill yourself with the scene, is, perhaps, still more pleasant.

My walk from Old Fort Bay to Bonne Esperance was undertaken

in honor of the day. Here I was, in a lonely out-of-the-way region of the globe, midway between the temperate and the arctic zones, and snowed and iced up, so to speak, from the rest of the world; to this, add the fact that I was upon English soil, and you understand my feelings. I shall never forget in this connection (though I mean no offence) a passage in one of Jules Verne's works, in which he recounts a dispute upon the naming of a point hitherto unreached in the unknown lands in the polar regions. The parties were an Englishman and an American; both had come together unexpectedly in search, the one of the northwest passage, the other, of the north pole; the name of Cape Washington was given by the American. The Englishman angrily asserted, "you might choose a name less offensive to an Englishman;" to which the other replied, proudly, "but not one which sounds so sweet to an American." I am afraid that my English friends shared a touch of this sentiment, at least the former part of it, as I maintained the national honor of the occasion and fired a salute of four guns to the memory of the day; for, on coming to breakfast, I was greeted with a sharp, "what's that for?" and an explanation only elicited a shrug of the shoulders accompanied by an *humph!* as if of no consequence to them and entirely unnecessary on my part.

After breakfast I prepared to carry out my scheme. It was a fine morning, the air was cold and clear, scarcely any wind, the roads in tolerably good condition as I supposed, and all nature invited me forth. In return for the reception my patriotism of the morning had received, I determined to pay my friends by not telling them where I was going — having but one object in view all the time; many were their solicitations, but I was firm. The dogs seemed unusually happy as they frisked about and around me, and it seemed good to get out in the air; so putting on my rackets, with my gun in hand, I started off. At first I had to walk on the level bay about a mile and a half to the headland on the left. The walking would have been called good by a native Labradorian; to me it was terrible, and I stumbled along over ridges of drifted snow and patches of smooth ice, on which as with the schoolboy it seemed as if for every step forward I took two backward, and that it would have been much better to have turned, as he did, and walked backwards; but at last the difficulty was overcome and the snow reached again when the travelling was smooth for some distance.

The wind had as yet hardly sprung up, yet the clear but rather cold air was unusually invigorating. The hills on either side looked quite fresh and clear in outline against the sky, and the day gave promise of being unusually fine. Everywhere, snow! snow! snow! It seemed as if the elements combined to make bad travelling for the sledges, for it is hard work for the dogs to haul the komatiks through the snow on the bay, especially when the salt water penetrates the ice, or rather the partially thawed top of the salt water ice, which, it must be remembered, requires a much lower temperature to freeze than fresh water, alternate with the deep ridges of soft snow; but with rackets the case is different and these snow heaps were just the kind of material for good walking. I soon struck for the highland on the left and was just approaching a little opening between the mainland and an island—such openings are called here by the name of "tickle"—when a gust of wind from the northeast, and in the exact line through which I was to pass, struck me fiercely. The snow was piled in deep, uneven ridges; cakes of ice had been thrown upon each other by a recent partial thaw blocking the way before me; and the wind, added to these hindrances, almost forced me to abandon my design. The gust swept fiercely through the narrow opening, and I was glad when safe on the other side and once more set out across the long stretch of bay between me and the island half-way to my stopping place.

The hills on the coast receded on the left in an outline of undulating crests far eastward; on the far west was the ridge of high hills that formed the entrance of Old Fort Bay; beyond lay innumerable islands, often so close together that they seemed to form a band of mainland in the distance of several miles that separated them from me. On ! on ! The scene was one of strange beauty, while words are utterly unable to portray its grandeur.

The ice and snow of a winter on the hills and plains of northern latitudes cannot be described to a dweller in city, country, or town. The few houses of the region, miles apart, hidden by surrounding cliffs; undulating hill tops and deep gorges; isolated knobs, now high, now low; near ridges looking far, and far ones looking near, the effects of refraction in a clear, northern air,— all unite with an irregular plain of level bay in being covered everywhere with snow, snow, snow! A dull glare of ice, and occasional bare places or peaks on the rocky masses of hill — for I can call the whole coast by no other name — relieve occasionally a monotony of snow; while the clouds above add white masses of *stratus* to the scene. Tell me, now, how can pen describe what sight and sense almost fail to appreciate? Arctic travellers (not that I dare assume a place among them) tell of the sights that everywhere greet them and which are indescribable; yet few believe them until they likewise catch a glimpse of a similar display of nature's arctic grandeur. In the narrative of explorers, we read of one by one who return to give evidence to their truth and attempt to describe similar experiences.

The process of walking on rackets is one easier to describe than to attain to perfection. The large size of the rackets occasions an unusual difficulty in walking. The feet must be kept quite wide apart, and usually the proper step requires the leg to be swung in a semicircular direction around the racket of the other foot. The effect to the eye is very peculiar and ludicrous to one observing it for the first time; and, in fact, to me it always appears ludicrous to see a man thus easily, though apparently awkwardly and with difficulty, laboring his way along, claperty-clap, as the big pads fall in their proper step places on the snow, and the person wearing them advances rapidly along.

By this time the novelty of such a scene as that I was gazing upon had begun to wear away and given place to uneasiness regarding the distance ahead rather than of that already travelled. The walking, now that the open bay was reached, began to be anything but good; for while the lighter and more crispy—for I can think of no other word to express the condition—the snow, the better the walking, the case is quite the contrary when a partial thaw sets in and renders the walking watery and sloshy. At such a time every hole in the sieve-like interlacing of deerskin, which fills the interior of the racket, is filled with the sticky snow, and the bars covered also; soon, by frequent pressure, the upper side is covered with the same, and so with the weight above, and the sticking of the snow beneath, the foot must fairly drag such a mass of cloggy matter along with it and the racket, and soon renders one unused to this kind of walking quite weary; but there is no help, and on, on, through the slosh and snow a fatiguing tramp is continued. It is almost useless to stop and rest, as, strange to say, the best rest is to keep on walking. I do not know just how to explain this apparent contradiction; the truth, however, is revealed by a practical test. At length the walking is so bad that I take off my rackets and try my dogskin boots alone, though the condition of things is hardly improved until the walking is bettered by an approach to the island before mentioned, where a layer of snow materially helps the matter and forms a pleasant change from the sticky material that I leave behind.

After pressing on with renewed courage I soon reached the other side of the island, and could see Bonne before me about three miles ahead with a small point of mainland between us. The walking was now good, but the weather had changed. The wind blew hard from the northeast, and the cold was biting. Soon the clouds began to gather, and, almost before I knew it, the at first gently falling flakes of snow had agreed with the wind and came drifting down in perfect sheets; harder and harder came the blinding storm, fiercer and fiercer blew the wind, heavier and heavier became the rackets upon my feet, and then the feet themselves; but there was nothing to be done but keep up the spirits and march along. I have heard of fierce storms quickly arising in these arctic regions, that frequently bewildered the best of even native travellers and turned him astray from an almost straight road. I have, no doubt, frequently seen such from some house or safe harbor without fully appreciating its intensity; but I then saw it and felt its full meaning, though I was too near a shelter to be lost, unless overcome by fatigue or bewildered with fright, neither of which seemed probable though of course possible. The wind blew the snow in fine dust all over my clothes, and the cold penetrated even the thick cloth of which they were made. It was a terrible walk to the mainland, but I soon gained it, and sheltered myself in the fish stage of one of the establishments on the east side. Here I rested while watching the storm. There was a struggle in my mind as to whether to proceed at once across the small bay to my friend's house a distance of about half a mile, or wait until the storm had passed; a determination, however, to brave the worst; and, perhaps, a sort of feeling that it was better to conquer the elements, than be conquered by them, took possession of me, so I braced on the rackets again, buttoned my coat tightly about me, and with an extra pull to my cap I started off. How the wind did blow! how the blinding snow beat over and around me! that half mile seemed longer than all the other seven that I had gone over combined. At last the other side was reached, the well known place gained, and in a few moments I was in the presence of the nicest and most pleasant family on the coast of Labrador, without exception, while the weariness vanished as I was greeted by friends and sat down with them to a capital venison dinner.

Any one who has been half starved for the space of several weeks (almost months) on bread without butter, and tea and coffee without sugar or milk, with any kind of meat save salt pork out of the question, will appreciate a meal of good food when they get it. The case was mine exactly; and the savory smell of a good venison stew with some large mealy potatoes as an addition, as it was put upon my plate, clouded my vision to all other surroundings, so that I had eyes for this and nothing else, while I lost all sense of the outer world in contemplation of that delicious plate of food that was being passed to me. The tea with both milk and sugar — for Mr. Whitely's is one of three families on the coast that keep a cow — proved an excellent beverage; while a real currant pudding presented an additional feature that was wholly irresistible. My friends must have thought me a barbarian and half starved at that; the latter I was without doubt.

Few changes had occurred at Bonne since my visit there in the fall. The ice had frozen in the bay in front of the house, and snow still topped the summits of the island; big drifts lay about here and there, showing the general direction of the wind in heaping them up, but no one had attempted to dig through them, and it would indeed have been labor lost since the wind would surely have filled the paths in a single night to their former height. The male portion of the family occupied their time chiefly in most interesting conversation about deer and deer hunting, and some eighteen or twenty men had already gone off into the country on a hunt; the unusual abundance of these animals had fully raised a deer craze that attracted nearly all the eligible young men of the coast. Already some thirty deer had been killed, and others were reported every day. I saw a beautiful head and horns of a young buck shot by my friend, and it truly was a beauty. One man twice killed two deer with a single ball; this is remarkably fine shooting and shots of this kind are only made by a good hunter and one of steady nerves and eye. The deer, it is said, are very tame; but a man must stand a great deal and be able to walk many miles a day if he would become a deer hunter in this country; and though I do not suppose I shall attempt a trip of this kind, I can yet hope that chance may throw me in the way of shooting one of these fine animals. This has been the only fresh meat that the people about the river have had this winter, excepting the small piece each received of the cow that was killed late in the fall.

All game has fled, and the only fear is that the cupidity—I can call it nothing else—of the successful hunters will overcome their natural good feeling and prevent them from making that distribution of their spoils to the unsuccessful ones that they otherwise would. There is a strong spirit of selfishness among some of the inhabitants of the coast who have risen to comfort solely by their own hard work, for many that are now poor might also have become comfortably off by their own efforts, had they possessed courage to press forward to the work.

CHAPTER XII.

80° in winter — Trip eastward — Starting — Esquimaux river and island — Salmon bay — Bradore bay — Caribou island — Five leagues — Middle bay — Belles Amour — Over Bradore hills — L'Anse and dunes — Blanc Sablon — L'Anse Coteau — L'Anse Clair — Forteau — Amour.

THURSDAY, March 3. This was a remarkable day — though such a day as does at times occur in this region. The thermometer went steadily up, higher and higher, until about two o'clock it reached 80°, and hot enough to make us all wish for summer clothing. Soon it began to descend as rapidly as it had risen, until in the night it must have reached zero, or very near it, again. This, I believe, was the hottest day that I experienced on the coast; summer or winter.

On Friday morning, the 4th of March, I started on my long expected trip from old Fort Bay to L'Anse Amour, a distance in a straight line of only about thirty-five miles, while, by the way we were obliged to go, along the bays and points of the coast, it was nearly, if not quite, fifty miles. It took us two days to go, and as many to return, while a stay of the same time at different places on the way consumed the greater part of the week. It was a pleasant trip, and the time seemed only too short, while it was quite impossible to see all the numerous sights and go to all the attractive places awaiting us on every hand. The weather was most beautiful, and the air in a continual state of exhilarating freshness. Only one or two small flurries of snow passed over us, while, for the most part, the sky was of a cloudless blue. Occasionally a light haziness concealed the sun, and once a dark gathering in the southwest reminded one forcibly of the coming on of a thunderstorm as we frequently see it at home. Once, also, a light fog arose. I mention it simply because our guide said that it was very rare to see a fog in the month of March. The cool breezes were mostly from points from north to south by east. The cold was not intense, and at no time did I find it necessary to wear an overcoat over the heavy clothes that I had on though it proved a very convenient cushion for the komatik. I think there was but one day when the sun thawed the snow; but the roads were good all the time. Over hill and on bay, wherever we went the travelling was good, for dogs properly shod, and there was no reason to complain of it. We did not need rackets, and the snow was good and firm, while a beaten path most of the way united with everything else to make my journey a most enjoyable affair.

In starting upon a journey, in these parts, little or no provision is made for food upon the way, unless the distance to be passed over contains no houses; for, as I have frequently observed, to refuse hospitality even to an enemy is considered the worst crime of which a man here can be guilty. That important matter settled, the articles to be carried are carefully selected. As it requires no great time to select the articles for such a trip, one is, so to speak, ready at any time for a journey.

Friday we were awake and about bright and early. The day was fair, and it was not long before a hearty breakfast was awaiting us. After our simple meal we hastily got together our effects and lashed them to the komatik. They presented the appearance of of a rather high cushion, and could be easily taken for a seat prepared for the occasion. Large sacks of rough bagging for carrying articles which might be picked up on the way, such as food or meat for the dogs, etc., we added two such bags to our list, and with our overcoats, a pair of rackets in case such should be needed on account of the roads, and my gun, the equipment was as complete as it was simple.

The harnessing of the dogs did not take long. The early hour, and the unusual stir seemed to show them that something out of the ordinary course of proceedings was in order, and they too showed their delight at the prospect by their gambols and frolics. It was really somewhat difficult work to harness them. They would allow themselves to be caught only with great difficulty, and then would soon manage one way or another to break loose just when we thought we had secured them, and were off again barking at us from behind the woodpile some yards distant. It is a matter of no small difficulty to "rig" a komatik for a trip, getting all the lashings and the ropes in proper order, especially when seven dogs are to be caught and harnessed separately, their lines fastened to the *petook* (if this is the proper spelling, which I could not ascertain certainly), being what we call the rope to a sled. The coldness of the air chilled our fingers; the dogs provoked us with their uncalled-for gambols and frolics, refusing to be caught, though they seemed to regard it as great sport. At last the three large dogs and the three puppies, which latter had lately been broken in were all harnessed; the effects mentioned were tightly strapped on the sled, and all was ready. It is a curious sight to see the dogs thus harnessed striving to start the sled, each on his own account. When the last one is harnessed, if the team is a good one, each dog starts off with a run in a separate direction; it needs a good driver to control them or hold them in, or I should say hold the sled in, until he is ready to start. The effect presented reminds one much of the directions in which the five fingers point when the hand is spread out to its fullest extent. Each dog starts off with a rush, brings up at the end of his harness with a *thug*, as the narrow but short sealskin thong tightens, and the dog is elevated several feet in the air. The driver stands holding the komatik back with both hands by main force, while he shouts at the top of his voice to the dogs, with very little effect, to stop them or hold them in until he is ready. It was a cold morning, but we had not long to wait. Hurrying out of doors, and waving good-bye, we were off the moment the *hi, hi, hi*, told that all was ready.

When a team of good dogs first starts off it is almost, and one might well say quite, impossible to guide them. They will start off in any direction of their own accord, perhaps towards the very opposite side of the bay, and it is not until the first rush is over, and they have somewhat abated their eagerness, that the driver's guiding words are heeded at all. At last the head dog minds the voice and gradually turns into the right track, when the others follow a little behind, and the trip is really begun. It was thus with us, when at five minutes past eight o'clock we started off in the face of a good cool breeze from the north, in a clear air, with a bright sun shining on us from an almost perfectly cloudless sky, for our trip to the eastward.

The road from Old Fort Bay to the river, the same which I had gone over in komatik and on foot so many times, was not changed much this morning; of course one would hardly expect it to change, except by accumulation or disappearance of snow and the thawing and freezing anew of the ice of the bay. The same level platform of thick ice (broken only on the sides of the bay near the foot of the hills, while its surface by a slight recent thaw was covered with innumerable sharp needles of ice pointing upward occasioned by a smart frost in the midst of the thaw, rendering the going anything but good for the dogs' feet) spread before us for about a mile and a half to the first *portage*, or path over the low hills, to the nearest pond over which one is obliged to travel. As we rode through this long, narrow cleft of the hills, I could not but think of the mighty force that had here been at work for centuries to render the place what it is; as also of the process by which indentations were made that left a succession of peaks separated by partial valleys on either side, from the mouth of the bay to the bottom, and extending forward and inward in successive chains far into the interior; and of the gorges and individual shape of each crest, bending gently down to the water from the upper end of the bay, while ending generally in rather abrupt, low, and yet often nearly perpendicular cliffs or cliff-like rocks on each side. Then the probable agency in polishing the rocks, often quite smooth, and in rounding off the peaks—for it is seldom that you anywhere see a pointed hill top—and apparently shaping the whole general appearance of hills, valleys, and surrounding elevations and depressions.

Thus thinking, we rode swiftly and pleasantly along the bay; we crossed the first portage, over a low bank, with hills on either side, at a little to the right of the bottom of the bay, where a rather high hill slopes to the water and forms its boundary line, and descended to the first pond. This pond is on the same level as the bay, and separated from it by only a low ridge of land from which the rock of the region crops out on all hands. It is nestled in a hollow with hills all around it while the outline, more or less circular in form, encloses an area of perhaps a half a mile. Across this we go, and then slowly glide along the second portage which, like the ridge containing it, is nearly on a level with the pond. On the right, the low, rather swampy looking level is covered with the gnarled trunks and stems of the dwarf birch so common in this locality, the *Betula populifolia* of the botanists, and the best fire-wood that the region affords, while on the left we pass close to a long, perpendicular wall of rock that, rising some six feet and extending some fifty in an even line, abruptly ends the ridge in this place; its surface is as smooth as if polished by some mighty force, and yet I saw no scratches, or even signs of cleavage anywhere upon its face. The extent of this portage is about the same as that of the one we had recently passed.

We now descend a little to a second pond; a very small stream of good drinking water (to which a large hole has been made through the snow) runs along this path. This pond was soon passed, and after ascending a low bank similar to that we crossed in going to the first pond, and like it a low ridge between hills, we descended to the river. Esquimaux or St. Paul's river, as it is called —the latter being the proper name, though it figures upon the charts as the former,—is peculiar in many respects. Its mouth is quite large, and with several flexures or bends; while Esquimaux Island lies directly on the right hand, leaving only a small, narrow, and almost straight passage to the open sea beyond. About seven miles inland the river narrows, passes some rapids, then enlarges again to the next series of rapids, beyond which I have not been. The waters are covered with ice the greater part of the time from November to June. The broad bay-like portion, on which we now entered, is everywhere surrounded with high hills which resemble those inland. Several deep indentations, formerly the sites of one or more houses, but which have been abandoned from unknown causes, are to be seen on the left, as we enter the western side and observe Esquimaux Island in the near distance in front of us; while the water reaches the sea on the right, and the tops only of several little islands appear to relieve in summer the otherwise open sea, and in winter the level ice. It is a wild scene,—nothing but snow-capped hills, in the distance, above and around, while huge heads of rocks jut out in long, stubbed, and rounded points of land, dividing the bay-like river bend into several smaller pond-like bends or bays. We skim along over the ice, in our hobgoblin team of dogs with sled, enjoying the beauty of nature thus opened to us in her icy realm, and drink in the fresh, yet not too cold, air that stings our ears and gives us ruddy faces.

The usual path to the mission is soon traversed, and we pass on our right the long, even, low sloping ridge on the north side of Esquimaux Island with rather higher crests on either side, extending still further north, the whole looking as if it might once have been the terminus of some glacial mass that swept over it, as well probably as of most of these regions, and on our left the group of some eight or ten houses which, with the church, constitute the winter quarters of the inhabitants of the neighborhood. Now we enter a small bend in that side of the river directly ahead of us, which leads to a gorge-like opening between either two very high hills (high for this region) or a single hill cleft in twain by some mighty force, the latter of which is more probable, and begin to climb the steep bank above covered with short spruce and fir trees, by a narrow and winding portage. Up, up the bank we climb, at least the dogs climb while we get off the sled and walk, at the top of which we still see the hills apparently four times the distance we have reached above us; a walk of a few hundred rods brings us to the opposite slope. On our left the huge mass of rock that forms the greater part of the hill has been broken off or rent asunder with the greatest nicety, presenting huge columns of granite, more or less square, on a nearly perpendicular face of rock. If you take a piece of paper (stiff writing paper is the best) fold it backwards and forwards in creases about three-eighths to five-eighths of an inch thick alternately, it will give you a very fair representation of the cliff as I saw it: nor did I see a corresponding rent anywhere in the rock on the opposite side. We now descended the slope and entered the pond-like arm of the river, or *lac salé*, as it is here called, which signifies a salt lake, or a salt water lake-like bay of the sea or river, which latter it is in this case. We had a nice path across *lac salé*, as, in fact, we did on nearly or quite all the ponds between there and our journey's end, and on this little arm of the sea, not a mile in uneven extent of coast line, we saw hills, cliffs, and wooded slopes on either hand around, nor was the passage through which we were to pass visible anywhere before us. It was a complete picture, and worthy the pencil of an artist.

We crossed a small pond directly after passing the salt lake just mentioned, and enclosed, like it, with high hills on either side. It was about on the same level with the water which we passed. Between *lac salé* and this pond, we found a long, narrow pass, where the rocks came close to the passage with their abruptly broken sides and edges gently sloping upward to low, rounded crests on either hand. Through the pass thus formed flowed a small stream of water running over rocks, the bed of a brook, and evidently broken pieces from the neighboring hills. It formed a pretty sight to see this little stream in such a natural and yet rather unlooked-for place, and the broken ice above showed the quite clear water as it flowed gently beneath.

Soon these scenes of picturesque beauty began to be familiar to us though we never tired of them; while the new scenes or new variations of old scenes repeated the picture in a more beautiful manner and added the charm of freshness and expected change to those which were to come. The long, narrow portages soon gave way to wider and broader tracts of country through which the way wound as before. The hills were reduced to low crests, and open field-like slopes on ridge and high level plains appeared in the distance. We soon crossed Salmon Bay, coming out of a long arm-like expansion of the neighboring lands, and which formed the centre of three, all similar expansions, the right and left of which appeared more like sort of bays or rounded arms, as one looked back upon the view from the opposite side of the bay. One or two houses were visible, the first seen since leaving the river, a distance of some five or six miles behind us. And here we came to another of these strangely formed places or ridge-like openings in the valley, between hills so often seen in different places all along the coast, and which remind one of artificial, though they are in truth quite natural, terraces. The height of this formation is about thirty feet, its top is nearly level. On the left, looking towards the sea, are the high hills of Bradore — though I do not mean the Bradore hills so called, which are over eleven hundred feet in height and situated some way back in the country, while those of which I speak form the boundary of Bradore Bay on its extreme western side and are only about four hundred feet high — with a rather abrupt slope to this ridge. On the right a rather low crest separated it from the sea. The ridge itself slopes to the water on each side, at an angle of about 30° on the Salmon Bay, and by a gentle rather than abrupt slope on the seaward side. The ridge points in a northeastward and southwestward direction as do most other similar ridges where I have seen them, and the direction of the slopes, and general appearance of the top of the plateau suggest to one's mind the final resting place of some arm of the mighty Labrador glacier before or rather during the final plunge of its huge mass of ice into the sea. Surely these well-defined and peculiar shaped plateaus are of glacial origin, and being in all cases, so far as I have seen them, of pretty much the same form and shape, the suggestion is of a common glacial one. Before we leave the subject a few words about Salmon Bay may be of interest. Salmon Bay, like the majority of the long, fiord-like bays so numerous on the coast east of it, is a long, rather narrow inlet, about four miles in length, extending into the land in a northwesterly direction. At its mouth Caribou Island, a little island a mile wide and a mile and a half in extent, occupies the greater part of the western side of the entrance; beyond a small pond-like piece of water, about three-quarters of a mile in either direction, is nearly enclosed by the small points of land that reach towards each other from the opposite side of the basin which admits one to the bay proper. In summer this is the seat of one of the largest fishing posts on this portion of the coast. Some eight or ten establishments here employ about one hundred and fifty men, and seven cod seines valued at twenty-five hundred dollars are used in the fisheries.

I must not forget that the country to the east of Salmon Bay, and before reaching the high cliffs and bluffs just next the river, is rather low, and made up of rounded crests of hills covered here and there with a scanty vegetation, presenting something of the appearance of a hilly New England farm lot. The tops of the hills were strewed with a few loose stones either broken from the rocks themselves or left there by some agency of ice or water. The same general features existed in most parts of the bay on both sides, and as I looked upon the scene I could almost imagine the mighty force that, slowly pushing itself and creeping onward by its own plastic mobility down the channels from some interior region, gradually ground off these hill tops, and scattered these stones, while it levelled the feeble barriers that attempted to confine it to the land, and buried itself in the sea.

From Salmon Bay, across a narrow plateau-like ridge, we descended to the sea again — frozen in a mass of icy needles that flashed and glittered in the sun, most treacherous and cutting to the dogs' feet, the precursors and frequent occasion of that malady, so terrible in these regions, snow blindness — and continued our course — with a glimpse of the far-off shores of Newfoundland, towards which spread an icy plain with a distant channel of open water, at our right, and the shore, skirted with the broken and fantastically shaped blocks of ice that lay piled, in all sorts of positions, on or against each other often several feet high, like tide marks on the left, — across the three full miles of Five Leagues Harbor to Five Leagues Point, the residence of a well known and thrifty fisherman and seal-catcher. Taking a cup of tea here, we continued our way to Middle Bay, on the east side of which, with another friendly acquaintance, we took our dinner and nooning before continuing farther. As we had made full sixteen miles since morning, both the dogs and ourselves needed and enjoyed this rest. After our dinner, which consisted of bread and tea, the latter a concoction of the twigs or rather boughs of the spruce, which are often used as a substitute for the real article and so carefully prepared that it is sometimes hard to distinguish from an inferior quality of it, we harnessed our dogs, and were once more on our journey.

I cannot quite recollect the exact position of the house of this hospitable fisherman, or of a large, old-fashioned, red-painted, country looking house that we passed somewhere here, which looked more like a comfortable establishment than any I had seen for a long while, and which, though I did not stop there, no doubt would have fully equalled the expectations excited from the outside appearance. Behind this was another of those peculiar ridges such as have been mentioned as occurring in other localities. As the direction of Middle Bay is about north northeast, this narrow ridge barely separates the eastern baylet — if I may use the word — of the bottom of the bay, from the western baylet of the opposite or Belles Amour Bay. The intervening neck (the ridge I have mentioned) extends outward on either side and forms a square block of land nearly two miles each way; on this are one or two fishing establishments that yield or ought to yield a good profit to their owners, but I sadly fear that industry is greatly crippled here as in other places about the Labrador coast, by a feeling that says let well enough (which is sometimes poor at best) alone, and hinders any real progress either in wealth or desire for cultivating the intellectual qualities.

I have been struck with the really musical and pretty names which appear all along the coast, and bear the marks of that society language—the French. Belles Amours signifies something like loves or passions of beautiful women, and undoubtedly took its name from some conquest of love by or over some fair inhabitant of the place.

We now descended to the famous Bradore bay, the "Brest" of the early inhabitants when Cartier discovered the St. Lawrence, when Cabot discovered Newfoundland, and when Corterel is said to have discovered Labrador. The shape of this bay is very nearly that of an acute angled triangle — the upper side, extending due east by north, in an almost straight line for nearly seven miles ; the other side (which I shall call the outer side) due north by slightly west (the centre part bulging out giving to the whole side the appearance of a bent bow with the end slightly recurved) for six miles ; while the base, or a straight line from the extremity of Stony Point its western, to the extremity of Grand Point its eastern, boundary, the distance is eight miles. The only island of any account in this large bay is called the Ledges Island and is about a mile wide by a mile and a half long only. It is about a mile from shore near the centre of the outer side, and, with a few scattering rocks, forms a mass of dangerous shoals in this northeastern end of the bay.

The little island near the land on the extremity of the outer side, and quite near Grand Point, is Paroquet (also spelled Peroquet) Island. It is a very small island, a mere rock rather than island scarcely half a mile in either direction, but small as it is it is as noted perhaps in its way as any of the larger islands on the coast. As its name would indicate, it is the abode of the paroquet or puffin, the sea parrot as it is called, or the *Fratercula arcticus* of the ornithologists. On this small island thousands of these plump little birds, with their huge scissors-shaped, horny bills, collect in the summer and breed in large companies. Their nests are made in holes in the ground, which is tunnelled with their burrows in every direction. A great trick of the inhabitants with strangers who visit this island is to get some person — the greener the better — to put his hand into the hole when the bird is within sitting upon its eggs. If you could but see the bill, you would readily understand why the attempt is never made a second time. Imagine a huge pair of horny scissors, two inches long, two inches high at the base, and half an inch thick yielded with force, and no wonder one does not care to repeat the experiment.

As the ice in Bradore bay was not all quite fast, that is, as open water appeared on it in many places, we were obliged to take to the hills and cross by the land. The hills and high cliffs which everywhere skirt the north shore, sometimes almost perpendicular to the water at their base, sustain a plateau extending far back into the country. A mass of hillocks crowns its summit, varying from two hundred and seventy-five to three hundred and twenty-five feet above the sea-level. The whole plateau, if I may so call it, spreads out for a long distance inland, and forms nearly or quite all the country upon the upper side of the bay line. During our whole ride over these hills the constant sight of something new, the unlooked-for contrasts presented here and there, rendered the trip across them a source of pleasure and delight — one well worthy the express journey of some geologist or glacial specialist, who should read to us the sermons these rocks contain. Now a long and wide (almost level) plain with its rather uneven surface would end in a row of low crests of unequal height, beyond which the slope would carry us some fifty or seventy-five feet to a pond; beyond a varied plain and hilly patch of ground would often give place to another pond, almost at a level with the surrounding hillocks. Snow covered almost everything, and only the rounded or broken hill-tops, and the rough pieces scattered from their place in the rock thus crushed, or scattered over the slopes by some mighty agency, here and there, rather evenly though sparingly deposited, alone offered a glimpse of the appearance of the surface beneath the snow. These blocks were for the most part very angular, often nearly square; occasionally a rounded one appeared, and I saw one huge, almost round stone, nearly two feet through each way, balanced nicely between two upright rocks, while on the opposite side an almost perfect and solid block cube of stone was nicely balanced upon the fine point of a small upright chip of rock, from which but a slight push would have dislodged it,— as also the rounded stone opposite — showing that the force or agency that left it there could hardly have been a convulsive, but rather a slow-moving and methodical one. At the northeast corner of the bay we took to the ice again, and finding it firm and hard we skirted along the edge of the outer side, and crossing Grand Point — where the formation begins to differ from what I have just described, and to take on the aspect of the whole plateau this side of Bradore and extending to Forteau bay, a distance of some eleven miles across, being a sandstone deposited in regular layers of which I shall speak soon — we landed at Blanc Sablon, the eastern termination or boundary line of the Province of Quebec.

Beyond, the whole broad plateau or table-land of Labrador proper extends. It exists as a dependent of the provincial government of British Newfoundland, to which Labrador pays duty and tribute in the shape of revenue on all goods received within its boundaries.

I will now speak of a little cove on the southern end of this eastern side of Bradore bay. I am almost certain that it is that portion marked in the charts where the water encroaches upon the land in a semicircular-like baylet almost directly opposite Paroquet Island. I discovered here a beach of pure sand, extending backward into a series of regular hillocks of sand or sand dunes, as they are called, which rise above the level of the surrounding country back of them. That they appear in this place, marking as they seem to do the separation between the Bradore granite and Blanc Sablon sandstone, and running away back in gentle slope to what seems to have been once a bay of the sea with its nearly level extension between a high plateau on either side, is perhaps rather remarkable, and of geological interest. The peculiar name given to this place of L'Anse aux Dunes, would seem appropriate were the word *dunes* in French translated dunes in English — the word *anse* signifying a small bay or cove. Here five or six men set some nine nets for seal in the spring, and also catch a few salmon and cod in the summer, but it is only a small station at best. Near the water the beach was strewn with shells, especially of the razor-billed clam as it is often called, and a variety of sea animals, while huge drifts of seaweed, like that so common in many places on the coast here and on the Atlantic generally, were entangled with blocks of ice and lay around from nearly one end of the beach to the other. That night we spent at Blanc Sablon, having travelled a distance of twenty-five miles, nearer thirty by the route we took, since leaving home in the morning; accomplishing the whole, including stops and all, in a little less than ten hours. The distance would have been gone over in much less time had the dogs been properly shod; but, as it was, the ice cut their feet so badly that blood flowed in nearly each print in the snow or on the ice, while the poor animals were quite stiff and lame the next morning.

Of Blanc Sablon I shall say very little, as I had so little time here to visit the place. On all sides of the harbor the country was one mass of stratified deposit of sandstone, as is the whole plateau, as I have before called it, between this place and Forteau. On the western side of the harbor the deposit is much broken, numerous hill-like elevations and broken ridges cover the surface everywhere on the tops of which a scattered vegetation flourishes; on the eastern side the deposit forms a ridge that extends for some distance in a north and northeasterly direction. For a mile or so in a northerly direction the water, retreating, has left the hollow occupied formerly by the sea so perfect that but little imagination is required to trace the former outline of the harbor. With the place itself I was much pleased. It is a busy looking station, and from its geographical position, large size, and importance as a fishing locality, it is often called the Boston of Labrador. It contains perhaps a hundred buildings on both sides the harbor and the adjoining islands, of which I shall speak presently, and some three hundred inhabitants, increased to twice that number in the summer and fishing season. The "large room," as it is called, contains an abundance of articles for sale or trade in exchange for furs, fish, and other articles used as a fair medium of exchange, at their current price either in trade or cash. The stock is owned by merchants from the isle of Jersey in the English channel — whence a great number of people come who live on this coast — and now in charge of a smart, gentlemanly clerk already some eight years in the companies' employment though still in his teens. The fishery connected with this same firm, employing some ten men in winter, and eighty in summer, is perhaps the largest in the place, and no wonder this young fellow clerk who oversees the whole is called the young master, while he still holds his position and retains the confidence of his employers as well as his employés. The two important islands, just outside the harbor, are Wood (*l'île au Bois* as it is usually called) and Greenley Islands. The former contains several fishing establishments, and another shop where various articles are bought and sold, and is the larger of the two being about two miles long, of triangular shape, with the apex pointing northwest, and a base about a mile wide facing southeast; the latter the light island, where the lighthouse is situated, one of the only two upon the coast from Point des Monts in the river St. Lawrence, eastward. It lies west and a very little south of Wood island, and is scarcely three-quarters of a mile either long or wide. To give a little, perhaps rather dry detail, I find the light described in the report of the Canadian government, somewhat as follows: "light upon the S. W. part of the island, latitude, $51° 22' 35''$, longitude (west of Greenwich), $57° 10' 50''$. Single light, revolving white for $\frac{1}{2}$, then red $\frac{1}{2}$, then white again $\frac{1}{2}$, blank $1\frac{1}{2}$ minutes (three minutes for full revolution). The tower octagonal, wooden with dwelling attached, 100 feet high, the light visible fifteen miles. It is an established light of the second order, and a fog gun is fired every half hour."

Taking a good rest at the house of the friendly people with whom we had taken up our quarters for the night, we gave ourselves to the enjoyment of the clear, cool, evening air, and soon after supper retired to sleep. The people in many places along the coast where I have visited, at least the men, have a habit of closing their day's work in winter with their supper. At that time all the work of the day is supposed to be over, and after the meal the principal occupation is visiting one's neighbors and either there or at home spending the evening in chatting, and smoking very poor and bad smelling tobacco, which, however, seems to be the best the coast affords. What would at home be thrown away as worthless is here sold in large quantities for a high price. I mention this fact to show the imposition often practised upon these people who are unable to help themselves, and who must either put up with it or go without; strange to say, most prefer to put up with the bad article, and hundreds of hundred-weight boxes of bad tobacco are used each season. Nearly all of the men on the coast smoke, and it is very rare to find a man, old or young, to whom the pipe is a stranger, or who does not use tobacco in one form or another. Even the young boys smoke as soon as they can secure the necessary articles. It seems to be a matter of pride with them here as elsewhere, and the fellow who can begin the earliest and smoke the most tobacco is the best fellow, and takes the lead among his comrades and companions.

The houses here are much like the houses elsewhere, a huge kitchen and sitting-room with a small bedroom on the ground story, and a loft with two rooms reached by a ladder leading to a small aperture about two feet wide in the floor above. The bed or bunk is roughly made, and more often the mattress simply lies on the floor. The people with hardly an exception are fishermen, and the best off are poor compared to what they might be should a spirit of economy and industry take possession of them and drive away the spirit of procrastination. The occupation during the day is chiefly that of mending and netting nets and seines, or laying plans for and chatting with neighbors on the next season's work among the fisheries. The fishing season is usually from the first of May, the opening of spring, until the first of September, the beginning of cold weather, but during these four months all is stir and excitement both day and night. Men in boats are out fishing all the time, and every device thought of is put into operation for the securing of a good "catch," as the work of the season is called. Labor is cheap, and none but lazy persons fail to enter into the full excitement of the occasion; these well deserve the poverty brought upon them by their own idleness and want of exertion. I have known whole families to exist on the charity of their neighbors with perhaps only a single or at most two barrels, one of flour and the other of meal, during the long six months of winter; but the idle always have their own reward, at least on this coast where no one is rich enough to supply such persons at their own expense, even if they were so disposed.

Early the next morning we tackled our still lame and tired dogs and proceeded on our journey. The dogs went badly at first but they bravely overcame the tendency to weakness, caused by their lame feet, and soon trotted along at so brisk a pace that, but for the occasional drops of blood left in their tracks from wounds made by the sharp ice cutting their feet, one would scarcely notice their tendency to fatigue. We soon climbed the steep, high hill directly back of the houses and the ridge or rather long, low granite mound — if one may so call it — and found ourselves on an uneven plateau of sandstone, the upper surface of which looked much like that of the Bradore granite; but while the vegetation on the Bradore Hills was scant and poor, here dwarf spruce and fir trees showed occasional green tops and branches from beneath the snow; while broken and cut sticks, appearing in all directions, showed where the ground, once completely covered with these trees, had been cleared for fuel, and left to again grow over, probably for the same ultimate use. I could not but reflect that I was riding over a mass of stratified sandstone, extending miles in three directions with the sea at the south, and once a part of the ocean, which receded either by elevation of the land, by sinking of the sea basin, or a combination of both. With about the same slope that we ascend from Blanc Sablon to this plateau, we descended to the bay on the opposite side from an elevation of about four hundred and thirty feet, and, as I later observed, the slope was nearly the same on the southern side also, though the distance passed over here was only about three miles.

The ride was so full of interest that I scarcely realized when a view of the little inlet of St. Claire or L'Anse au Claire Bay came upon us quite unexpectedly, and the ride down the hill and along the western bank of the bay afforded a fine view of the surrounding beauties of nature. Here we took dinner with a most excellent family, and the pleasant conversation of both host and hostess, who were great friends with my guide, proved most interesting. The gentleman who had for a long time resided here as a fisherman — and certainly a very intelligent one — gave me much useful information about the country, and stated the fact that he had, from personal examination, found that this same sandstone formation continued beneath the sea, as he found from soundings while fishing for cod, and appeared again on the Newfoundland shore, which is here about fourteen miles across its nearest point. I saw here, also, that this little bay partook of the same general character of so many other bays along the coast here, and distinctly showed the former extension of the sea in its basin beyond, while the limestone cliffs and hillocks appeared in all directions, to the right, to the left, and directly ahead. After our dinner and a little time allowed for resting ourselves we continued our journey in a cool, bracing air, across the bay. We ascended the opposite ridge, a continuation of what we had just passed over, and with a similar height above the sea, only perhaps with a rather more even surface, and crossing several large ponds, continued our way over these hills in a triangular direction to the height above Forteau Bay, a distance of five miles, passing through a slight snow fog, a peculiarity of this district perhaps (though I am assured of rare occurrence in the month of March), which, barely lifting, gave us a hazy view of what was around. We now descended, in a tremendous hurry, the famous steep Forteau hill, that is situated here, to the bay; the dogs could not keep up to the sled in spite of double drags, or huge rings of thick rope, thrown over the runners, fall between them and the snow and form a powerful resistance to the forward motion of the sled,—yet we reached the bottom in safety.

As this is another of the important indentations of the coast, it may be well to give simply an outline of the principal points of interest connected with it. If then we measure the distance between Point Forteau on the western and L'Anse Amour on the eastern extremity of the bay, we shall find a straight line between these two places to run in a northeast by easterly direction for a distance of nearly four miles. The outline of the bay itself is triangular; the apex from the centre of the mouth of the bay lies inland in an almost exact northwesterly direction. The western side of the bay is nearly straight, while the eastern represents the figure 5 with the dash at the top off, and the curve at the bottom of the bulge not quite reaching a point exactly below the straight line above as it necessarily does in a well made figure of that character. Of course there are many little irregularities of coast-line, but the general form is quite as I have described it. At the extremity of Amour Point stands Amour lighthouse, the other of the two lights on the coast, and which will soon be described. Strange as it may be, Forteau Bay basin shows still another of those plainly marked, former extensions of the sea to some inland point; and, as this peculiar sandstone formation ends at the beginning of the bulge, on the eastern side, the whole forms an even plateau from Blanc Sablon to this point. A formation of more or less stratified limestone then begins, whose eastern terminus I have not yet ascertained, though it is said to extend under the sea and appear again like the sandstone at L'Anse Claire, on the opposite Newfoundland shore. The whole thus presents an interesting field for future investigators, as it forms an additional link in the chain of points of interest, whose combination forms a culmination of great geological importance in reading the former history of the region. It was quite fortunate that at about five o'clock in the evening we were so near our journey's end, for it would have been an easy matter to have tracked us across the bay (Forteau Bay I mean) on the ice by the blood alone from the dogs' feet. We had six dogs in our team, three full grown and three young ones. As there were not enough shoes for all of them even when we started, and as we had not been able to procure a sealskin or any canvas to make others to replace those already worn out, by this time most of the dogs had one or two shoes only, while one had none. We had driven him without any all this distance, nearly twenty miles, because having a full set of four nice shoes, he had turned to and pulled them off with his teeth and eaten them up at our last stopping place, and his punishment was tying his mouth up tightly and driving him as I have said. This fellow bled from all his feet, and nearly all the others showed drops of blood in each footprint; but there was no help for it, and so we kept on as well as possible until our destination was reached.

Forteau Bay is the first bay of any importance on the Labrador peninsula, and though the principal port on this part of the coast is Red Bay, twenty-two or twenty-three miles farther east, the former is not without its objects of general interest. Each side of the bay is lined with buildings, — houses, shops, and fishing store-houses — to the number of some twenty or thirty. On the eastern side of the bay a neat little church, well built and painted white, rears a small but homely looking, short, square steeple with a small spire upon it against the dark background of the ridge beyond; by its side stands a tastily built parsonage, silently awaiting occupancy by some quiet and practical Christian people whose "charity shall begin at" this their village "home," and end there also, which, wisely administered, "shall cover" for the people "a multitude of sins." And truly the people here need such a family, for they are sadly deficient in intellectual ideas, neighborly charity in little things, and personal virtues, though there are many exceptionally fine families among these plain, rough, good-hearted people.

It was just about dusk when we reached our destination on the extremity of L'Anse Amour, and being Saturday night we looked for a quiet rest on the following Sunday, both for ourselves and our sore-footed dogs. It was a nice old-fashioned couple that met us here, and, sending the boys to take care of our team and the articles upon it, they invited us into the house, where, after cordial greetings (for the guide was well acquainted here) they placed before us, for refreshment, cups of hot tea and buttered graham bread—the first I had seen on the coast. The large house, with its low studded ceiling and ample apartments, presented a cosey and homelike appearance. The kitchen served as a dining-room and place of general assembly, and there we all met together, — those who smoked did so, and those of us who did not made ourselves comfortable and looked on, while we all chatted pleasantly together until supper time; this over, we spent the evening in chatting pleasantly and familiarly with our host and hostess.

Sunday, March 6. Two pleasures fill me to-day, the oue that I am here in a new place with the beauty and freshness of new scenes before me, the open bay in front, the sea with a distant view of the Newfoundland coast at the left, and a huge bank of limestone containing unknown treasures in the shape of new and rare fossils behind the house and not a hundred rods away: the other the prospect of a good, quiet, homelike Sunday with pleasant people who greet me most cordially, upon my appearing at the breakfast table. The simple but relishable meal over, the morning was spent in talking, walking, and in reading. The dinner disposed of — an equally satisfactory repast — all hands were invited to take a walk to the limestone cliff and see its attractions. This we did, and were soon examining this mound ridge of sea-deposit which appears to stretch a long distance in a northwesterly direction, though just how far I could not tell. The edges of the cliffs, here some seventy-five feet high, were exposed, and presented a most uneven, and irregular jagged surface, facing the sea; below, the broken pieces that had tumbled down by weather, wind, frosts, rain, and their own weight, strewed the ground everywhere in a sloping pile of fine chips — like slate rock — and stones of various sizes with occasional huge bowlder-like lumps of solid rock. I picked up several well formed fossils, and accepted our host's kind invitation to spend a week or more with him in the spring, when the snow and ice should have disappeared, in examining the place with reference to its geology and for specimens.

A rough climb brought us to the top of the ridge, and gave us a fine view of the surrounding sea and country. We had been followed by eight or ten of our dogs, and it was an amusing sight to watch their efforts to follow us in our climb, and their repeated tumbles and consequent slides down the icy slope some fifty feet to the bottom of the descent. At length we are all safely landed, and a brisk walk in the strong wind and rather cold, bracing air brought us to the road. On our right was the lighthouse, but we did not visit it. It is situated on the extremity of the point, and we learn from the reports that it is in latitude 51° 27′ 35″, longitude 56° 50′ 55″. It is a circular lighthouse, height 155 feet, built in 1855. The light is of the second order, and visible eighteen miles ; it is fixed and white. A whistle sounds every ten seconds in foggy weather. This and the light on Greenley Island are the only two lights on the coast ; no doubt another will soon be built, perhaps near the rocks upon which the Edward Cardwell was so lately wrecked. There at least ought to be one near that point of the coast, though Beacon or Old Fort Island would seem to be the best place for it. Our walk home was soon accomplished ; the afternoon and evening passed away quietly,— a sermon read by one of our number occupied the latter part of the evening, and we all retired to rest early.

Monday morning we left these kind-hearted people, with many expressions of cordiality on both sides, and were soon travelling towards home again, as this was the end of our journey. It was a bright and clear, cool morning, and the dogs spun merrily along, well shod and apparently quite over their lameness and sore feet. We returned by the same road as that by which we had come, as far as L'Anse Claire, and then, veering to the left, followed the coast to the strangely located abode of another hospitable and well known family, at the foot of the central point of the sandstone cliff here situated midway between L'Anse Claire and Blanc Sablon ; this is called L'Anse Coteau, and occupies a little niche in the coast just east of the extreme eastern end of Wood Island, which is seen just beyond the point. The ride around this cliff presented somewhat the appearance of our walk around the limestone of L'Anse Amour. The sandstone, everywhere broken, showed us plainly the layers or strata, and its various colors of brown, red, and gray. We stayed here over night and continued our journey the next day. Returning by Bradore bay, which was now quite frozen over and safe to travel upon, I could now see the appearance of the granite at this point. Several huge and irregular dikes, apparently of trap, marked the surface of some of the rocks. Most striking irregularities of breakage, in some cases amounting almost to cleavage, appeared in the cliffs and in the pieces broken off and tumbled to its foot. Some of the bowlders were cleft by frost and weather, while everywhere evidence of most interesting structure prevailed; but I had too little time to spend here, so continued my homeward journey. The rest of the return trip was pleasant and delightful; the air cool yet comfortable, with a clear sky. The dogs, though weary, seemed to know that they were going home and trotted along quite rapidly. Soon darkness began to close in upon us, and in a short time hearty home welcomes and a nice hot supper were the entertainments of the evening. "Early to bed and early to rise," says the old proverb; we tried the former part of the saying and soon drowned our cares in peaceful slumber.

CHAPTER XIII.

Canadian porcupine — Picking fall berries in spring — Carrying wood to summer quarters — Anticipating Fourth of July — Summer quarters in winter — Capsized — Fox hunt on rackets — A mile of soft snow without rackets.

THURSDAY, March 10, I spent the day in skinning and stuffing a porcupine, that was brought in to me by one of the neighbors, and a most difficult task I found it. The Canadian porcupine (*Erethizon dorsatum*) is quite common all along the coast, and in the interior of Labrador. It is an animal more or less peculiar to this region, and is generally found in winter by following, on the newly fallen snow, the impressions of its feet which look much like the imprints of a small child's foot. It is found more frequently in winter than in summer, when it comes out from its hiding places, which are in caves, under rocks, and often in the hollows of trees, and travels about for food. It lives on berries and the bark of trees, gnawing them in such a manner that the hunter knows at once when one of these animals is about, after having found its cuttings. The animal returns to the same place each day to feed until its supply ceases, when it seeks a new place. Though naturally a sluggish animal, the porcupine, when pursued, takes at once to the tree-tops and is then very spry and agile. When caught upon the ground it immediately rolls itself together into a sort of ball, and with spines erected meets the intruder. Only the belly, and extremities of the animal are destitute of these spines so that it can be safely attacked only on these parts. The Indians kill it with a blow from some stick which they carry for the purpose, or, if

TRIP TO OUR SUMMER HOUSE. 215

it ascends a tree, they cut the tree down and then soon dispatch the animal. It is a formidable object, when thus on the defensive, for other animals to attack, as to touch it detaches many of the spines which work their way into the flesh causing terrible wounds. It occasionally utters a sort of plaintive cry, and this, with many other circumstances, has won for it, by the whites along the coast, the name of "Indian papoose." The Indians regard its flesh very highly. One can easily see that it is no small job to skin one of these animals, and that the quills, liable to be lost, afterwards cause serious trouble should they get into the foot or hand. The Indians when they wish to use the quills for fancy work, as they often do, carefully pick them out and arrange them to form mats, or various ornaments of one kind or another; when the flesh is to be eaten they are generally hung up over a flaming fire and singed to the skin, thus burning off all the chaff of the quills. The young are covered with long, black silky hair with whitish ends.

Friday the 11th. This afternoon the snow, melted by the hot sun, having partially disappeared from some of the elevations, we picked a dish of nice, fresh berries for supper. Here the snow covers the red berries and keeps them in a perfectly fresh condition until the ensuing spring when they are picked and eaten in large numbers. They taste very fresh and nice.

Saturday, March 26. This day, looking to be a fine one, with wind south and a mild thaw, seemed to invite a tramp; so accordingly, as the men were to carry out a load of wood to the summer house on the island — only about four miles distant — I determined to take my gun and follow them; the report that a large, white owl had been seen there, helping materially to decide me in the matter. The men started off quite early, directly after breakfast, for the woods, with their dogs and komatiks, to get their load. If the going is bad, or the dogs are obliged to wear their sealskin or canvas, pocket-like shoes, only a light load is put upon the komatik, but if the ice is smooth, and the going good, it is an old saying that you cannot "load a komatik;" that is, the sled slips along so easily when once it is started that you can pile on all the weight that it will hold, and the dogs will draw it with ease. I have known a team of four good dogs to draw a load of nearly a thousand pounds of iron for eight miles, and the roads not in the best of conditions.

While the men were piling the sleds with wood — we had two teams — to carry across to the summer house, I put on my warm clothing and prepared to accompany them on foot. It was a clear, beautiful morning, and after walking some little distance the bracing air seemed to give me renewed spirits; but soon a misfortune quite dampened them again, and rendered me unfit both in body and mind to enjoy fully the sport of the day, or rather the sport that might have been during the day. This was the loosening of the stopper of my powder flask, so that before I could stop it, the horn had swung behind me, mouth downward, and the powder, to the amount of about half a pound, was instantly a long, black, snake-like train on the snow beneath. Strange to say, my first impulse was (thinking that the snow would soon wet it, and that it was impossible to collect any again) to utilize the waste; so imagining that it was Fourth of July, or Washington's birthday, I cannot remember which, I hastily drew a match and touched the train. With a whiz it exploded and a long burnt track alone remained to tell the story. I had then time to think that but a single load remained in my gun; and that the sleds were fast overtaking me.

It was very nearly as far home as forward to the island, and the thought that a single load will often do the work of a dozen impelled me forward rather than backward. By this time the sleds had arrived, and together we went forward at a medium pace, a fast walk, over the not very good ice toward the island. When I say not very good ice, I mean bad for the dogs' feet and the easy running of the komatik, yet not thin. We did not come to thin ice until the point of the island opposite us was reached, and here we came upon a narrow platform of thin ice, with the water close to us on each side, over which we must pass. The water rippled up to its edge in a treacherous manner, and the surface looked dark, thin and wet. Thinking that we could clear it, with a shout the driver urged forward his dogs, and with a rush we made for the opposite side, but crack, crack, crack; the dogs stood still and looked to see what was the matter, only for a moment, but that moment was enough; the ice gave way and the komatik and its load of wood, on top of which were several jackets, and my powder horn and gun, slowly sank into the water. To spring from cake to cake to the firm ice, and to reach down and seize the above mentioned articles as they were slowly disappearing, and before they had reached the water, was the work of a moment; but the precious articles were saved.

Then came the work of picking out the sticks and reloading the sled. Fortunately wood floats, and the sled had not been broken or otherwise damaged (they are made very stout), and soon we were again on the move. Luckily, nothing was lost, while both myself and friend, the driver, escaped most miraculously, not having even wet our feet. Arriving at our stopping place, we left the wood at its destination, and went up to the house.

How changed the place looked from what I had seen it in the summer! It was then fertile and flowering; it was now snow, snow, snow everywhere. I took my gun, with its only charge, put in on leaving home very luckily, and started for the hillock on which the white owl had last been seen; but, alas! he was not there. I climbed to the top of the crest, but could see nothing; on the crest beyond, still nothing of the owl; but on the third crest I espied a fox trotting off at a slow gait up the ridge before me, not two hundred yards away. With my telescope, I could see that it was a red fox, and that he held up his left front foot, using only three feet to walk upon, as if lame from being caught in some trap or otherwise, so I determined to chase him; no quicker said than done. The fox was about three hundred yards away from me when the chase began. I saw him through the glass for a moment as he trotted along the snow ahead of me, and then taking up my gun, started after him; he was just behind the ridge, and I had hoped to gain upon him, but a fox is a cute animal if he has but three legs to run on, and by the time I had gained the ridge, he had heard me coming and was now far to the right and still out of gunshot. On I pressed,

14*

occasionally losing sight of the game altogether and now having the stimulus of seeing him before me, either tracking the snow with blood from the wounded foot, or slowly climbing the hillock in front. Sometimes he would make a turn to the right, expecting to throw me off the scent, and often to the left for the same purpose; but the island was small, and the ridges so far distant, comparatively, that it was impossible, now at least, for him to gain his object. On we went over hill and dell, sometimes one gaining and sometimes the other. At last the end of the island was reached, and the fox was running across a narrow pass, covered with ice, between this and another island; I had gained on him and he was now less than two hundred yards away, so I determined to fire. Hastily kneeling behind the crest of a hillock, and resting on a stone there, I fired; the ball reached the fox but did not hit him; and, though I had already run several miles across the island, and had shot away my only charge, I started in pursuit again, across the pass and away over the next small island. Here comes the strange part of the chase; the footing led plainly across the snow for a short distance, and then, mingling with another recent one, diverged; but which was which I could not tell.

The island was hilly though small; upon gaining the summit of the crest the fox had disappeared. Following the slope downward towards a small point of land to the westward, I soon came across the bloody track of the fox again; it disappeared when I reached the front, then appeared again along the edge of the rocks quite near the ice of the bay and below the rocks. This was a cute trick to escape detection, but the next step was more so. The tracks disappeared all of a sudden in the centre of a patch of snow with moss around it, and not a trace of them could be found anywhere. I carefully searched the narrow point over, and looked behind each rock, ascended each crest, examined each old fox footing, partially filled with drifting snow, so that I could not have mistaken it, and not a sign appeared. The fine fellow had played me another of the many tricks for which Sir Reynard is noted, and left me, four miles from home, heated with running, cross and hungry. Vowing vengeance, home I started, awaiting the next pleasant day for another hunt.

The next day, though more or less snowy and otherwise uncomfortable, we went out to the island with another load of wood. I took my gun, hoping to see some signs of game, and started a little ahead of the loaded sleds which soon caught up to me, when we proceeded along together. It seemed as if we never went so slowly, and though the loads were not large, the previous day's thaw rendered it treacherous travelling. We plodded on cautiously, beguiling the way with conversation until within a short distance of the island, when sharp eyes detected, on the slope of a low hillock (of which there were several), among the stones and rocks, a small moving object. A few steps nearer decided the question of what it was, and no doubt remained in my mind but that my friend the fox was making another tour of the island, perhaps searching for me for the fun of another chase. Several crows, or rather ravens, hovered occasionally over him, and vented their spite in repeated dashes and dabs at his head, wishing, no doubt, that they could enjoy a good meal from his carcass, or refresh themselves with his eyes; but no such fortune for them occurred, and we saw him slowly disappear over the ridge, trotting in the direction of the komatik and ourselves, whom he evidently had not yet seen. Seizing my gun, which was lying on top of one of the loads, I started on the run to head him off and try and get a shot.

It was hard work running on such snow, and I sank to the knees at nearly every step; but passing over the ridge I saw the fox climbing the opposite slope ahead of me. He had turned, apparently, and started off in a new direction; so I started off after him. Soon he disappeared over this second ridge, and when half-way up the bank, chancing to turn around, I saw a fox just crossing the path by which I had come. For a moment, and only a moment, I hesitated which one to follow—then, turning, I started for the nearest and one last seen. The fox used only three feet (the other bleeding from some trap wound) and did not run fast; yet I was obliged to do my best to keep up with and not lose sight of him. At last I gained perceptibly. I could see his black tail and stern—

it was probably a cross or patch fox — and soon, making for a huge rock in the centre of an almost level plain, I had a chance, long shot. The ball sped swiftly along and missed; but it struck so near as to bewilder the animal, who, for a moment, seemed undecided which way to turn, but quickly disappeared over the ridge. I followed him until too tired to run farther, and was obliged finally to give up the chase and returned to my companions quite crestfallen, yet ready for another trial.

Sunday, the 27th. We are alone, the family having gone to visit a neighbor about eight miles away, and it does seem a relief to be quiet — to hear no noisy children, and no rough, coarse scoldings or threats of violence to them in case of disobedience. The day was pleasant, and we all enjoyed it; it seemed more like Sunday than any similar days we had passed, to me at least, while on this part of the coast. The evening came before we really knew it.

Monday the 28th was a damp, snowy, dismal day; we all remained in the house and amused ourselves as best we could in reading, and writing, or netting nets and winding twine. Towards evening several of the neighbors, whom we knew well, came in to chat with us, and thus this day passed like many others.

Wednesday the 30th. To-day I took a tramp with two or three others, inland over the ponds: but we carried no rackets and found the walking terrible. In many places we sank to our armpits, and we were obliged to progress Indian fashion, that is, crawl on the hands and knees, using a long, round stick, with which to press upon the snow while extricating ourselves from the drifts. It was a most tedious and difficult work. We would walk on the treacherous crust for a few steps, then sink in with one foot up to the knee, recovering our position only to fall in with the other foot and again to sink nearly to the armpits. The stick then kept us from sinking farther — the snow often being fifteen feet deep beneath us, — and we would slowly and with difficulty crawl out and onward. Thus we soon were obliged to turn back, and though having gone scarcely a mile we were completely tired out when we reached home. I shot several species of birds, however, which paid well for all my trouble.

CHAPTER XIV.

Preparing the summer house to live in — Moving out — A spring rescue — Seals on ice — Larks — A home scene — Spring duck shooting — Repairing the boats — Visit to the Indians — Indian canoes — Netting nets — Labrador mail — Natural scenery of Labrador — Repairing canoes — Visit to Eskimo graves — Ornithological notes.

DURING the early part of April the weather still continued cold and disagreeable, while it snowed more or less the whole time. About the middle of the month we could spend the greater part of the day at the island in refurnishing our cabin, and soon had the roof finished, the inside ceiled, and the partitions put in their proper place, while new flooring was laid down up stairs. While this was in progress, the boys cleared up around the house outside as much as possible considering the amount of work in progress, and a couple of good, stout men wielded a large saw which converted several huge logs, from a large pile of similar pieces a little to one side of the house, into boards for the use of the carpenters inside. All hands worked hard, and one could see the improvement from day to day, as affairs progressed and drew to completion. Towards the end of the month the sun got high enough to allow us to move out again, and the almost new house furnished very comfortable quarters. There is one peculiarity of the Labrador climate that I must mention. There is, strictly speaking, no spring in Labrador, and though the ice does not begin to disappear much before the end of May — while large masses often remain until July, and icebergs float through the straits even in August — it goes very suddenly when once it really begins. In spite of all these drawbacks there is a certain mildness in the atmosphere that takes the place, apparently, of spring proper, and accordingly it thus becomes possible to move out of "winter quarters," and into the summer house in its more exposed situation, from the middle to the last of April; strange as it may appear, the time set generally falls on the week after Easter.

The process of moving out is much like that of moving in, though in the latter case you go by boat, and in the former by sled; as the baggage consists principally of provisions and boxes there is not much to move. Of course in this region trunks are seldom used, being replaced by the sailor's chest or carpenter's box which holds each individual's goods. It was a glad day when we turned our backs upon the house we had occupied throughout the long, tedious winter, and finally landed, with our "goods and chattels," at our summer house. It was a beautiful morning. The air was keen and sharp with the freshness of the still lingering winter, though the absence of that intense cold, so usual at this time, was marked as quite a pleasant change. The sky was clear, and towards noon the sun came out warm and nice. The hills were still more or less covered with snow, yet here and there a suggestion of a much greener foliage than could have been seen a month earlier even had made its appearance. The greatest change, however, occurred in the inroads which the waters of the sea, owing to the previous mild weather, had made upon the ice of the bay. From a point of the mainland we could see that half the pass between the two islands was already open, and far onward and outward we could view an open sea. I say open sea; yet though the ice had broken up, leaving the water visible, there were still large masses of drift, or as it is called *shee-shee* ice floating up or down with the current or drifting about at the mercy of wind and tide, and no boat could yet be safe far outside. As we stood viewing the waters, with their distant long lines of drift ice, which resembled the pictures often seen of arctic winter, we would occasionally see short, round bodies upon it, that upon inspection proved to be seals. We could with our glass often see these animals sporting in the open waters of some lagoon-shaped mass of ice, and occasionally notice both old and young seal together on the blocks. We could only look at them, however, since the ice prevented us from launching the boats, and they were too far off to be reached by either rifle or shotgun. The distance appeared to be about two miles and the inhabitants considered it as about such. When tired of watching the seals, we turned our glass to the loom of the Newfoundland coast that appeared in the distance like the rising cloud of a heavy bank of autumnal Newfoundland fog. Then again, nearer home, the open water in the bay reminded us that soon the ice would disappear and the boats could be launched.

I was much impressed with the beautiful song of the larks (*Eremophila cornuta*), which everywhere greeted us. Sometimes they would send forth distant trills as they flew past the island high over our heads, while at others they would sing the most beautiful carols as they rose in spirals high into the air; at still other times they would hop about the dooryard free from distrust while they fed upon the scraps scattered for them, for which they had chirped a few notes of thankfulness before finally taking wing. About this time flocks of snow buntings filled the air, and lit upon the snowy slopes of the crests and knolls about the island, hotly chased by the boys who kill them with stones, or catch them in snares. These birds are generally tame and unusually fat, which renders them delicious eating. The yard was now full of busy men; the doorstep of happy children; and the house itself with the industrious housewives—all intent upon putting things in order for present comfort and future summer use. Meanwhile the dogs and little puppies enjoyed themselves romping over the island, while I remembered the two pussies as they stood in the doorway, or rubbed about the doorsash, or stood their ground against some venturesome dog who mildly poked his nose into and inquired who was within the door. The whole scene is painted on my memory as one of delight, as the approaching season wafted its breezes to a house and yard full of delighted beings who had been cooped up for six long months in the inmost recesses of a most piratical looking harbor where no one would have suspected that such a thing as a house ever could exist. Soon the ducks began to fly, and then such sport as we had. The king eider came first, then the common eider; the former is called the passing, the latter the laying, duck. The birds at first fly in large flocks, often thousands in a flock, and generally the different species do not mingle. They have a certain course which they pursue, and the shoals over which they fly are called the "gunning points." Here the men and boys congregate, and, lying low, behind some rock or cake of ice, await the flight. Some days the birds fly thickly, others rarely any pass. The people see them at a great distance, and often hear the beating of their wings before they see them. The birds fly over or along the side of the station, and the minute the head of the flock has passed the first or head gunner, he rises or turns and fires when all hands do likewise, and the slaughter begins. Often twenty or thirty birds are thus knocked down by a party of two or three persons with double barrel guns.

My first spring ducking was in the afternoon of Tuesday, the 12th of April, when several of us drew one of the small, flat boats over the ice to the clear water beyond, and, launching it, started for the gunning point. We brought home a good bagful of birds that night, and you may be sure that they were well served, and well disposed of the next day.

After a few days' work the house was prepared both outside and inside for our comfortable abode. A coat of blubber—or the remains of the livers of the codfish, after the oil has been boiled and tried out of them—as a final touch was put on to the roof with an old broom, and the whole declared to be water-tight, as a hard rain soon proved it to be. We were now comfortably settled, and viewed with satisfaction the progress made each day in the destruction of the bay ice, and the lessening of the snow on the hills beyond and the ground about the island, by the rays of the sun which gained strength each day as the season advanced.

The men now turned their attention to the boats, and began repairing them for immediate use when the ice should break up enough to enable them to be launched.

Monday the 18th. I visited the Indians this afternoon, and

completed a bargain for the purchase of an Indian canoe. These Indian or birch-bark canoes are getting to be more and more valuable all along the coast. Formerly the bark grew in abundance in certain localities on the Labrador shores, but the call for it lately has been so great, since both boats and huts are made of it, that the home supply has become exhausted, and the Indians now send for it to Anticosti, and even Gaspé on the south shore of the St. Lawrence, whence the greater part is now obtained. The *Betula papyracea*, the tree from which this valuable product is obtained has, strange to say, in these regions at least, become nearly extinct. Of course, the stripping of a tree of all its bark or outer covering at once kills it. The great danger is, that soon the probably already limited quantity south of the St. Lawrence will also become exhausted, when, unless considerable growths are found upon the island of Anticosti, where the Indians were recently engaged in searching for it, the supply will become entirely exhausted. At present the Indians, and those whites who are so fortunate as to have bark on hand, are very sparing of it, and will sell only for cash to those parties with whom they regularly trade.

An Indian canoe is apparently (to use an American slang phrase) a most "cranky" affair. It is light, weighing according to its size from seventy-five to two hundred pounds. The ordinary canoe is about twelve to fifteen feet long, and two feet and six inches wide in the centre, its widest part, while the depth is about three fifths of its width. From the middle both ends taper, cigar-shaped to the bow and stern. Each end is slightly elevated and pointed; but it is needless to describe further the shape of an Indian canoe. Within this apparently frail craft the natives go from place to place —of course seldom venturing far out to sea—with the utmost freedom. I have seen them rocked about near shore in the surf when it seemed as if the waves would overpower them at any moment; and then again I have seen a canoe with a single individual paddling as easily and regularly through a narrow pass against high waves that had appeared too dangerous for many of the older boatsmen with their wooden boats. In these small canoes, that appear to toss and rock about so frightfully to one not acquainted with their use, whole families of Indians, often comprising three men, two women, and several small children, will go from island to island or harbor to harbor miles apart, in most squally weather; when thus moving about they carry their luggage with them. What, then, would be the surprise to see, as is often the case, a canoe literally and absolutely loaded to within three to five inches of the top with a family moving, in fine weather, to some location miles farther up or down the coast. In a number of years there has come but a single instance, that I can recall, when a load of this kind has been swamped and any of the family have perished.

It, of course, takes some time for any one to become an adept in the use of these canoes, and though I finally purchased a good second-hand one, I made little use of it save to paddle about around the islands where we were staying, and over to the nearest island beyond, where neighbors resided, a distance of perhaps a quarter of a mile from point to point; but it was most excellent exercise, and I enjoyed it heartily. The price here of a new canoe that will hold say four people and their baggage, and eighty odd pounds, is somewhere in the region of from £7 to £8 of Newfoundland money, or, being four dollars to a pound, some twenty-eight dollars, varying two or three dollars either way. There are generally but one or two Indians in a tribe that can make a first-class canoe, and these have their hands full the greater part of the time.

In the evening we lashed the canoe that I had purchased to our komatik and started for home.

The next two or three days were spent in netting a net with which to capture seals. A seal net is an immense affair made of stout salmon twine, and netted in meshes usually about six inches from knot to knot, the best size being apparently twenty-seven meshes wide, with a length of about forty-five fathoms, or about two hundred and sixty feet. The process of netting is one that cannot well be described. The needle that holds the twine is of peculiar make. The meshes are made by doubling the thread over a small card of the required size, while the knot is tied and the whole is drawn tight. When made the knot comes on the ridge of the card and cannot be slipped; this forms a string of loops into each one of which the needle is passed while a new series of loops are knotted on the card just below these. In this way the netter proceeds with twine, or needle or card, of any size, and fashions a tightly knotted network of any size he may desire. In this way all the cod seines, nets or traps, are made, while the six inch seal mesh, and the quarter or eighth inch bottom to the dip net or lance seine, undergo the same process. The work, however, is quite easy and most fascinating.

Wednesday the 20th. Great has been the joy of all hands to-day. The mailman has at last arrived with news from home. Our last letter bore the postmark of Sept. 23, and here it is over seven months since knowing whether those we left at home are dead or alive, or our country prosperous. How eagerly those letters were read, and the papers studied, I will leave you to imagine. It was indeed a joyful day.

The winter mail for the coast of Labrador arrives, usually, some time the latter end of March, by special carrier. This man starts from Bersimis, which is a small village about one hundred and forty or fifty miles from Quebec, and for which place the mail starts from Quebec on or about the first of February, about the fifteenth of that month. He travels on foot with snowshoes—sometimes by komatik—with the mail upon his back in a stout leathern bag, and makes daily marches of from fifteen to thirty miles, according to the weather and the travelling. Though the distance between Bersimis and Esquimaux Point, the end of the route generally for the first carrier, is only about two hundred and six direct miles, it becomes at least a quarter to a third more by the route taken, since there are bays to go round and rivers to cross; so that often instead of ten it takes twenty days to accomplish the distance. It is forwarded to Bersimis from Quebec, I believe, by coach, this being the stage limit; should it be late, however, the time is extended so much. As there are houses every few miles apart all up and down the coast it is an easy matter to drop into one of them for the night, and along the route the mailman is always welcome. Strange to say, there are branch post-offices at stated places along the line, and at these places only is the bag opened, while the carrier takes the letters to the various people to whom they are directed on his homeward trip; and even this is done by courtesy, since it is required by law, I believe, that the letters shall only be delivered to those to whom they are addressed by the lawful mailman; the carrier, being only a paid messenger, has no responsibility but to deliver the bag containing the letters and papers in safe condition to the postmaster at the end of the route, who takes upon himself the responsibility of sending them along the line by the returning carrier—thus making himself liable, while trusting only in the good faith of the carrier, to damage for any losses sustained. At Esquimaux Point, the mail is taken by another man who has travelled up the coast while the first man was travelling down. The carrier from Bersimis returns to that place with the return mail, while the one from Bonne Esperance, who has thus disposed of the up mail on its way to Quebec, returns to the former place with the down mail. This is taken in the usual way, but more frequently by komatik, since the bays are generally frozen over by this time, and travelling upon them is infinitely better than over the deep snow-clad hills which here begin to line the coast. I should have said that the mail first stops at Mingan, a post of the Hudson's Bay company, where one of that company's agents is usually an authorized mail agent also. From Esquimaux Island the mail goes to Natashquan, the next regular office, a distance of about one hundred miles, and from that place, through a tract of country the most difficult yet travelled, especially in bad or mild winter weather. The carrier is often obliged to go over high hills, away inland, to cross creeks or bays that are not yet frozen over, and which are scarcely a mile or two across, and at St. Augustine, much out of the regular route, to cross the deep and irregular cut of Shecatica Bay to Bonne Esperance. The whole distance, thus reckoned, is about two hundred and fifty miles. Thus from

Bersimis to Bonne Esperance, a distance of about seven hundred miles, the mail is taken by the carrier who tramps the distance generally with snowshoes or rackets at the rate of from fifteen to thirty miles a day, as I have said; hence, though the mail generally starts from Quebec on the first or second of February, it seldom reaches its terminus before the last of March or the first of April. A long time to wait for one's letters, you will say; and indeed it is, but you hardly mind it when your news from home does come, especially if it be good news.

After reaching Bonne Esperance, a special carrier is sent on to Blanc Sablon, eighteen miles farther down the coast, with the remainder of the mail. The peninsula of Labrador proper beyond receives no mail until the lighthouse steamer, a small vessel which is sent yearly by the Canadian government at Quebec to supply the lighthouses along the coast with provisions, oil for the lights, and coal, brings a second mail, in the early spring, as soon generally as open water will allow passage. In the summer, the mail comes and goes, several times in the course of the season, by the traders who bring it from and return it to Quebec; while another also arrives from Natashquan, *via* packet from Gaspé on the south shore, twice a month which is taken up by some authorized trading vessel— most every trader stops at this port—and carried onward; and still another mail comes from the States *via* Newfoundland, by a mail steamer, employed at one of the fishing stations, that makes bi-weekly trips from St. John's to one or two localities on this part of the coast. In this way the people on the coast of Labrador receive and send their yearly mails. A cable runs from Anticosti to Quebec, by way of the south shore and it is soon hoped that one will be laid from that island to Mingan, at least, the post of the Hudson's Bay Company before alluded to, if not farther down the coast,— but there is yet much to hope for on this score.

The weather now began to be fine, and the warm sun to melt away the snow, and turn to green the brown winter-killed leaves of the plants already brought to light, in the damp mosses on the hill tops and occasionally on the plains. The birds were becoming abundant once more, and apparently sighing for their mates, while all nature began to rejoice.

I cannot describe the characteristic aspect of a Labrador scene. It is one peculiar to the region itself and must be seen and felt to be appreciated.

The extensively broken coast line affords you a varied view of now sea and now land, in the shape of some island or promontory of the mainland—the former being more usually the case. High and low hill tops crown the immediate coast line, in the majority of places, while often their somewhat distant outline reminds you much—if you close the view in other directions—of our own eastern United States scenes of hilly outline in the distant horizon. A spring month, to one situated on one of these little islands, is always most delightful. The novelty of busy preparation for the summer season combined with the animation which all nature presents as well as the balmy air and the peculiarities of situation and surrounding objects, cause one to feels a freedom scarcely to be imagined, since care is thrown to the winds and you immediately find something that occupies you pleasantly, almost without knowing it; while each day, as it passes, adds to the pleasure felt.

My joy can easily be imagined when, one day, towards the latter end of the month, one of the men, knowing how I sought for birds and other natural objects, brought me a robin which he had shot a short time previous outside the yard, and not far from the house. It was the first real home bird that had greeted me, and was all the more appreciated for that. The robin does not appear abundant in Labrador; though a few breed here, inland and along the rivers.

This week I rosined the bottom and sides of my canoe. In this operation, as generally performed by the Indians, the seams of the canoes are covered tightly with spruce gum and rosin, while should any leaks appear, they are covered over with a different preparation usually made by the Indians, thus: a quality of rosin is put into a tin can, and a small portion of oil—seal or whale, usually the former—is added to it, with a very little paint,—white lead—the whole is then put over the fire and heated. As it melts, oil is constantly added, a little at a time, and the mixture stirred with a stick. As soon as the substance will drop from the stick, instead of running freely from the end, the pot is taken off the fire immediately and the leaks in the canoe are thickly coated with it while yet hot. An Indian finds a leak in his canoe most ingeniously. After rosining all the apparent cracks, he goes all over the boat again applying his lips to every suspicious looking place, and, exerting both suction and pressure, soon discovers the places where air is still admitted ; these he rosins, and then his canoe is launched and tested by paddling a short distance or rolling and rocking it violently from side to side. If, after a sufficient time, water appears, the bottom is again examined, and redressed with rosin until it is tight. When an Indian has finished with his canoe for the day, he takes it out of the water and turns it bottom side up, and, if possible, throws spruce boughs upon it to keep the sun from melting the seams ; if no covering can be obtained he leaves it bottom down upon the softest place he can find, that the bottom may be protected from scratches. A canoe is always lifted, as so much dead weight both from and into the water.

One of the peculiarities of a Labrador spring scene is that of drifting or "banquese" ice. This is ice that breaks up in some northern locality, and flows, in greater or smaller masses, through the Straits towards the Gulf and open sea, generally melting by the time it reaches the Magdalene Islands. The "banquese" ice often lies a mile or so off shore, and, to the naked eye, appears to be covered with logs and sticks, apparently from some wreck. A good glass will show the mistake at once, and you find, with surprise, that they are so many seals, both old and young. If they are abundant, boats are put off and the seal-hunting begins.

Tuesday, May 3d. I spent most of the day in examining several Esquimaux graves, but found only a few old bones, and a substance resembling seals' hair in each case within eighteen inches to two feet of the top of the mound. The graves were five in number, but everything had disappeared so that nothing of any worth rewarded my work.

Wednesday the 11th. I started off on a trip down the coast, but not before having secured a specimen of the pintail duck (*Dafila acuta*) that one of the men shot while it, with its mate, was feeding in a shallow bay of the sea, in front of the house. It is very rare in these parts, and seldom seen here, though not uncommon, I believe, in parts of Newfoundland.

Thursday the 12th. Passed into Blanc Sablon to-day; the bay, at its entrance, was full of birds of all kinds. I noted several species of gulls and terns, including several jaegers, or what are often called hagdowns or shearwaters, while ducks were plentiful, and the puffins or paroquets abounded in tens of thousands. Greenley Island, at the entrance of the harbor, has always been a noted place for these birds. They breed here in vast numbers, covering the ground everywhere with burrows. There are now only two or three places on this part of the coast where the puffin breeds in any numbers, and Greenley Island is one of them; another place is the Parakeet] Islands, in Bradore harbor. The bird seems now more abundant at the former place. Though I visited the island, and made personal observations there, I find that the ground was so well and thoroughly gone over by Dr. Elliott Coues, some years previous, that I give his description of this species, as covering the ground in so complete and natural a manner that I am sure it cannot fail to interest. Though I have seen and identified nearly all of Dr. Coues' points here given, a few of them are new however. He says:— "The habit of collecting in immense numbers at particular localities during the breeding season, so characteristic of the whole family of Alcidæ, is a trait exhibited in the highest degree by the species now under consideration. With scarcely the exception of the common murre, no bird of the family shows so preëminently gregarious a disposition as does the Arctic puffin. Collecting, as it does, in thousands, on particular islands of small extent, it becomes a matter of astonishment that food can be procured in sufficient quantity to sustain them, so that each pair can find a place to deposit its eggs. The pertinacity, too, with which they cling to the immediate vicinity of their breeding place is remarkable. But a very short distance from an island where there are thousands, it is a comparatively uncommon thing to see a puffin. The most extensive of these breeding places appears to be an island near the harbor of Bradore, visited by Audubon in 1833, of which he has written so graphic and instructive an account. The one, however, that I had an opportunity of visiting cannot be much behind it in point of the numbers of the birds breeding on it; and during a stay of three days I had ample opportunity of examining the island and noting the manners of its curious population. My visit was on the 25th, 26th, and 27th of July. Let a short extract from my journal describe our approach to the island.

"We were now within less than a mile from the island, towards which all eyes were anxiously turned, and still not a bird met our gaze. But a few minutes more, however, and they commenced to appear, flying around the boat or resting on the water; all were 'parrakeets,' and 'tinkers,' except now and then a solitary ' turre.' They were tamer than I had ever seen birds before, almost flying into our little whale boat; it was hard to restrain from firing. As we rounded the island close to the shore, they came tumbling out of their holes by hundreds, and, with the thousands we disturbed from the surface of the water, soon made a perfect cloud above and around us, no longer flying in flocks, but forming one dense, continuous mass, and yet not a gun had been fired.

"The Parrakeet Islands are three in number, lying along the western shore of Blanc Sablon Bay, just at its mouth. The one I visited is the innermost as well as the largest, though the others are equally crammed with the birds. It is about a mile in circumference; in shape almost a perfect semicircle, with two points stretching out and inclosing a snug cove, where only can a landing be effected with safety. It is abrupt and precipitous on three sides, the fourth sloping gradually down to the cove. The top is nearly flat, and covered with a rather luxuriant growth of grass, the soil being

15*

enriched by the innumerable droppings of the birds. The three sides in which the holes are dug are so steep and precipitous that it requires considerable agility to scramble along them, the danger of falling into the water being increased by the slipperiness of the soil, worn smooth by innumerable feet, and continually moistened with ordure. The sides are composed of soft, loamy earth, with rocks of every size and shape jutting out in all directions, and afford the most favorable possible conditions for the excavation of the burrows. The fourth side between the two points is composed mostly of masses of rock, in the crevices of which the auks chiefly deposit their eggs; they very often appropriate the deserted holes of the puffins.

"The holes in the ground in which the puffins deposit their eggs (a habit, as far as I am aware, entirely peculiar to the genus in this family of birds) are excavated by the birds themselves, an operation for which their powerful beaks, and long, strong, and sharp claws admirably adapt them. They extend nearly or quite in an horizontal direction, and are semicircular in shape, with the diameter scarcely larger than is necessary for the free passage of a single bird. They vary much in length, but the majority are not so deep but that the egg may be reached by thrusting in the arm to its full extent. Their course is seldom in a straight direction; they curve and wind in a most tortuous manner, many burrows being connected together by winding passages. The entrances to the holes are worn flat and smooth by continual paddling from the feet of the birds, and, as well as the whole sides of the island, are moist and slippery with the ordure. The sides of the island, just above high water mark to the very top, are perforated with innumerable holes, but on the top itself not a single burrow is to be seen.

"At the further extremity of the hole, which is usually a little enlarged, the single egg is deposited, always a slight bed of dried grasses being first arranged to keep it from the moist earth. I have indeed found eggs lying on the bare ground near the entrance of the burrows, whither they had apparently been dragged by the bird as it hurriedly made its exit; but in no instance did I find one in its usual position at the farther extremity, that was not upon a layer of grass. I noticed this fact the more particularly since Audubon especially states that no nest whatever is formed for the reception of the egg. Without for a moment doubting the accuracy of that great naturalist's observations, the present case is only additional proof of the extent to which the birds' habits are influenced by circumstances; the position of nests, the number of eggs, etc., varying much, and the food changing in a measure with every change of locality. The eggs measure two and a half inches in length, by one and three-fourths in greatest diameter, varying very little from this standard; in shape, which is rather rounded ovate, they differ in being more or less obtuse at the smaller end. The greatest diameter is nearly opposite the middle. The shell is usually more or less granulated, but differs much in the extent of the granulation. The color is white or whitish, varying from nearly pure to a brownish hue, the latter color being in the shell, and not caused by soiling or discoloration. They are marked with obsolete, almost imperceptible dots, spots, and lines of light purplish, mostly concentrated into a ring around the large end. There are sometimes a few irregular splashes of very light yellowish brown. Audubon is clearly in error when he states that they are simply 'pure white.' At that date (July 25) they all, with few exceptions contained young about to be hatched."

A great trick of the Labradorians is to get a greenhorn to stick his hand into one of the burrows of this bird when the bird is supposed to be within. If you carefully examine the bill — of horn, nearly two inches in length and about the same in height — one will see that a most alarming species of forceps may be thus put in motion, and, as the bird is one of the fiercest of its kind, can readily imagine why the victim never repeats the experiment.

The number of birds that I saw on Greenley Island was simply immense, and could easily have been a multiple, and not a small one, of ten thousand. I have often seen the water covered with a clustered flock, all engaged in making a hoarse, rasping sound, not unlike the filing of a saw; this is also done both by the "murre," and the "turre," and at such times, which ever species is present, they receive from the sailors the name of "guds," from a fancied resemblance to that sound. When on the wing I seldom if ever saw them mix with other birds. Though they appear in large numbers, at stated times, they disappear, or rather disperse after breeding, almost as suddenly as they came; yet stragglers do not leave until the harbors are blocked up with ice. At Greenley Island although there is a large fish-curing establishment, houses, and a light-house on the northeast end of the island, the birds occupy the other side unmolested, and are seldom interfered with by gunners; yet the island is scarcely three-quarters of a mile long in its longest direction, and even less than half a mile wide. Though I have used up much space for this bird, I can but finish Dr. Coues' most interesting description of this strange species of the feathered tribe, especially as it accords so nearly with our own experience. He says:—

"Hardly had our boat touched the shore than we leaped out, guns in hand, and at once scattered over the island. As we wandered along the sides, the affrighted birds darted past us like arrows, issuing from their burrows beneath our feet and around us, and all making directly for the water. Those already disturbed flew in every direction above us, while thousands rested on the water in a dense mass at a little distance. I took my stand on a flat rock, and in less than an hour a pile of puffins, more than I could carry, lay at my feet. Shortly after I commenced firing the birds formed themselves into an immense circle, of a diameter of perhaps a third of a mile, one point of which just grazed the island. It was astonishing to see with what precision this circle was preserved, each bird flying directly in the wake of the one that preceded. I had merely to stand facing the advancing birds, and no better opportunity for continual slaughter could be desired. I now realized what I had been told, but had found hard to believe, that a wagon might be filled with the birds by a tolerably expert workman, shooting them at just such a moment that they should fall into it. The poor things seemed not at all aware of the nature of the danger that threatened them; flying so close past me that I could almost strike them with my gun. During the continual firing the birds would emerge from their holes every minute or two; and after shooting for half an hour on one spot I was not a little surprised to see two or three start out almost from between my feet, and in a great fright make the best of their way down to the water. On emerging from their holes the birds generally looked around for a moment to see what was the matter, and then, in great haste, fluttered and tumbled down to the water below, in which they immediately dove, and, swimming swiftly under water, reappeared at some distance. From the countless thousands around me I did not hear the slightest note of any kind; they flew in perfect silence.

"The flight of the puffin, when once on the wing, is firm, well sustained, very swift, and performed with short, quick, vigorous beats. When it takes wing from a rock, whence it can project itself into the air, it at once supports itself without difficulty; but when on the water, it is obliged to flap over the surface for several yards before it can rise on wing. When getting under way, the feet are extended backwards and outwards on each side of the tail, which is spread, but they are soon drawn up, and the tail closed. When shot at and not touched, like the auks, they swerve from their course, open and shut the tail, and extend the feet. When standing on a rock at the entrance of their burrows, where they alight without the slightest difficulty, they present a peculiar grotesque appearance, such as is afforded by no other bird.

"When taken in the hand the puffin utters a loud, hoarse, croaking scream, at the same time fighting furiously. They are capable of inflicting a very severe wound with their powerful bills, easily drawing blood. Their long and strong inner claw is also an effective weapon, so that by dint of scratching, biting, and struggling, they proved difficult customers to manage." With regard to this same claw he says:—"I could not but admire the beautiful provision of nature with regard to furnishing this bird with the means of excavating its burrows with facility. The inner claw of each foot is very long, much curved, and excessively sharp. To preserve it so, when not in use, it always lies perfectly flat, so that the point does not rest on the ground. In digging and fighting, however, it is held upright, and then becomes a very effective weapon."

With regard to the razor-billed auk, the "tinker," or "turre," while on the subject of auks, I will say that I have noticed them breeding on a small island in almost as large colonies as the parrakeets. At the Fox Islands, off Kecarpwei River, they are very abundant; several of us landed, and had about the same sport Dr. Coues mentions as having had with the puffins; I noticed them in thousands about several other small islands also, and am informed by the inhabitants that this species was always very abundant about this locality while much rarer and replaced by the "murre" farther northward. They breed in the crevices of the rocks, long, deep, and narrow ones being preferred. I did not find but a single egg, but was repeatedly told by the people, that if I took the eggs, the bird would lay again the next day. The inhabitants systematically take all the eggs they can find on a given island regularly twice a week throughout the breeding season, and find the birds so wonderfully accommodating that the last batch taken is nearly as numerous as the first. The "turres" associate both with the "murres" and the black guillemot. The latter bird lays its eggs, smaller, and otherwise distinct, in similar situations and often the two are found breeding side by side, but seldom in any quantities.

With regard to the foolish guillemot, or "murres," I found them breeding in similar situations and together with the razor-billed auks. The egg is noted for its variable size and the nature of its marking. I have taken them all the way from *pure white*, through an endless series of blotches, and waved lines of black, purple, and brown, to an almost pure green, and blue, and even a delicate pink barely spotted or marked at the larger end. The people on the coast cannot tell whether either the *turre* or *murre* lays more than a single egg, or whether they sit upon their eggs or allow the sun to hatch them. I have been told, on apparently good authority, that they do sit upon their eggs, and consequently are furnished with a large, bare place upon the lower belly where they have picked the feathers from themselves in order to make the proper hollow in their downy covering for the egg to rest in — but I failed to notice the spot upon any of the birds shot. I could not ascertain, either, the period of incubation.

CHAPTER XV.

Blanc Sablon again — Northern limits of the bittern — Return along the coast of Natashquan — Spring scene in Red Bay — Other places — St. Mary islands — Cormorants — At Natashquan — Ramble about the place — Appearance of the birds — The Dark Day — Arrival at Mingan.

AT Blanc Sablon we anchored for the rest of the day and night. I landed, and walked along the beach to examine the general structure of the place, and found the prospect much more pleasant than it had been in the winter. I caught sight, for a moment only, of a small sparrow, which, I distinctly saw had a black cheek and face. The bird was about the size of a chipping sparrow, and yet I distinctly noticed a large black patch either on the cheek or chin, which I could not tell certainly, as he hopped past me into the rushes beyond the sandy beach, and thence flew quickly to the other side of the creek. Here, also, I found a person who informed me that, a short time previous, one of the men had shot " in the marshes a bird with a long neck, long bill, and long legs." The American bittern (*Botaurus minor*) is probably not rare here, being in fact the only bird of the family which we know as venturing so far north as this region, and undoubtedly this was the bird referred to.

In the afternoon I took a short walk around the shore. I crossed a shallow streamlet that, flowing through a rather wide bed of sand and small pebbles alternating with patches of muck, of which material neighboring lands are largely composed, empties into the salt water at the head of the bay. The beach here I found to consist of yellowish white sand.

Leaving this sandy beach we next came to a beach of rocks and débris from a sandstone ridge close by. After passing several ridges, all broken and crumbling on their face towards the sea, we came to a long stretch of mucky meadow, nearly if not quite level with the sea at high tide. Soon these marshy lands gave place to long ridges of glacial-worn, rounded, rocky elevations, which run into the water in the direction of Greenley Island. This singular formation of rock reminds one much of an immense table, of longitudinal and transverse elevations and depressions of several acres in extent, which slowly fall to the sea easterly on both sides.

Several houses and sheds were perched here and there with apparently little beneath to support them, while the rock itself furnished a natural "fish flakes," upon which fish were spread to dry in the sun. The direction of these ridges, as they fell off into the sea, was almost exactly north by east to south by west, and, as they entered the water, they were pointing directly for Greenley Island, where a grand confusion of broken rocky débris would undoubtedly tell the geologist its history. Everywhere were present rounded tops, and cleft sides of rocks while I was confident I found upon their surface several glacial scratches lying in about the same general direction. The whole mass reminds one of an immense checkerboard, where the boundary lines between the squares were deep clefts and the very top of the squares rounded hummocks, covered with glacial marks. There is hardly another such location "on the Labrador," as it is here called, that presents so unusual and decidedly remarkable an appearance.

Friday, the 13th. The wind has played us one of its tricks, today, and left for parts unknown. We tried all day to get into Forteau but were unable. We consoled ourselves however, as well as possible, with roast duck, and waited for the wind. What little breeze we did have was dead ahead. Finally we returned to Blanc Sablon, and prepared to send letters home by a small schooner that we found leaving that afternoon for Gaspé. Saturday it was foggy, and we were unable to proceed but a short distance from the harbor. The gun at Greenley Island lighthouse, and the steam whistle at L'Anse Loup, kept up a continual hooting, while, near to, we could hear and almost see — several times we actually did see them—the whales as they sported and spouted close to our vessel, in spite of the foggy weather. We afterwards found them very abundant in this vicinity, and often saw half a dozen of them within a short distance of the vessel in different directions, all spouting at the same time. They were probably of the species called finbacks, since the "spout" corresponded to this class of whales more closely, being a single stream sent upwards ten or twelve feet in an almost perpendicular line, falling back again as spray in nearly the same place. The sulphur bottom, the Greenland, and the hump-backed whales, it is said, all blow a double column of water rather obliquely backwards; the finbacks, a high straight stream some twelve feet directly upwards to fall back again to the same place as spray; while the sperm whale shoots its single stream somewhat forward, the spray falling forward and beyond the head. Whether this distinction holds good in all cases I do not know, but the seamen insist that it is invariably the case.

During the night the wind sprang up and we drifted nearly to Newfoundland. In the morning we found ourselves in sight of houses two miles off the land; in a short time we would have been on shore. About daylight the wind started up. The outline of the Labrador coast, the fog having cleared away by this time, showed plain and clear. The various buildings along the coast, and the highlands of Bradore, L'Anse Dune, Blanc Sablon, L'Anse Loup, Forteau, and L'Anse Diable, appeared in rapid succession. We noticed particularly the difference between Black or Pirouette River, with its receding slopes, on the east, while the ridges of the west coast extended away back into the country in the shape of huge rows of hills, that, though well wooded, appeared barren and desolate enough.

On we sailed: from the correspondence of the coast line to the position of Red Bay on our charts, I felt we must be near that place; and soon Saddle Island appeared ahead of us, and, with a glass, we could plainly see the church on the hilltop, and the houses on the slopes below. The passage to the harbor of Red Bay is between Saddle Island and the mainland. It is very small and narrow, and scarcely perceived until you are close to the west of it. The island appears like a part of the mainland. It is probably one of the most secluded harbors of the coast. Our surprise can be imagined. We had supposed ourselves at least twenty if not thirty miles farther up the coast, when we had taken our first reckoning. When close upon Saddle Island the opening begins first to appear. The water is deep in the passage — as everywhere in the harbor — close to the very edges of the land on either side, and though the passage was small we beat in without the slightest difficulty, running so near the rocks that our boom nearly touched the rocky ledge ashore as we tacked ship. Here we entered a new region: I wish I could picture it to you. The air was clear, fresh, and crisp. The sky was almost cloudless. The hills presented most charming natural pictures with their coverings of already green foliage. Close to the edge of the water nestled the houses with the stages and workshops of some twenty-five or thirty families.

When once in the harbor we were shut in completely. The high top of the crests on Saddle Island prevented even our mast from being seen, while we were easily led to imagine ourselves in one of those strongholds of ancient piratical romance,— always so well chosen and impregnable. In the evening we went ashore and heard a good, earnest Christian, of the Wesleyan faith, lead a good old New England service of evening prayer. We afterwards occupied some time in calling upon various people dwelling here, and found them very hospitable.

Red Bay is the Newfoundland headquarters, for this part of the coast, of trade and of the traders. It is a very old settlement, and contains several very aged native inhabitants. Though there are one or two large fisheries here in summer, there are twenty-one families only that winter and live here the year around. A. M. Pike, one of the oldest inhabitants, told me that he had lived on the coast for thirty-two years, and that the place was never larger — except during a little while in the summer — than at present. Of the twenty-one families, seven are named Pike, three Pennie, and three Ash. One old gentleman showed me a sample of lead ore which he said had been taken from the neighboring hills, and also informed me that mica, in large sheets, was abundant not far off; but no one could inform me as to Labradorite, which, however, occurs as a bright green and as a black, glittering, scaly variety in several places along the coast.

As a short description of the harbor may be of interest I will try to give it. From Twin Island, the eastern boundary of the eastern mouth, which is shaped much like a carpenter's square, we approach directly to Saddle Island, which stands in the very centre of the mouth of the harbor, so that, in approaching, neither the eastern or western entrance is perceived until one is directly upon it. This island is about twice as long as it is broad, and lies about southeast by northwest. There is a hill on either end one of which only contains a beacon. The island is almost wholly rock. The depression between these two crests reaches nearly to the level of the water and yet it contains a pond of tolerably good water where the people obtain their usual supply for daily use in the summer time. In what is known as the outer harbor, the water is deep on both sides close to shore, while the eastern entrance is more shallow than the western; so that while men-of-war vessels often pass in at the western, and anchor within the second or inner harbor, only small boats can pass through the eastern entrance. The western entrance enlarges into what is called West Bay. The shores of the outer harbor gradually approach each other to within almost a stone's throw, and yet there is ample room for the largest man-of-war vessel to pass safely and anchor, as the revenue and other vessels that often enter here do, within the inner harbor.

Close to shore the inner harbor is shoal, yet in its centre, it is very deep. In the farther end of this peculiar hour-glass are situated the winter houses of the inhabitants, at the foot of high, receding, unevenly sloped and gorged hillocks that look like a vast amphitheatre. Near by, on the east side, is a little brook; here plenty of fresh water is always to be obtained, while the slopes of the hills furnish abundance of firewood, if one will only cut it. Taken all in all, this is a most beautiful place, and well calculated to excite the enthusiasm as, likewise, the envy of all lovers of beautiful scenery. While in general outline the eastern side of the harbor is low and marshy, the western is composed of granite hills from four hundred to nearly five hundred feet in height, coming down to within a few fathoms of the sea. Again on the east the little elevation, on which stands the church, is only seventy-eight feet above the sea, the hill immediately behind it one hundred and seventy, while the highest and next in order is only two hundred and ten feet. From this elevation I could see beyond low earthy and granite hillocks. Immense ridges and bowlder-like rocks of granite were lying about us in every direction; beneath were bays, ponds, and low marshy spots reaching in succession nearly to the sea level. The formation is so much different on the opposite sides of this harbor that it is quite remarkable. On the west red feldspar predominates, in large cliffs, whence the name Red Bay, while on the east the rock is almost entirely granite or gneiss. Saddle Island, so named from its resemblance to a saddle, contains a most peculiar phenomenon. In the low marshy depression between the higher extremities of the island is situated a small pond. Though this pond is within a few feet of the level of the salt water, it is so sweet and fresh that the people use it for drinking water. The pond is very deep, yet with no apparent inlet anywhere. The outlet runs continually, yet the supply does not appear to diminish.

I shall never forget the clear, beautiful, varying shades of green on the slopes, and the dark outlines of the houses, as the sun sank behind the western hills, overshadowing them for an instant, the first night of our entrance into this charming little harbor. We could see the people all along the shore, wending their way to church; while in place of the well-known music of the church bells, the robins, here equally abundant as at home, and the "russingels," or fox sparrows, sent forth a perfect medley of harmony that accorded well with this scene.

Give me the rustic harmony of a woodland scene like this, and I will defy the best laid argument of philosophy that would attempt to prove that such people, if sincere in their worship, have not reached the outermost circle of heaven's horizon. I care not for pompous argument, and flowery speech, that would attempt to convince one by its mighty utterances, when the glimpse of such a scene as the one I represent is before one's very eyes. Surely such a scene as this produces a quietness, peace, and serenity of mind that no argument can prove false, and no philosophy can shake. It is in itself at once the reality of both argument and philosophy, and presents to us an end, which, having reached, calms our fears and bids us drink and live.: drink in the beauties already fading with a falling sun, and live in newness of revived hope to return home with a satisfaction such as no mere sermon could give.

From Red Bay we retraced our steps along the coast, calling at various places on the shore. I will try to give you an idea of the coast about here. From Saddle Island (Red Bay) to Carrol's Cove is five miles. Carrol's Cove is a sort of carpenter's square attachment of the main coast, which here consists of high cliffs and hilltops. It is low and scarcely above the sea level at high tide. The extremity points in an easterly direction; the shores everywhere are narrow strips of pebbly beach; while the point itself consists almost entirely of rocks. The bend in the land forms a sort of harbor that, in mild weather, is not an altogether bad one. Here some eight families live in about as many houses. Many of them are quite intelligent, and some of them have sons or daughters that are now residing in different portions of the states, and I was often accosted with the question of, "Do you know my son living in such and such a place?"

We soon passed from Carrol's Cove to Eastern Modest a distance of four miles where eight families reside; thence to Pirouette River, three miles and a half, where there are five families (this place is also called Black Bay and the river at the head of the bay Black River); thence to Western Modest, nearly three miles farther, where seventeen families live; still farther up the coast to Cape Diable, about opposite which is Capsan Island, one and one-half miles, where there are five families; into Diable bay, or L'Anse Diable which is, perhaps, some two and a third miles farther, where there reside seven families. We continued our journey three and one-half miles to L'Anse Loup where we found eight families residing; from the bottom of L'Anse Loup Bay to Schooner Cove, the property of a merchant from Newfoundland a Mr. Watson by name, the distance is a mile and three quarters; and from here to the lighthouse, at Point Amour, two and one-half miles farther. We did not anchor at either Capsan Island or L'Anse Diable, since there is no good ground to anchor there, and vessels generally remain either farther up or down the coast, while the travel is in small boats between these two places. Thus from Red Bay to Point Amour, a distance of about twenty-six miles, following a straight line from settlement to settlement, there live about eight families and four hundred people.

The census from Pt. Amour to Blanc Sablon could be estimated in about the same proportion, while the latter place is perhaps the largest, with its surroundings of Wood and Greenley Island, east of Esquimaux Point and Natashquan. Strange as it may appear, nearly every family of this little colony keeps fowls and domestic animals, and it is no unusual sight to see thirty or forty of the former running about the settlements, the hens picking for food here and there, and the cocks crowing continually. We were able to purchase about eight or ten dozen fresh eggs for the nominal price of a shilling (twenty cents) a dozen. We would willingly have paid twice that amount.

I will not stop to describe all the scenes along the coast here, but will simply say that some of the places were gems of loveliness. Some were backed by tablelands of sandstone, others were peculiar formations of granite. Most of these places we had only time to see from our vessel as we passed by them, yet they presented a panorama of loveliness. When opposite Pirouette I could plainly hear the pipings of the marsh frogs in the swamps of the river beyond, and have no doubt but that, as one of the inhabitants told me, they are very common there. Several of these places appear to have a formation much different from that of the country around them, and I have no doubt but that most interesting results would be obtained by careful study both of the fauna and flora, as well as of the geology of the region.

Thursday night we reached L'Anse Loup, passing the Battery as it is called and Red Cliffs. The Battery consists of a plateau with perpendicular, stratified cliffs in front, about three hundred feet high, though I did not go ashore to measure it exactly. It forms a most striking, and grandly beautiful feature of the surrounding scenery. I am informed that in winter it hangs with masses of icicles, that, from the strata of colored rock and soil back of it, forms most beautiful and almost dazzling reflections of colors of all sorts and plays. It must truly be a grand sight to see this huge mass of rock showing forth crystals of water in such mingled brilliancy.

A path runs below the overhanging cliffs, narrow, but distinct even at high tide. In winter, when blocked with snow, the people are forced to scale the height and travel with great difficulty over instead of beneath this platform of rock. Though travelling below is much more dangerous, the danger is generally laughed at, and the space crossed as quickly as possible. Several very narrow escapes from serious accident have been recorded here. At one time a huge rock, of several tons weight, fell directly between the dogs and the komatik, as the sledge was hurrying along at its utmost speed; no one was injured, though all were very badly frightened. At another time a sledful of several young ladies had just passed one of the most dangerous parts of the road when a shower of rocks fell behind and between them and the next komatik which was but a short distance behind, yet nobody was injured. Soon we had passed this place and were snugly anchored in L'Anse Loup Bay for the night. The morning gave us a good view of the bay, which is a simple indenture of the coast, about as deep as it is wide, and nearly a mile and a half in either direction. The eastern and western sides are ridges of hills, while their slopes are rather pretty and picturesque. A small stream enters the foot of the bay, wide but shallow; while west of this is a huge, low ridge of rocks, and farther west still a beach of pure, clear sand. The extension of country beyond appeared as if it might once have been a part of this same extension of bay, as it no doubt was.

Forteau Bay is very similar to Loup bay. It is about twice as deep, and more triangular in shape, while the eastern extremity bends inward much like an inverted comma, giving the appearance almost of a second bay infringing upon the first. The eastern side seems to have been formed by the washing away of the limestone ridges which are here several hundred feet high, and extending far back into the country. The western side is principally of limestone which recedes to the top of the cliffs beyond, at a height of about four hundred feet. The bottom of the bay is mostly a sandy beach, except where occasional outcrops of rock appear. There is a small stream here also, as in nearly every bay along the coast, that seems to drain the remains of some former extension of this same bay, from the low and extended valley beyond. I noticed particularly the cliffs on the eastern side, which reached almost to the sea, and were nearly perpendicular; whose stratifications were apparent even from our vessel, and whose uneven fractures presented the appearance of ruined towers or castles and temples. I plucked several sweet-scented spring flowers; and saw with pleasure signs of the springing into new life of evergreen as well as alders, shrubs and closely clustered vegetation everywhere abundant.

Our stay here was short, however, and a fair breeze soon brought us again to Greenley Island. I will describe it.

Greenley Island is a low island, scarcely seventy feet, at most, above the sea level. The northern part is short and wide, the southern point long and blunt. Several rising hillocks mark the centre of the island; from these the land slopes on one side close to the sea, on the other to the western portions of the island which are covered with rocks and bowlders as if once the terminal moraines of a glacier, yet much waterworn; while the water beyond is clear and sandy. On the east, and I think also the north side of the island is sand; on the southwest the rocks extend but a little distance into the water, while on the east point is an immense flat table of rock, seamed, scarred, and rounded by the water, which covers it at low tide. This is a curiously formed ledge of granite, and does not appear to have been broken excepting by the scars of time and water, yet it appears to form the underwork of this part of the island.

Upon the island is an occasional outcropping, apparently of this same rock, though for the most part the ground is soft grassy and mossy muck, with occasional fresh water ponds. Here and there are strewn angular blocks of coarse, poor, grayish-yellow granite, quite different from the predominant rocks on the island. These are more or less square in outline and varying in size from two to five feet. The tops are flat, and the edges all clean cut, and hardly if at all water-worn, being distinct from the worn edges of the bowlders, which were common near to the water's edge. These blocks I have mentioned are scattered at irregular distances all over the southwest portion of the island, being more abundant near the table rock before mentioned, and west of the lighthouse. All the beach on that side of the island which faces Wood Island is sand, while the high point here seaward is mostly of the same origin so far as I could ascertain.

The lighthouse is situated on the southern extremity of the island. It is an octagonal wooden structure, marked like stone or brick, and painted white upon the outside. The apparatus for illumination consists of an iron framework fastened to an upright revolving rod, that moves by a simple arrangement of wheels; one of these is heavily weighted while a handle is furnished for winding the weight and keeping the apparatus in motion. Another small upright rod with an upright screw attached keeps in motion a patent governor, for regulating the time of each revolution. This governor is a crossbar, on each end of which is a sort of fan, of brass, which turns in a perpendicular or horizontal direction to indicate slow or fast. Ordinarily the governor turns one hundred and twenty times in a minute, and the lamps are four minutes in making a complete revolution. The speed is regulated by government authority. The top of the tower has twelve large, double plate glass windows, each a quarter of an inch thick. The lights are twelve, arranged to shine as four, three being white and one red, which flash as they revolve at given intervals far out to sea, warning the sailors that the coast is nigh.

We were very cordially received and shown around by the light-keeper, who, being a French gentleman, however, understood very little English. There is here also a fog gun, fired every half hour in foggy weather. That, with the five minute steam whistle at Point Amour, near by, renders it quite lively here at times, and furnishes much amusement to the natives, especially those, who, coming from a distance, hear these things for the first time.

Monday the 23rd. At last we have a breeze, and hoisting full sail we are soon sliding through the water at the rate of about six miles an hour. By night we are far on our way to the westward.

Tuesday the 24th. Though the wind has slackened a little it still holds good. The air about us is perfection itself, so clear and bracing is it. At eight o'clock we were just off the St. Mary Islands, having gone about eighty miles in twelve hours, and, counting the curvature of the coast, a full hundred and sixty in the last twenty-four; and yet on we go,—dashing through the water. We pass Shag rocks, a long row of bare rocks, without vegetation of any kind, where the cormorants, or shags as they are here called, breed in large numbers upon the ledges of bare rock; they use their own guano deposits for a nest. There are two species of cormorants here, the common cormorant (*Graculus carbo*), and the double crested cormorant (*G. dilophus*); both are called shags, but the latter are generally designated by the Indian name which is, if I am informed correctly, *Wapitougan*. Both species breed equally abundant apparently. I have seen thousands at a time lining the rocks. They sit upright, in rows, upon the edges of the rocks, and seldom one sits behind another, so that, to accommodate them, every edge of each crag presents a trimming of cormorants; a lively looking trimming just as some shot is fired that sends all into the air. The eggs are two to three, and, though really bluish white in color, are invariably covered with a calcareous deposit that renders them exceedingly chalk-like in appearance.

At a distance these rocks present the appearance of being covered with snow, but a nearer approach shows that this is a covering of guano from the continual droppings of the birds; while the tops of the rocks are thickly embedded with an accumulation of guano from the same cause, firmly stamped down with the continual pattering of numberless feet.

Tuesday the 25th. We anchored off Natashquan. Here we obtained a bundle of newspapers, mostly Harpers' Weekly, the first we had seen for nearly seven months. Natashquan point is a little better than a sand bank, with an overgrowth of low spruce and fir trees, and but a poor attempt at vegetation. At its extremity are placed the houses of one of the Hudson's Bay Company's posts, and one or two native huts, while on a small island opposite is a very neat house belonging to a trader, who passes the greater part of his time between this place and the neighboring shores and Quebec trading along shore. The water all about the point is very shoal with dangerous sandbanks in every direction. I saw the hulk of a vessel of about eighty tons, that several days before had run aground here; it had become stuck fast in the sand and was now a total wreck. A few miles almost direct east takes us to the mouth of the river where the settlement is. The harbor, even here, is full of sunken ledges, most of which appear only at low tide. Vessels cannot approach near the shore even here, since the sandbanks again interfere, and the water is quite shallow even at high tide. A little distance above this is another river, and the intervening space is a picturesque little peninsula, of coarse and fine granite of feldspar, over which a scanty vegetation forms a groundwork with dwarf spruce and fir trees extending far back into the country.

In the bushes, just back of the few houses that line the stream, I saw large numbers of birds. The white throated sparrows sang their well known *pea-body*, *pea-body*, *pea-body*, prefaced by their usual whistle, from nearly every prominent tree-top, while I amused myself for nearly an hour watching the robins as they flew or hopped about on the lawn, or in and out the wood-pile and other debris in front of the houses, enjoying the bright sun which shone down, warm and gladdening, upon the ground just springing into greenness again, wet with the moisture of melting snow. I saw quite a number of other birds, and recognized the white crowned sparrow, and also a shy Maryland yellow-throat (*Geothlypis tri-*

chas), who appeared several times, for my express benefit, I suppose, in plain sight, before finally disappearing into the underbrush at the right. The remainder of the forenoon was spent in examining the glacial rounded rocks, on which I found several well defined *scratches*, and in following the stream for a short distance to the meadows, or low marshy districts just beyond the houses; walking all the way on shelving rocks that, nearly level with both meadow and stream, sloped off in large platforms into the water. This river, I am told, is navigable only for small boats, and for only two miles from its mouth, though I believe that the Indians travel somewhat farther in their canoes. As the people living here were mostly French I could glean but little from them. The harbor, however, is a mass of shoals even to the mouth of the river, whose eastern bank is sand, while the bed of the stream partakes somewhat of the character of the harbor, as far as I saw it, at least. I here heard the Canadian "russingel," full of most tuneful melody for which it is so noted throughout Canada. On the right bank of the river, and bordering the beach, are quite a number of houses, while a small island near by contains a cluster of as many more; altogether quite a settlement for this region. One large fishing establishment has about forty boats and two hundred hands engaged in the fisheries, during their season; while there is a postoffice which receives mails to and from Quebec, Bonne Esperance, and the South Shore by packet, via Gaspé, touching at Anticosti, between which latter places a submarine cable has been recently laid, to give warning of the shipwrecks which are so constantly occurring on this island.

Saturday the 28th. It was to-day, if I remember right, that we experienced the first of the two noted dark days of 1881. We were about half-way between Natashquan, the point we had just left, and Mingan, a post of the Hudson's Bay Company, to which we were bound. Early in the morning the wind left us, and soon the atmosphere was clouded over with a dull murky and yellowish smoke-colored light, that almost hid the sun. We could only see a faint light spot where that luminary was protesting unsuccessfully against such an infringement of its illuminating powers. By eleven o'clock the sky was like the lurid smoke of a furnace, and about as yellow, the air was so heavy as scarcely to be breathed, while the sailors all turned at once to Mother Shipton's prophecy, and believed, for sure, that the end of the world was about to approach. I afterwards learned that as far down the Gulf as Bonne Esperance, and even at L'Anse Loup, the lamps were lighted at various times from eleven in the morning until four in the afternoon, while nearly all along the coast, some part of the day presented for a short time, an appearance nearly as black as night. I will mention another circumstance and its interpretation by the captain and crew that appeared most striking. As we drifted along we passed successively, long waves of a fine, yellowish dust powder that lay upon the surface of the water often so thickly as to cover acres of water at a time. It looked precisely like a deposit of sulphur. Part of those spoken to on the subject declared that it was a deposit from the smoke of several forest fires, which we afterwards know to have raged on Anticosti, as well as several places on the mainland. I believe they said that they had seen something like it before — at least it did not particularly surprise them; while another class declared that it was the dust or rather pollen from the innumerable alders that line the banks of the rivers all about the coast. The extent of these patches was remarkable, whichever explanation was true. The patches were often over a mile in length, while we passed over many acres of it before leaving it.

Several whales had played near us during the night, and when first seen, the ridges were declared oil from the whale blowings,— which, often indeed, cover the water for miles; but during the night all passed off, and in the morning we had passed Esquimaux point, a Roman Catholic sealing settlement of about one hundred and sixty houses, and soon reached Mingan, a most beautiful little harbor of clustered islands, where the varied figures of the tide ripple in the shallow water are one of the most remarkable displays of the kind along the coast.

CHAPTER XVI.

Mingan and surroundings — Hudson's Bay Companies' buildings — Mingan River — Indians of this region; their habits, religion, etc. — "Montagnais" and "Nascopies" — The Indian trade at the various places along the north shore — Romaine or Olomanosheebo — Natashquan again — French steamer and salmon freezing — Jewelry peddler — Agwanus, Nabisippi — Terns and gulls — Codfish "schooling" — Esquimaux Point — Indian names, etc.: St. Genevieve Island, Watcheeshoo, Manicouagan, Saddle Hill, Mt. St. John, Washatnagunashka Bay, Mushkoniatawee, Pashasheeboo, Peashtebai — Shooting at the Fox Islands — Mutton Bay, Great Mecattina Islands — Old Fort Island again at last.

I can well remember the morning when our little schooner headed for the well sheltered harbor of Mingan. We had started from Esquimaux Point, off which place the vessel had been anchored during the night, about nine o'clock, and, passing the point with its low extension of sand beach and its one hundred and sixty houses,— some of which were of quite unique pattern and pleasing outward appearance,— had fallen in with a light breeze which took us along right merrily through the tide ripples and shallow waters between the long chain of islands seaward, and the mainland on our right. Early in the afternoon we sighted a long, low point of land in the distant horizon, where a small white dot was plainly visible, representing the buildings of the establishment toward which we were fast approaching, and which was our destination. There are times when the motion of a contrary tide against the sides of a vessel appears to show that one is fast gaining, when in reality losing ground; there are also times when such a tide is in the vessel's favor, and a swift, yet almost imperceptible motion, carries her on at a rate of five, six, or even more miles an hour. At times our vessel had each of these motions, now going swiftly, now slowly, as the case might be, while the low and sandy, or the high and cliff-like sides of the neighboring islands grew nearer and nearer, to fall slowly behind us and grow dim in the distance, as the point toward which we were aiming grew each moment plainer and plainer.

We were between the mainland and a few low islands on our left, when suddenly we struck a most remarkable "tide rip," as it is called. The rippling of the water, with low, even lappings, sending forth music like the laugh of "Laughing Water," extended all around and about us, a mile at least in each direction. Cross currents made long furrows here, while there, broad sheets presented the same even ripple as far as the eye could reach. On through this charming and fascinating little place we slowly glided, as we listened to the merry waters and feasted our eyes on the playful ripples, watching our sure approach to the harbor now so near us. Flocks of ducks, hurrying to and fro, passed us on our right and left, while gulls and other birds sported around and above us, or floated on the surface of the water, often a few rods only from the bow of our vessel as we glided along. At last we reached harbor, and were soon safely anchored.

Mingan harbor is a narrow but deep stretch of water open to the sea on the east and west, with the mainland on the north, and Mingan Island on the south. Of Mingan Island I can say little; it is a low piece of land, long and narrow with a foundation of sand which is visible here and there along its surface. The main body of the island seems to be composed of a series of rocks deposited in layers one above the other, and forming low, irregularly faced cliffs, with slate-like cleavage and fracture, which are nearly or quite perpendicular in outline. The upper surface of this mass bends in various directions, while its height is twenty to forty feet above the sea. Low, stunted firs abound everywhere, so that the island forms a not unattractive sight in this really romantic little spot.

On the mainland, or Mingan proper, contrary to what might be expected from the appearance of the island opposite, an entirely different formation exists. Nowhere along the coast, for a considerable distance at least, does a rock of any size appear, either in place or loose as bowlder, stone, or pebble. Strange to say, as will be shown further on, the rocky precipices, or rather steps of the rapids in Mingan river, some three miles from its mouth, seem to be the first indications of rock formation in this locality, while these are simply the eastern and southeastern boundary of a tremendous mass of high rocky ground that extends inland for miles, perhaps thousands of miles.

The coast and its beach, as the whole country to the rocks inland, is everywhere low and sandy. On the beach itself the sand is dense and very fine. Farther in shore there is a very scant, occasional streak of low vegetation where are pastured a few heads of cattle and goats that graze on the lawns, here and there, where they can find food. A few acres of good grass are fenced in, and this supplies an excellent feed for the animals during the winter, which here is neither so long nor so severe as is usually the case farther north, at Bonne Esperance even. From Mingan west to Long Point, a distance of about six miles, this low sand beach extends almost without a single rock, I believe, while the east beach is entirely of sand. The river itself passes through a ridge of this same material which forms a high bank on the left and a low one on the right, as one passes inland, while the whole land rises directly from the sea then falls in a northeasterly direction, and the trend of greatest height, here, as nearly everywhere along this part of the coast, is in a northwesterly direction. In the background, the distant hills rise to a height of at least a thousand feet, while dim outlines of others, of perhaps greater height, appear in the horizon. This is the picture whose charming outline at once attracts and captivates one upon entering the harbor of this sequestered little spot. Exhilarated by the sharp, fresh air we land, and soon count our trout from the waters where few but the Indians have preceded us.

Mingan has been for many years a post of the Hudson's Bay Company. Thither the Indians from the interior resort to sell their furs, for which they receive in exchange provision, clothing, ammunition, and those useful articles of which they may be in need.

Mingan is situated about three hundred and sixty miles from Quebec, in a straight line, while it is only twenty-five miles from the opposite shore of Anticosti and is a little east of a point opposite the extreme southwestern portion of that island. The attractions of the place are only its fishing and the houses of the company's post with that of the *Guard de pêche*. From your position on board your little vessel in the harbor, you can see them all; the long plank walk with the net shop at its eastern extremity has near it the officers' house with a cosy little office close by; farther down are the storehouses, wherein are the provisions, clothing and such like stores with which the general trading of the establishment is done, while bundles of fine fur hang suspended from cross bars and nails in the lofts above. Just around the bend, the walk continues to an old unused wharf where it terminates; being a distance of one-tenth of a mile. I say one-tenth of a mile,— many is the time that this plank walk has been paced, while sauntering for pleasure or to pass the time away, undoubtedly by each individual dweller of this establishment. A few barns or outbuildings, of one sort or another, placed here or there as the case may be, complete that portion of the post which has been built up to the present time. Most of these buildings have been tastily painted, thus presenting a neat and attractive picture to one viewing it from the vessel in the harbor, or the deck of the little steamer, that, plying between here and Quebec, touches all the important points along the coast for a distance of some few hundred miles. If you visit this charming little spot, you are sure of a cordial reception from the gentlemanly officers of the post, who are only too pleased to welcome strangers amongst them.

If there is plenty of time at your disposal, hire, for a small amount, a guide and canoe and make a day's trip up the river. The Mingan river flows in a west varying to southeasterly direction, and enters the Gulf not far from the Romaine river which flows from nearly a contrary direction. At the mouth of both rivers are shallows and accumulations filling the water with ridges that control strongly the current at this point. These sand bars are constantly

17

shifting, while in places they have overrun each other and piled up small islands of sand which becoming overgrown with grass or scant vegetation have become the nesting places of gulls and ducks, thus supplying the people with birds and eggs in large numbers whenever they are desired. Following up the river you will find sand and sand banks on either hand, and extending, with scant vegetation, far inland. Soon we approach the rapids, where the river widens into a baylike expansion of water bounded everywhere by granite cliffs, which, rising to a height of three hundred feet extend in undulating billows of uneven height, far towards the dim outlines of the hills beyond, while tangled vegetation, and bowlders and loose rock lie mingled in confusion on all sides.

In front of the rapids, and just before reaching them, we came to a partial clearing, on our right, in the dense mass of fir and spruce trees here grown so closely together, where a party of pleasure seekers from "the States" had built a "cabin" which they used as a rendezvous during the summer sporting season. The rapids, directly opposite this charming spot, consist of a body of water pouring over a series of rocky ridges running from shore to shore, and which form a regular pair of steps of fifteen to twenty feet in height. The opening of the river is between perpendicular walls of granite which have apparently been worn down and crumbled away by time and the water so constantly dashing and splashing over it in its path to the ocean. Above the rapids the stream is narrow but deep.

To the left of these rapids formerly existed a narrow pathway which, ascending to the height above, led to a position whence the descent to the river again was comparatively easy. This path was once much used by the Indians who sought the interior of the country by this route, but it has long since been discontinued. I ascended this path with the guide for nearly two miles, but the walking was so difficult, the pathway often so obscure, and the whole surface of the plateau exhibiting such a sameness of general feature that we soon gave it up as a bad job and returned with difficulty the way we had come. I found in the rocks several small veins of magnetic iron, and also of lead, while a few sheets of mica several inches in either direction were also picked up, but the nature of the formation precludes the probability of finding much of value in the mineral line either here or anywhere else upon the coast.

The Mingan river, like many if not most of the other rivers along the coast, extends inland about twenty miles when it reaches a pond; it is then connected by a series of ponds to some lake whose altitude usually exceeds that of the surrounding country, and whose waters, descending in a contrary direction, form gradually a second river which flows to the sea by a similarly circuitous route to that of its congener.

We descended the river much more rapidly than we had ascended it, the current being very swift in places, and the wind also being in our favor. From the shore we could see the summit of Mt. St. John's, lying some fifteen miles inland in a northwesterly direction, which mountain is said to be a little over fourteen hundred feet in height. Directly inland the country is said to rise in successsive steppes — if one might use the word in this connection, — to what is termed the "height of land," some five hundred miles inland, where a chain of mountains, peculiar to the whole lower St. Lawrence region, and northern Quebec, with peaks varying from one to three thousand feet in height, continues in an eastern trend towards the sea, which it reaches at the extremity of the Labrador peninsula, near Ivucktoke, or Hamilton Inlet.

I had intended saying something further here upon the subject of the Indians themselves, of this locality, but they do not differ greatly from those of the whole coast, and all agree in the same general characteristics. Mingan is the camping ground, so to speak, for all of this class of people for several hundred miles of coast and as many inland. Their chapel or church is also situated here, and weekly worship is conducted by their chief, except at such times as their priest makes them a special visit.

The religion of the Indians seems to be of a sort of Roman Catholic order. I am told that it is quite similar to that of the

French Canadian Roman Catholics, though having a distinct Indian characteristic which marks it at once as peculiar to that class of people. Their church, at Mingan, is a low, wooden affair, very plain, and with only the necessary paraphernalia connected with their worship within it. Outside and near to is the burying ground, and above each tomb, — at least the majority of them — a simple cross of stained wood marked the head, the size of the cross being the sign of the importance of the individual in his tribe and village. Back from the burying ground, and some distance in the neighboring woods, was a large cross, and a bower of fir boughs a little distance from it, representing some further ceremonies in their mystic religion. Here, I am informed, the people go to bow and reverence the cross, and to dance or weep within the bower, as the occasion may require. With regard to the Indian religion, Mr. Butler says:—

"The worship of the Indians at Mingan is in accordance with the teachings of the Romish church, I imagine. I have never heard of any separate form of their own. The cross and bower you speak of are, I believe, a sort of memorial or votive shrine. There is a story connected with it but I have forgotten what it is." Mr. Butler has thus touched upon a genuine relic which, could it be recalled, would probably interest every intelligent reader in the United States and abroad. He further says: "I suppose their religious ideas, apart from the Roman Catholic Church, are very vague." Much to my annoyance, the attendance of strangers was forbidden rather than bidden to these their mystic rites, and I was unable to observe them at their worship, although their priest visited them and performed services while I was there.

The respect shown by the Indians to their dead results in a species of religious superstition, peculiar, perhaps, to all communities of their race and color, that the bodies of their dead friends must, at all hazards, be protected from anything that would defile, or in any way injure them, while any relative of the deceased remains alive. They regard their burying ground their final home, and even from far distant camping grounds they are said to send delegations on long trips, both in summer and winter, for the purpose of making sure that intruders have not disturbed the remains of their friends.

Although for the most part, these Indians, both as a tribe and as individuals composing it, are quiet and peaceably disposed creatures, on no occasion, probably, would one of them kill a white man, or one of another tribe, more quickly than if in any way interfering with the bodies or burial places of any of their tribe. Socially, the Indians are quiet and peaceable, if treated with respect and kindness, though they are quick to take offence at one who attempts to "bully" them or infringe upon their rights.

Of the Indians of Labrador I will now say a few words. There are two principal tribes of Indians, not counting the Esquimaux of the extreme northern portion of the plateau, who inhabit this region: the Montagnais who inhabit the coast, especially of the river and Gulf of St. Lawrence, and the Nascopies who dwell principally inland and whose visits to the seashore are periodical and chiefly to secure supplies by selling their furs and obtaining credit on their probable winter's catch. Of the origin of these tribes it is not necessary to enter here into any discussion. The Montagnais are probably a part of the Algonquin, and the Nascopies are undoubtedly a sub-branch of the same stock.

The "Montagnards," or "Montagnets," or "Montagnais" are found in abundance chiefly along the shores of the lower St. Lawrence, and they extend more or less abundantly from Quebec, even, as far as Mingan, while stragglers occur even farther down the coast. Tadousac was formerly a great trading post of theirs in the St. Lawrence, and even as early as the middle of the sixteenth century when Jacques Cartier visited this region these Indians flourished and were friendly, as they always have been, to the French colonists. The Montagnais were always active in war, and not so retired as their neighbors of the interior. From their residence on the coast we hear more of them and their exploits as we also know them better. The Montagnais were one of the first Indian tribes to subscribe to Christianity, though nothing has induced them to give up their nomadic existence and settle permanently on reservations which have been offered by government. They showed aversion to agriculture, and preferred to live in idleness rather than to cultivate the soil, though many of their neighbors of other tribes reared five plantations of maize. They were early beset with Jesuit missionaries who labored in vain to civilize them. Perhaps no one thing tended to demoralize the Indians then, as now, more than the traffic in spirituous liquors, which was everywhere encouraged rather than discouraged.

The " Ounadcapis," " Ounascapis," " Naskapis," " Naspapees," " Nascopi," " Naskupi," or " Nasquapee," as they have been variously called, formed at that period a distinct people inhabiting the territory lying north of Lake St. Johns and extending towards Hudson's Bay. In a communication from Mr. J. H. Trumbull, of Hartford, Ct., regarding this tribe he says : " They speak a dialect of the Cree language, nearly like, but not identical with, that of the Montagnais Indians, of the same stock. The word " Nascopi " is properly the name for an " Indian man" (*i. e.*, *vir*) in their dialect, and that, in all Algonquin languages, the name for " man " and the verb " to stand erect " are nearly related." In about the year 1674 the Nascopies came in great numbers to Tadousac and intermarried with the Montagnais, though since then the tribes in general have been hardly distinct, yet a few of each race still retain the peculiarities of their tribe, so that there are still direct descendants from the pure stock. In relation to the name Nascopi, I found it in common use all along the coast for a pile or heap of stones thrown up into some form several feet in height and usually placed on top of an island or neighboring height to mark some position, or important spot or event. These heaps occur everywhere, and are known, as I have said, by the name " Nascopi," by the natives, also " American Man " by the sailors. They are common everywhere. The name does not occur in any of our local dictionaries or encyclopedias that I can ascertain.

The Indians traded with the French as early as 1504, both Basques and Normans frequenting their chief post at Tadousac for this purpose. In 1871 a census of the Montagnais Indians along the north shore of the St. Lawrence resulted in 1,685; there being 190 at Seven Islands, 552 at Bersamis, and 560 at Mingan alone. For the Labrador division exclusively there were 1,309. In 1877 the Nascopies of the lower St. Lawrence numbered 2,860, though doubtless through error, 1,860 would have probably reached nearer the truth if indeed there were so many as that. In that same year (1871) there were estimated in Labrador and Quebec to be 2,500 Nascopies, and 1,745 Montagnais. Since that time the number of families have constantly diminished. Some have renounced their trading and trapping voyages and settled in comfortable cabins and are turning their attention to farming and the raising of such crops as potatoes, turnips, oats, etc., and secure about enough hay to feed a few head of cattle during the winter, but the traders are fast undoing what has been done, and sell them goods as well as liquor largely on the credit principle so that, so to speak, they are demoralized almost as fast as, if not faster than, they are moralized.

Godbout river was formerly a great Indian station and gathering place; not more than a dozen families now reside there, and they only in the summer time. Farther down the river, at Seven Islands, about five times that number gather in the summer, descending by the Moisie river, and strive to recuperate from the half famished condition in which scarcity of provisions in the winter time has left them. Moisie itself, at one time quite a rendezvous for these families, is now almost deserted for this place (Seven Islands). Mingan, now the favorite resort of this tribe, is a good location for their wants. It has been previously described. The Indians meet here in the summer, and have a general resting time. Many of them, if the season's " catch " has been good, buy them boats and barges for $80 to $150 and make hunting excursions both up and down the coast, or to the island of Anticosti thirty miles distant across the channel. In the year 1878 there were about 80 families and 375 people, young and old, stationed here for the summer. The year I was at Mingan there were about the same number. Natashquan is another station of these Indians during the summer, here being a post of the Hudson's bay company here also, though at the extreme point of the mainland on the east side of the channel. Their settlement here is entirely by mishwaps arranged for temporary accommodations only during the summer months, and rarely more than fifty families and two hundred people, old and young, assemble here from their inland excursions to sell their furs and to recuperate. Musquarro, though formerly a great Indian rendezvous, has now become deserted for Romaine or Olomanosheebo, which is really a most delightful and picturesque place,—at least so it seemed to me as we entered its snug and quiet harbor one beautiful evening, and viewed it with the lights and shadows of the sun's last rays upon it. Romaine river is now a great highway for the Indians who visit the interior or those who descend to the seacoast.

St. Augustine, about thirty miles to the westward of Bonne Esperance, was formerly the great resort of the Nascopie Indians. Here for a long time the Hudson's Bay Company kept a flourishing post, which was afterwards deserted by them, and a generous, honest dweller of that region was allowed to take possession of it, who now supplies the Indians who come from the interior, to this, the only post of the region, for a distance of many miles in either direction. Many of the Indians wintering here came directly across the country even from Ungava and the shores of Hudson's Bay itself. About 1871 there were as many as one hundred and twenty families of Nascopies at this place, with about a third as many Montagnais; the two elements are so intermingled now that the numbers are pretty evenly divided between the two tribes. It has been said of the Nascopies in general, that "although intelligent they are yet very superstitious, believe in dreams, in their 'jougleurs,' or medicine-men," etc. Of late years the Indians have encamped largely in the islands and mainland near Bonne Esperance where Mr. Whiteley and others furnish them with supplies to continue their hunting and trapping in the interior the following winter. There are thus about three hundred and seventy-five families, and 1,700 people leading a nomadic existence, and dwelling about and around the various resorts and islands from Quebec to Belle Isle. These Indians are seldom if ever worth over a few hundred dollars, their furs are *not* abundant, they themselves being thus obliged to eke out a miserable existence, starving to death in the winter to procure food for their families, and secure enough furs to pay for their summer's provisions, at which season they are usually obliged to glut themselves to gain sufficient strength to pursue their hunting the next winter, else they would surely starve and die in the midst of plenty, from their previous winter's want.

Another great source of misery to the Indians is credit. This effectually bars them from enterprise, and prevents their advancement in every possible respect. They cannot consider themselves free when once they have become involved to any trader or dealer. The uncertainty of their business makes it all the worse. If a year comes when game is scarce, and little fur can be obtained, they come from the interior disheartened, for who will give them provisions if they have no furs? At last some one furnishes them with enough provisions, to keep them from starving, on credit of the next winter's "catch." These are soon eaten up, and the same trader finds himself obliged, to save himself, to fit them out for the coming winter, with the proviso that he shall be paid from the results of that catch. The Indians are obliged to promise or starve. The next year is a poor year also. The Indians take little fur, and, knowing that if they go to the trader who fitted them out they must give him all they have with no prospect of any return, they come to some other part of the coast, and try the same experiment with another party; thus they go from place to place, leaving debts wherever they go, with no prospect of ever paying them, and the fear that soon every avenue will be blocked to their approach. The traders, equally in despair, are but just opening their eyes to the situation, and finding the only solution of the difficulty in a compromise in which each side shares.

When the ice breaks up in the spring, usually the last of May, the Indians seek the coast with their furs to trade and to recuperate. Many of the traders practise all sorts of arts whereby to deceive the Indians both as to the quality of their furs, and that of the articles which they offer in exchange for them; the majority, however, ask only a fair price in exchange for cash, and the charges seem exorbitant only as the proposed credit is large or doubtful. Flour is generally $7.00 to $9.00 a barrel; lard, 20 cents, butter, 30 to 40 cents, and ship biscuits, 10 cents per pound; pork a barrel, $25.00 to $28.00; cotton, 25 to 40 cents per yard; molasses, 60 to 80 cents a gallon. In exchange, beaver skin is worth $1.50 to $2.50 a pound, martins $1.50 to $3.00 a piece, lynx, $1.50 to $2.00, bear, $5.00 to $7.50, fox, $1.50, silver fox, $15.00 to 30.00, cross fox, $7.00 to $9.00, and mink about $1.00. This will show the general average of the trade, varying slightly according to the season all along the St. Lawrence and Labrador peninsula.

The summer visits of these Indians are dreaded by all fishermen. They roam at will, fishing or shooting, visiting salmon and seal nets at night, and stealing the "catch" of their more fortunate white neighbors, while they scare away all species of game and render others as miserable as they themselves are, till fall again disperses them towards their winter hunting grounds in the interior of this wild, bleak, desolate country. In 1881 the value of their whole hunt was only about $20,000. The same year their numbers all told, from Quebec to Belle Isle, were about 11,000 young and old; this was probably too large an estimate by several thousands. One can thus see that the Indian population of this region is anything but an easy one to manage. They come down from the interior in small bands to the various places named above, in a half starved condition, and attempt to make up for their loss in hunting and trapping, by begging from any and all that are more fortunate than themselves, and by obtaining large credit from the traders. The government can do little to help them. If one year it sends supplies, the following year the Indians come down *en masse* to their rendezvous and loaf around doing nothing to earn their own living, while waiting for a similar shipment from the government. If this comes it demoralizes them more than ever, and if it does not come they have then lost all the benefit of the fishery, where they might have reaped a good harvest. A few of them are furnished with nets, hooks, and lines, and work industriously during the summer months. The soil, at the places where they remain during that season, is unfit for cultivation, and as none of the whites attempt cultivation, the Indians would be hardly more fortunate. One year the government sent them a number of bushels of potatoes to plant, as an experiment. The Indians cut them up at once, and thanked the agent for being so good as to send them supplies, hoping that they would send more the next year. Hunger has reduced them as a tribe, though a few are haughty and troublesome at times. It is impossible to civilize them to any great extent, and there are but few schools, and these only in the lower provinces where there are also a few reservations.

There has recently been appointed, by the government, an Indian agent who is now hard at work trying to better the condition of these poor, unfortunate people, and make it possible for each family to become sober and industrious and earn its own living in a thrifty way; but their nature rebels against most all treatment, and they prefer the nomadic existence of their fathers, or the uncertainties of the chase, and are delighted to roam at will and fish the stream, thus gaining an uncertain sort of existence from year to year until at last they disappear and are heard from no more. Disease very seldom attacks an Indian. Such diseases as smallpox and measles are the most prevalent,—for the former they are vaccinated freely by the government agent while he is on the coast. The aged and infirm are disposed of as speedily as possible, being left to starve and die or turned off upon anybody who will undertake to care for them. Often in the summer time large forest fires occur, but these are rarely caused by the Indians, as many seem to think. An Indian is very careful on this point, since it would be a great offence to be guilty of wilful destruction of the "hunting grounds."

I dare not say much concerning the dress of the Indians. They wear anything and everything. Old garments and new garments, thick and heavy, brown, white, or black; leather or sealskin boots, rubber boots or moccasins, according to the weather, state of their purse or their credit. The squaws wear calico, or woollen dresses of any shade, quality or pattern, and a peculiar, long, peaked cap usually of red flannel cloth. Dressed deer-skin waistcoats are common with the men and are very warm; moccasins of all sorts and shapes are made, and used or sold. But this extraordinary race demands far greater attention than has been heretofore given them, or that can possibly be contained in these fragments of their history, and it is to be hoped that the government which has so far acted judiciously in the matter will be able to do some permanent good to this unfortunate and destitute people.

Wednesday, the 8th. We left Mingan, on our return trip, yesterday, with a good wind and fair sky, and to-day we made Romaine river or Olomanosheebo as the Indians call it, another now deserted post of the Hudson's Bay Company. This location, Grand Romaine, as it is called, has recently become a great rendezvous of the Indians. The place was crowded. There must have been thirty or forty families camping there, just on the eve of their departure on a hunting excursion, so that we were too late to visit them. They were in the midst of a celebration of some grand fête day, and were saluting their priest, who had just arrived to conduct the ceremonies of the occasion. They continued an almost uninterrupted firing of guns for about two hours. In the evening all attended service; ten minutes after every Indian had left the place, and it was as still and deserted as if no one had ever existed there. Romaine is as pretty a place as its name is musical. It has a secluded yet snug appearance, while the hills form a sort of barrier within which the natural beauties of the place unfold themselves. The rocky islets on the outside enclose a safe harbor.

Tuesday, the 14th. We reached Natashquan to-day, and there found letters from home awaiting us. Here we found, surrounded by petty traders, a large French steamer that was coasting the shore for fresh salmon, which, first undergoing a freezing process, were packed, to be transported to the French coast where they are retailed at a large profit. The captain had had no cause to complain of the "catch," and all the men were hard at work curing and packing a lot of splendid large fish recently brought in by one of the fishermen from a short distance down the shore. The captain was an intelligent and excellent appearing fellow, and extended to us the usual courtesies, for which the French generally are so well noted, when he found we were Americans and strangers; and I should do him injustice did I not make particular mention of the excellence of his table, to which he cordially invited us, and which invitation we as cordially accepted. After dinner we were shown all over the steamer, and she was indeed a beauty. She was almost new, and her engines in perfect trim, while all her appurtenances showed the signs of newness and solidity. Her tonnage was a little over one thousand. Though the captain showed us everything freely, he would not describe to us the new freezing process to which he subjected the fish he preserved, claiming it to be a new invention and not that of vaporization of ether or any kindred process in use at the present time. One of the steamer's tug boats was put at our disposal for an excursion the next day, but the rain deprived us of this very great anticipated pleasure.

Saturday the 18th. Quite an excitement was caused this evening by the arrival of a jewelry peddler. He had sold a large quantity of this artificial and counterfeit material, and now was eager to get away from the village by the quickest possible conveyance, and I cannot wonder if a sample of his goods that came under my eye is a fair sample of all of which he disposed to this honest-hearted community. It was that of a very poorly plated ring worth about a shilling that was sold for ten shillings. The young fellow who purchased it intended it for his young lady, but, finding that it tarnished the first night his rage may be easily imagined.

At Natashquan we obtained a fresh supply of provisions, and a few pounds of most excellent fresh maple sugar; it was put up in square cakes of five pounds each and sold at the surprisingly cheap price of ten cents a pound.

Our next stopping place was at Agwanus river, twelve miles above Natashquan and but a few miles below Nabisippi, which latter place we could plainly see with the naked eye. Agwanus is a very pretty place. A beach of quite pure sand is crowned by a number of grass-plats upon which several houses have been built while the whole is backed by the cliffs and crags of the neighboring hills. We sailed by a number of small, low islands or rather rocks, for there was scarcely any vegetation upon them, the breeding place of innumerable terns (probably *Sterna macroura*), which fairly swarmed everywhere we went. They took good pains, however, to keep just out of gun-shot, so that we did not procure any of them.

It was dusk when we passed through this region, and as we slowly glided along the channel among the rocks, we watched the beauties of the scene. Low patches of green topped the brown rocks, and were set off by the display of the darker green of the spruces farther inland and the shadows on the still darker green of the cloud-shadowed rocks still farther away. Soon we came upon a small cabin, snugly tucked away in a sheltered place among the rocks near the shore. Close by here we anchored, while at our right another small island swarmed with gulls and terns at which we practised shooting until dusk. This place we learned was Washtawooka bay. The harbor protected us perfectly on all sides, and here we anchored for the night.

Thursday, the 21st. Although the longest day of the year, we to-day made our shortest run, being but six miles, only to return to Nabisippi, another now deserted post of the Hudson's Bay Company, for the night. We spent part of the time lying to about a mile off shore and shooting at the gulls, of which large numbers surrounded us. It was the species known as Bonaparte's gull (*Chræcocephalus philadelphia*) which abounds about the shoal waters and fishing grounds everywhere along this part of the coast. We saw here a most beautiful but rare sight,— it consisted of large body of codfish "schooling," as it is called, in reality playing, upon the surface of the water. The water would be covered for acres with the heads or bodies of these fish as they dashed madly about or scooted forward on the surface of the sea, often in perfect line and in perfect time. Again they would disappear as suddenly as they appeared. I have seen them at times leap several inches clear of the water. Again they would form in long ranks and rush through the water with such velocity as to make it actually hiss as it closed behind them. Sometimes they would suddenly disappear and again as suddenly appear headed in some other direction and proceed with their "playing" as before. They often sport in this way for hours, appearing in thousands and tens of thousands, and then disappear as suddenly as they came not to be seen again during the season. At this, the "old salts" say " they have taken to deep water again."

Wednesday, the 23d. We started off early this morning with a fine breeze, on our return trip. (We had visited, but did not stay long, at the Roman Catholic settlement of about one hundred and sixty houses, at Esquimaux Point, about twenty miles east of Mingan. I simply mention the location as it is an important one in sealing industries, though otherwise it does not, I believe, attract particular attention.) Farther to the eastward the small island of St. Genevieve (pronounced here *genyurve*) forms a prominent landmark, as does also the locality of Watcheeshoo (pronounced *watch-a-shoe*) which is near Manicouagan bay. Close by is Saddle hill, the highest part of this neighboring coast, being about three hundred and seventy-five feet above the sea, and about sixty-five miles to the north and west of which lies Mt. St. John, the highest peak on the North Shore at this point, being 1614 feet high. A few other Indian villages were passed, such as Washatnagunashka bay, or Mushkoniatawee, Pashasheebo, as also Peashtebai, and Appeeletat, all of which names, strange to say, really sound quite musical when pronounced properly by one acquainted with their Indian sound.

Friday, the 24th. We lay to, awhile this morning, off the Fox islands, and filled several pails and buckets with murres' eggs (*Lomvia troile*), while with our guns we shot about a hundred of these birds in less than an hour, and yet we left them flying as thickly over and by the island as when we had first landed. We boiled the eggs and found them excellent eating. They are not quite as rich in flavor as hens' eggs, but certainly fully equal them in quality. With this addition to our stock of provisions we had several new dishes, among them a most delicious rice pudding. In the evening we passed the highlands of Meccatina, nearly six hundred feet above the sea, and also those of Mutton bay, about seven hundred feet high, a small settlement where dwells a missionary who ministers to the people on this part of the coast; and anchored in the snug harbor of Great Meccatina, where we lay all night. Here we again saw the magnificent comet, we had occasionally seen before, in a northeast by north direction, and apparently about 30° above the horizon. It was about 11 o'clock p. m. that I made this observation.

In the morning we proceeded eastward with a fine breeze. As we passed, all the harbors were full of Newfoundland fishing vessels, many of them from Harbor Grace. Baie des Roches was filled so full that we could scarce obtain anchorage. I found on many of the rocks distinct and well defined glacial scratches, and noted other peculiarities of the location. We remained here all day on account of the intense fog everywhere. The next day we managed, after beating about for some time, to reach Old Fort island again whence we had started, after one of the most enjoyable trips I ever experienced.

CHAPTER XVII.

Affairs at Old Fort Island — The fishing season — Thunder storm — Arrival of vessel which is to take us home — Our trip in her to L'Anse Loup and scenes at intervening places — "Off for home " — Double reefed fore and main sails — Island of Anticosti — A hurricane — Quebec and home.

AFFAIRS at the Island had not changed much since I had left it, and everything moved on in the same quiet, well ordered style. There had been an arrival which pleased the children greatly, in the shape of a young calf, in the barn, and most of the day was occupied by them in watching its movements, which they did with the greatest of interest, reporting hourly at the house. There were three children in the family, but one would easily have imagined that there were at least thirty, by the succession of continual appearances and as sudden disappearances at the door, as each came to relate the dispatches from the barn. It, however, afforded them occupation, which was the main point.

The animals about the place, not counting in the dogs, consisted of a bull, a cow with its calf, and two goats — one of which was a billy. The goat furnished milk as well as the cow. Many people along the coast keep goats, and prefer the milk for the children to that of the cow. Both the billy and the bull were turned loose on the ground with simply a board before their eyes, and one of their fore feet tied to a rope passing around the horns. In this manner all roam together : dogs, children, animals and all.

It really seemed quite refreshing to be fed once more on good home-made bread and butter, to drink fresh, rich, creamy milk, and to have the luxury of real cream in one's tea and coffee. The gun still afforded the roast duck of the noon or evening meal; and many a morning have I been out before breakfast and brought home a bag literally full of plover and beach birds for the meal. Good cheer, and plenty of it, was never wanting now. Soon the men began to trim their boats for the fishing season, now nearly upon them, and all around us was activity and life. A curious example of how everything is turned to use occurred recently. There had been a wreck somewhere off the coast, and several dead sheep had been picked up just off shore. Of these the skin was carefully saved, the tallow melted down and turned into homemade candles, while the carcasses were salted down to serve as food for the dogs the ensuing winter. The candles were, to be sure, a rather poor apology for such articles, and their wicking simply pieces of cotton cloth, but they answered every purpose.

The fishing season was now well advanced, and a trip to Bonne Esperance assured me that the people generally along the coast were in "great humor" over the unusually large "catch" of fish which was everywhere reported; but our chief delight centred in the letters and papers from home which were found awaiting our arrival, and glad indeed we were to get them. In the evening we were treated to what at home we should call a mild thunderstorm, and were informed that it was "the most terrible one that had ever visited the coast." Such storms are, indeed, quite rare here, and there is seldom even what we should call a "hard rain." The next day the sky cleared most beautifully, and we had one of the finest days I have ever seen on the coast. In the evening one of the fishermen brought in a seventy-five pound cod, and it was an enormous fellow, the largest I had ever seen. The day following, as it was warm and pleasant, I took my first and last plunge bath and swim, off the dock, in Labrador water. It is safe to say, that in those five minutes there must have been a change of temperature in my body of at the very least one hundred degrees, in the shade at that. I never attempted it again.

Thus we pass away the time. Day follows day in quick succession, while all is pleasure both within and without; but all pleasures have an end, and too soon we find the vessel that is to convey us home already in the harbor awaiting us. The Captain is to make a two weeks' trip " down along " visiting, for purposes of trade, the various places over which we had been before, yet we preferred to join him, and so by evening we were packed and "all aboard " for our trip. We passed Salmon Bay, everywhere abounding in glacial evidences, rounded its trough-like hollow, which appeared as if gauged out from the land toward the sea, as it undoubtedly was, and noted everywhere its peculiarities and attractions. We visited Blanc Sablon in full summer activity, and saw, even now, early August, snow-clad hills in the distance beyond; while nearer to green slopes and verdure were everywhere scattered by Nature's profuse hand.

I took my gun and started toward the distant hills. I climbed the crests close to the beach, and at the head of the bay. They were huge sand heaps sparingly grassed over, and reaching to two hundred or more feet above the sea level. Again huge depressions, nearly as deep as the hills were high, lay before me. These elevated tablelands, and smooth even valleys everywhere intervening stretched forward and inland in all directions. From the highest of these tabled hills, what a view burst upon my sight! On one side a long extent of country (apparently rich pasture land for herds of cattle, though we searched for them in vain, and listened in vain for the tinkling of the cowbell) receded to the hills on the right, while all was enveloped in dark shadows upon the green groundwork from the hills and the clouds. The whole outline of the picture was that of a large funnel; the tube extending in the distance, and the mouth occupied, in greater part, by a magnificent large pond, the outlet of which, draining through the centre of the tunnel, followed the tube, and, lost in the distance, eventually found its way, dashing down the rocky Bradore heights, into the sea.

On the other side Blanc Sablon harbor and the sea beyond came in view. To the west were Long Point and L'Anse Couteau, while Wood and Greenley islands occupied the centre of the picture, and the fishing boats (I counted two hundred or more) everywhere dotted the scene, like flies upon the wall. My game bag was empty upon my return to the ship, notwithstanding several large flocks of curlew at which I might have shot, but my mind was filled with this glimpse of one of the most beautiful of Nature's pictures, so that I minded not the revilings of our captain at sight of the empty bag.

The next day we reached Forteau. A walk around the base of the hills and cliffs on the northern side of the harbor, through growth of tangled spruce and fir where an occasional bluebell or bed of cornell peered at us from some sheltered retreat, brought us to the house of a pleasant and homely family who cordially welcomed us. The following day I took a short walk inland, to what are here called "the deserts," which are elevations and depressions of low sand dunes, whose summits are more or less grassy. They are from ten to fifty feet high, with corresponding depressions of dry sand. We found in many of these hollows several well formed spear and arrow heads, and could have picked up a bushel basket full of "chips," which were everywhere abundant. The story is told, that when the Esquimaux were driven from this part of the coast by the mountain Indians, who at the time nearly exterminated that curious race, all this region was the scene of the Indian descent to the plains from the highlands, hence the chief place of the engagement between the two parties; here the Indians made and used their arrows and other implements. The chippings that we found were mostly of a white, chalcedony-like flint rock, not at all like anything that we could find along the coast, but said to be "common inland." A few quartz and ordinary flint pieces were found, but they were comparatively rare. But we were soon forced to leave this interesting locality. Returning to the house we spent the evening, while yet light, in watching the feats and gambols of one of the young dogs as it leaped into the water from a pier over fifteen feet in height, and even dove for stones thrown at it to a depth of nearly four feet, bringing the stones to the surface between and over its fore paws; then, as the evening had advanced, we returned to the house and retired to rest.

The next morning several of the boys joined us in a walk across the limestone ledge above the house to Schooner Cove, a small western branch of L'Anse Loup. Here one of the Newfoundland merchants has a well-to-do fishing establishment, as also a small storehouse for the sale of supplies for this part of the coast; here we were to meet our vessel which had preceded us by sea. The walk was over a fertile limestone ridge about two hundred feet high, where still further evidences of glaciers could be seen about us. I found the dry beds of several ponds as I walked, and in one place one small pond still existed. It was situated in a hollow formed in gradually sloping hillocks. Considerable vegetation grew around it, and it was altogether quite a picturesque spot. Our guide then told us its history. He said that the water of the pond was fresh, but yet so deep that after repeated trials no one had ever been able to reach the bottom with the sounding lead. It was supposed to have an underground connection with the sea; but, he further explained, that the water itself was not salt since the fresh water, the results of springs and drainage was lighter than the salt water, hence would and did not mix with it. At times, he said, the surface was agitated with heavy waves, and covered with a frothy substance like that which the sea waves cast upon the beach. The pond appeared to be about seventy-five feet below the height of the surrounding plateau which averaged two hundred and forty feet above the sea level.

Saturday, August 13th. We are fairly off for home, I mean our United States home, to-day, having left our farthest point northeast, and started towards Quebec. Oh, what beautiful evenings! What superb weather! How long will it last? Shall we ever visit here again? These were the exclamations and questions that escaped us as we ploughed on, — on through the waters towards home.

Sunday we reached Old Fort Island, received on board the remainder of our luggage, and in a few hours were off again. Towards night it came in foggy, and in the morning it rained quite hard. In this state of the atmosphere we missed the proper entrance to the sea that we should have taken, and passed on through what is called the little rigoulette, at the bottom of which enters Kekarpwei River, and where there is *no* exit. Never shall I forget the clearing up of the fog and the disclosing to us of one of those charming Labrador scenes, so characteristic of the locality; low shores, sandy beaches, grassy slopes and tops, and a forest of low and tall spruce and fir, intermingled with cliffs and rocks everywhere. The passage was so narrow we could with difficulty haul the ship around without her touching the boom on one shore and the stern on the other. Narrow and shallow as the passage was, we succeeded at last, and returned to the opening that we should have taken at first into the sea. I do not believe that there was a person, however, save the captain and the crew, who regretted the extra time spent in this charming region. At length we were once more out to sea, and right merrily we sped onward, with "*belle brise*," as the captain called it, towards Quebec.

In passing Whale Head, one of the numerous small fishing stations on this part of the coast, we found a small sail-boat of Indians following in our wake, a short distance off. The captain, wishing to send a letter ashore, produced a large bottle, placed the letter within, carefully corked it again, and, with gestures calling the attention of the Indians to himself, threw it into the sea. We watched eagerly, and soon had the satisfaction of seeing the Indians' boat secure the bottle. The captain assured us that the letter would reach its destination, and that messages were often transported in a similar manner from place to place, when a favorable wind rendered it impossible to stop the ship, and some sail-boat was near to pick up the bottle.

Night soon set in, and with it the breeze freshened so that soon the order was given to reef sails; this was succeeded by an order to double-reef both fore and main sails; and on, on we sped,— through the treacherous Gulf of St. Lawrence towards home, the water fairly sissing as we cleaved it, and the wind fairly hissing as it slid from our sails. I think our Captain told us that we had made better time, in a given time, than he had ever made before on any trip; I fully believe that it might have been true. Wednesday morning the 24th, we shook the reefs from our sails, and in the evening were anchored off Natashquan. A boat carried off the mail and returned with the up mail, and we were again moving. By evening of the next day we were off Anticosti Island, this scene of so many mournful wrecks and disasters.

The sailors about this part of the coast say that the Gulf of St. Lawrence ends and the mouth of the river begins just off the western end of this Island. Most writers make the dividing part at the bend farther up the river; which is right is not a point for us to settle. Off Anticosti the nearest land is Mingan, which has been so fully described. On the south shore its nearest point is Cape Gaspé. The island itself is about one hundred and twenty miles long by thirty wide. It is well wooded in portions of its surface, though it is generally barren and uninhabited save by a few bears and other wild animals. Very little and very poor water can be found upon it, while the two government lighthouses upon either extremity alone represent the life of the island. Indians occasionally hunt for bears and procure birch bark for their canoes along its shores and in its interior. Upon its southern side are dangerous reefs. Heavy gales occur frequently near by, and many are the tales of horror told of wreck and disaster upon its coast, but I hasten on. On Wednesday evening, the 31st, a gale struck us. Fierce and heavy it blew. Sharp thunder and lightning were followed by alternate puffs of wind, cold and hot as if from the mouth of a furnace. The squall fairly turned into a hurricane. Before we had gone to rest the gale subsided, the dark clouds gave way, the rain ceased, and the clear evening predicted a beautiful day for the morrow. The morrow arrived: it found us once more at Quebec.

CHAPTER XVIII.

Third voyage; summer of '82 — Puffin-shooting — Dredging — Bad weather — Main boom breaks — Chateau and Temple bays — Places of interest — Mines and minerals — Aurora and phosphorescence — Icebergs — Fox harbor — Battle island — Indians and Esquimaux — Indian vocabulary — Square island — Dead island — A water garden — Triangle harbor — Homeward bound — Notes on Dutch and Esquimaux settlements.

I HAVE now neared the end of my explorations. Yet, strange to say, I find myself once more embarked upon the perilous enterprise of again stemming the sea and stormy Gulf of St. Lawrence for a further extension of my researches upon the Labrador coast. This time I start from Boston, July 13, 1882, in a small schooner of about one hundred tons, the "Polar Star" by name, with a party of some dozen gentlemen, young and old, who, with me, are also bound for this bleak and rocky, yet picturesque coast. The party consists of ornithologists and mineralogists, conchologists and ichthyologists, photographists and pleasurists. All in an *amateur* sense however, except possibly the pleasurists, and they might almost be said to outweigh everything else and form the main feature of the party. In fact it was a pleasure party and nothing else, of which guns, ammunition, and fishing tackle formed the chief topics of conversation from the time we left until we returned.

I will not stop to describe our journey to Halifax where we procured a relay of supplies for our voyage; or of our stop on the Cape Breton shores, at several points of interest; or our journey through Canso to the stormy Gulf of St. Lawrence, where, after passing the famous Bird Rocks near the Magdalene Islands, just east of Anticosti, we encountered one of the shortest but severest gales that the captain had ever met, that nearly plunged our good ship with its cargo of precious souls into the bosom of the raging deep; but we will pass at once to the sights and scenes which seem of sufficient importance to induce us to add a single chapter to our already quite full account of the "men and things" seen and done upon "the Labrador."

And now I find that we go over a great deal of the ground already gone over so fully and often at great length in our previous pages. Our dozen pleasure seekers, however, gather a great many new facts, yet we find that the daily life of the native inhabitants does not differ essentially, as we progress east and north along the coast, from such as we have already described it to be. The houses grow smaller and smaller the farther north we go, yet the same general character of life everywhere prevails.

The time at our command for the voyage is limited, yet we reach to within a few miles of Rigoulette, the chief station on the east coast, if we except some of the Dutch settlements much farther north, and the mouth of the only river of importance in all Labrador. Beyond are the "Dutch settlements," the headquarters of the Moravian missionaries, who are supported in their work chiefly by the Moravians in this country at Bethlehem, Pennsylvania. Their headquarters on the coast are at Hopedale, Nain, Okkak, Port Manvers, Hebron, and possibly even at Ungava bay itself, though at the last named place I am uncertain whether there be an established station or not. Situated as we are, then, on a flying visit much farther north than we have ever been before in this most interesting country, with little time at our command for investigation, and with so many avenues open through which to procure facts concerning the places visited, I find myself compelled to assume the diary form of writing; and, instead of a systematic account of each place as we visited it, and an arranging of facts always in their proper connection, I give them as they were procured, being sure that, in this case at least, it is by far the better way, and will give more satisfaction in the end.

Our party first visited Bonne Esperance, from there L'Anse Loup and Forteau; at each of these places we spent some time dredging in the harbor, and filling our bottles with specimens and our cans of alcohol with fishes and other marine treasures. When off Blanc Sablon, we lowered a boat and all hands went for a hunt. Some went to Pigeon Island and some the next morning to the west end of Greenley Island: the puffins were as abundant as when described by Dr. Coues earlier in our pages. We had no difficulty in killing three hundred in a single day, and could have procured twice that amount without the least trouble. We found the island on this end literally tunnelled with the holes of this bird, and the appearance was much as if thousands of woodchucks had been at work burrowing the ground; there was scarcely a square yard of earth that did not have at least one burrow in it while more often there were twenty.

We lay in Forteau and L'Anse Loup harbors, becalmed, for nearly two weeks, during which time we used the dredge with great success and brought up from depths varying from six to twenty fathoms a large assortment and variety of marine invertebrates, which were carefully labelled and packed away to be sent to the Smithsonian Institution at Washington. The waters seemed alive with new and curious forms, however, and every haul of the dredge procured something that we had not before obtained.

I shall not soon forget our run to Chateau. We started with a fair breeze but it soon became so foggy that we could not see where we were going. We reefed sail and continued to beat about looking for some signs of the harbor. Suddenly we passed some fishing boats but as suddenly found huge rocks looming up directly in front of us. A shout from our captain, while he put the helm hard to, brought the vessel around, but so narrowly did we escape the rocks that as we jibbed we could have touched them with an oar. We put the ship about, and scud for the open sea. The waves were lashed to fury by the wind which blew abaft our starboard side; yet, blowing as it was in this howling tempest, we succeeded in signalling one of the small boats for a pilot, who boarded us with a great deal of difficulty, and again putting about we steered for the harbor of Chateau or rather Temple Bay, which is the true harbor at this point, but we did not part with the gale so easily.

As we entered the narrow passage to the bay our captain shouted to take down sail, but the pilot countermanded the order; at least, between the two the order was not obeyed, and, as we were running with the wind now almost dead ahead, though a little on our port, suddenly rounding the point of land on our left an unusually terrific squall struck us, and with a sound like thunder our main boom snapped like a pipe stem. Had the sailors not rushed to the ropes and instantly taken down the sail it would have been blown to threads in a moment. Our jib alone was now sufficient to take us to the safest position in the harbor, where we soon let down both anchors, paying out nearly all the chain on each. Here we stayed in imminent peril all night of being hurled upon the rocks the other side of the harbor, not forty rods away, at any moment. Thank Providence our good ship weathered the blast. The next day the sailors spliced the boom with spruce side pieces and about twenty fathom of a nice three-quarter inch manilla dredge rope belonging to our largest dredge; as we stayed at Temple Bay and about Chateau for two or three days, owing to bad weather, I will try to describe the place.

Chateau Bay is a small bay and comprises really the outer entrance only of a much larger inside bay. The larger is called Temple Bay, though it is often mistaken for Chateau proper. Henley Harbor is a small harbor outside the main bay and a little to the eastward of it. The point of land separating Temple from Pitt's Bay, east of it, is called Pitt's point, just outside of this is Whale island which fills the cove so closely that but a very narrow entrance admits vessels to the harbor within, yet the water is deep enough here for even large vessels.

Whale island is thus named from a most extraordinary resemblance to the shape of a whale's back. It can only be seen from a single position (the foot of a large hill said to be seven hundred feet high) in Temple bay and in a northwesterly direction from the island. The highest point on the hump of the back of this marine granite monster was carefully measured and found to be about three hundred and forty-five feet above the sea level. It would be a curious fact if the supposed basaltic prisms of Castle island should prove to be only a peculiar formation of rocky cliffs similar in origin with the other rock formations about this part of the coast, but close investigation seems to show this to be the case. The crouching figures represented in profile near this place are truly remarkable; they are figures of men, and could hardly bear a closer resemblance to the real objects if they were indeed genuine. One of them, especially, so nearly resembles a person in a crouching attitude as to deceive the keenest eye if watched in the most favorable light, and well do these stony sentinels maintain their ceaseless vigil, year by year, century by century.

The forts, located here, — remnants of the old wars which exterminated the Indians and Esquimaux residing on the coast, with the white settlers then temporarily residing here also, — are objects of great interest. At one time their outlines were quite distinctly traceable, and even their internal structure well planed out, but time has effaced nearly everything but the merest outlines of their positions, which are now barely sufficient to enable one to determine their site. The fort at Henley seems to be the larger, more important, and more distinctly outlined of the two; the one at Temple bay the more accessible. At the latter place we dug up canister and grape shot in abundance and could undoubtedly have procured a large variety of articles had we spent some time there. The situation of this fort was the summit of a huge hill the basal point of which was the separating line between Temple and Chateau bays. On the southeastern side of the slope we found and examined three caves, or rather clefts in the rocks, of which local tradition told startling stories of robbers, fierce animals and money, which were said to exist there. We found no difficulty in "finding bottom," and saw no cause for alarm, whatever others might have feared. Superstitions are abundant everywhere on the coast and there were undoubtedly those who believed the various stories of dragons, blackmen, and lobsters with terrible claws, who were said to guard treasures of inestimable value in these and other abodes of foxes and weasels. People told us of a large stone monument or house about three miles inland said to have been built by parties from a man-of-war who entered the harbor secretly, some years since, by night, and proceeded inland for some mysterious purpose. One man, I am told, declared solemnly, that they came for "buried treasures," and built this "stone house" to guard the remainder until they should come for it. Undoubtedly it was done by the sailors to excite this very superstition. They succeeded admirably.

Between the hill containing the fort and the opposite height westward, is a most beautifully formed glacial ridge and slide. Seaward it is more or less abrupt and precipitous though I should judge not over forty feet high. Towards the bay it slopes evenly and smoothly to the water. On this slope the houses are built. They are like other houses on the coast, with a single peculiarity in the shape of the fireplace. This was a hearth of some iron piece, usually the sides of an old iron stove, a back fireboard of a similar character, while the remainder of the chimney *was of wood and formed part of the house proper.* Why the blazing, roaring, crackling hearth fire that I often saw did not burn the house down I cannot well see. An iron frame, made like an old-fashioned steelyards, hung over the fire, the hooks of which could be raised or lowered at will, with two hooks (if I remember correctly) upon which were hung the kettles — here all the cooking of the family was done. One housewife showed me with great exultation, how nicely the bread kettle hung over the fire. I thought that if a modern mother was obliged to bake the quantity of bread weekly that this mother did and in such a primitive manner, she would show the arrangement with anything but satisfaction.

At one point in Temple bay I visited a mine of white mica that was just opened. It was romantically situated about 150 feet above the sea and by the side of a winding brook, that tumbled down among the confusion of loose rocks below and abounded in trout.

The mica, though very pure, was only in very small pieces. The rock in which it occurred seemed to be a gigantic bowlder rather than a rock in place.

While on the subject of minerals I will say that at Dead Island, some miles farther north, a party of miners boarded us, but did not remain long. On our whole trip along the coast we found quite a number of minerals, but none in quantities sufficient to pay for being worked. We found a mica mine at Dead Island, also, but it did not appear to be so good even, as that at Temple bay. At another locality one of the party found a quarry of very poor Labradorite of the black variety; we obtained a few pieces only. Everywhere granite rock predominated. In one locality veins of quartz and mica alternating in thin layers, one above the other, extended for some distance in several directions, bounded, I believe, by granite also. White and black mica were abundant everywhere, but in small pieces. Tourmaline of the black variety was not rare and several remarkably finely terminated crystals were procured. Some fine rubellite was also found. Copper pyrite was common, as was also iron pyrite; sulphide of iron was very abundant : several pieces of apatite were found; a large amount of galena and in one locality molybdenite, the latter probably in no very great amount. Poor labradorite in various forms and color; quite large but very brittle garnets; argentiferous lead in small quantities; quartz very clear and glassy; feldspar of various colors; and occasionally greenstone like Pike's Peak greenstone, wrongly called labradorite, was found. With this brief account of the mineralogy of the region let us pass to other and more important subjects.

At Temple bay we spent considerable time dredging, and brought up many curious and rare specimens from the bottom of the bay. A large, bright red holothurian or sea-cucumber, seemed particularly common to this bay, while the smaller varieties also abounded. Shells of many kinds were dredged without number and at every haul of the dredge the shrimps and crustaceans seemed equally abundant. I shall not soon forget a dredging party that took place one evening in this same bay. We started out from the vessel directly after supper, and rowed across the bay nearly to the opposite side, then, letting down our dredge, we began our work. That night we secured a most strange collection of objects. Our buckets were quickly filled with the profusion of material that was procured, and we were soon obliged to row back to the ship and get more pails and buckets. Occasionally, when too near shore, we would bring up a dredge, full to the top, of spiny sea urchins or echini among which an occasional star-fish or holothurian would be found; in such cases we were obliged to empty the net overboard and make a new haul.

In the midst of our work, when we had nearly filled our buckets and pails with rich material, to be looked over in the morning, suddenly a most brilliant Aurora gathered in the heavens. It gathered itself as if it were an immense snake, and with many undulations seemed to coil and recoil itself to make room for the enormous length with which it spanned the heavens and reached almost directly over our heads, from horizon to horizon. It was broad and of a most intense white. It undulated like a ribbon, and changed its form continually, sometimes concentrating much like an immense drop, then as suddenly lengthening again. Then its direction would change from northeast and northwest to nearly east and west.

While these contortions were attracting our attention in the heavens, another peculiar phenomenon was beginning to appear in the water, which suddenly became magnetized as it were to an unusual degree, and that most remarkable occurrence of phosphorescence began to display itself in a most intense degree. I have never seen it so beautiful and so luminous. We had now reached the side of the ship, and every dash of the oar sent large, whirling eddies of fire off at our right and left. The boat left a long, luminous wake, like the reflection in the water of the auroral ribbon above. A dash of the oar would cover the surface with bubbles of fire, while, occasionally, large disks of the same would sail by apparently ten or fifteen feet below the surface, we could not touch them with our oar, though that was twelve feet long. We all sat up some time watching these curious appearances, and each decided that they were the most beautiful that they had ever witnessed. We caught a huge ball of fire on our dredge rope, and hauled it in. It was placed in a small can of water and found to be one of the jelly fishes, with which, in the daytime, the water abounded. It was nearly an inch long. Is it possible that these animals, large and small, are luminous to such an extreme degree?

After remaining for several days in Chateau we left it for our next port north. We had no more than cleared the land and taken our course than the fog shut down upon us again, thick and heavy. We kept steadily onward, however, but soon found we were rushing into a tremendous ice mass. The vessel's course was changed just as an immense ice tower, between two and three hundred feet in height, surged by us with a velocity that would have crushed us instantly had we struck it; another and another followed, and we began to fear for our lives, but soon, by good fortune, the fog lifted and we sighted Belle Isle, turning our prow, then, to a similar course northward, to that which we had been steering eastward, we were, by evening of the same day, quietly anchored at Fox harbor, where we passed a most comfortable night.

Fox Harbor is one of the principal harbors of St. Lewis Sound, and just north of Cape Charles. It is a large indentation, and contains several very important harbors, the most so being Battle Island, often called the Boston of Labrador. St. Lewis inlet runs a long way into the interior of the country and is navigable nearly its whole length of some twenty to thirty miles, I believe. We did considerable dredging here, and produced capital results.

I think that it was on Saturday, Aug. 12, that we arrived at Fox Harbor, and glad enough were we to be in safe anchorage, once more, while the fog continued to settle upon us. The next three days were quite pleasant however, and we made the most of them. Everybody on board started in the boats for a tour of investigation on shore. Here, at length, we had struck a real semi-arctic habitation, inhabited by Indians, Esquimaux, and several half-breed families. The houses were similar, but poorer, than those we had seen all along the coast. The children were everywhere followed with troups of dogs, but they were not savage, being mainly pure Newfoundland and a race of large Indian dogs. Several of these dogs were brought home by various parties on board, and have since thrived well, excepting the two Indian hunting dogs, pure breed, which, I understand, have since died. A peculiarity of these dogs is said to be the fact, that they will gorge themselves, and carry food for a long time in their stomachs *untouched by the gastric juice*, disgorging it from time to time for their young. One man affirmed that he had known them to keep food in this way for two days, throwing it up in the apparently perfect condition of fresh meat, upon which young puffins fed greedily.

Our men returned to the vessel loaded with spears, bows and arrows, komatik whips, sealskin boots and mittens, and several finely spotted skins. One of the party procured the tusks of a young walrus, two of these animals having been killed by the natives the previous winter. They told me here that this animal though occasionally seen about this part of the coast was rarely captured. Upon inquiring I found that no white bears had been seen here for several years.

Across the harbor lies Battle Island, on the eastern side of which is Battle Harbor. It is a village of about fifty houses, and a place of much importance upon the coast. A mail steamer calls every fortnight and returns directly to St. Johns. It is a fishing community, and does not differ much from the settlements at Red Bay or Blanc Sablon.

We did some good work at Fox Harbor dredging, and this was the only place where we found squids, although they doubtless occur more or less abundantly at nearly or quite every harbor. Another peculiarity of our finds here was the immense number of small crustacea, sandfleas and worms, that were everywhere abundant under rocks and in pools of water wherever we searched for them. Here, too, as at other places, we dredged several *Terebratula*, but found them generally rare. One of our party secured a most beautiful and magnificent large salmon trout nearly two feet long.

Leaving Fox harbor we passed Mecklenburg harbor but did not enter it, as it was not of sufficient consequence; we also passed St. Frances harbor, the mouth of the Alexis River, navigable for about twenty miles inland, and said to present as beautiful scenery as any harbor along the coast, while the intricacies of its mouth being as complex as any river south of Rigoulette, and steered for St. Michaels and Square Island, the next place of interest, where we stopped over night. We anchored at the farther end of the harbor, and a most beautiful and picturesque little spot it was. This place is named Square Island from the large almost square island which nearly blocks the entrance to the harbor. We entered through a very shallow and narrow passage, crossed the harbor, and were soon anchored in a sequestered little spot safe from everything save those intolerable torments the blackflies and mosquitoes. The houses here looked more like the nests of an army of cliff swallows than anything else that I can imagine; they were perched everywhere on the high rocks close to the cliffs, and looked as if glued to them, so closely did they stand; and so near the color of the rocks were the weathered boards and boughs of which they were composed, while so snug was the harbor, that one might have hunted for weeks for the location, did he not know it from previous visitation, and then have passed it without discovering the entrance passage, while high cliffs everywhere surrounded it. A party went over to Nolan's harbor, a few miles distant, and met Capt. Fitzgerald, of Harbor Grace, Newfoundland, who oversees quite a fishery at this point; but one place so closely resembles another on this part of the coast, that the intricacies of bays, coves, islands, and narrow passages of water present every possible shape, size, and form of harbor. It is, in fact, like the "Bower of Fair Rosamond," in which one would easily lose one's self without the help of a most skilful pilot.

On Thursday we left Square Island and sailed to Dead Island, a few miles north only of our former position, and found quite a community of fishermen living here. The inhabitants were chiefly summer visitors from Newfoundland, engaged in the herring fisheries. They had quite a good catch, and were about preparing to return home with their cargoes. The majority of these fishermen, we found, were from Harbor Grace, Newfoundland, and we everywhere found them a rough, tough, but not ill-natured race, yet one with whom we did not care to deal any more than it was found absolutely necessary.

At Dead Island we produced some of our best results at dredging. The harbor was not deep, but the seaweed, with which the bottom was covered, was everywhere full of life, and covered with shells and minute crustaceans. In one small pass to the north of which we were anchored, I found one of the most remarkable nests of marine animals that I had ever come across, either on Labrador or in any of the harbors of Massachusetts. The water was from one to five fathoms deep, and clear as crystal. The bottom was one large, magnificent flower bed of anemones growing on a ground of red nullipore that covered everything. The extent of this growth must have been acres, and as we sailed along in our boat we could see the magnificent animals as plainly as if they had been before us in the bottom of the boat, and we could pick them with our hands.

The unevenness of the bottom furnished a pleasing variation of elevations and depressions. Choice nooks and hiding places, or plains were everywhere interspersed. Natural grottoes, and varieties of rock-work, all were there, and all covered with "red rock," or "live rock" as the people call this peculiar growth, probably the red nullipore (*Lithothamnion polymorphum*), and some so heavily incrusted as to represent miniature shrubs and trees even by their own incrusted additions. Over this growth the anemone (*Metridium*) grew as luxuriant as flowers reared in plant house or hot-bed, and a most gorgeous hot-bed, even of beautiful and rare tropical plants could not have excited more admiration. I hauled up, with a huge scoop of the dredge, specimens whose base measured ten and even more inches across, and whose expanded disk was nearly as wide. Fringed tentacle several inches in length would surround a disk whose neck was more often over than under six inches in length. When touched they would coil into a mass of leathery pulp as large as a medium-sized musk melon.

This fine floral carpet was everywhere interspersed with green echini, some large as a good-sized sunflower; myriads of starfish, with yellow, red, or brown backs were basking in some clear space or curled up to fit the surfaces of the rocks upon which they lay. Suddenly we came upon a single bed, it must have been nearly half an acre in extent, in the middle of the passage, where an almost perfectly level spot appeared so covered with these anemones that their waving fringes intermingled to hide the bottom and present a bed truly of the most exquisite and fairylike texture. Truly were I to be buried in the ocean, I could not nor would I ask for a more enchanting spot upon which to rest. I am sure that no Arabian Nights' tale ever pictured a more imaginative scene of splendor, than this simple bed of sea flowers — this "wind flower" of the water formed in reality.

We left Dead Island on Wednesday the 23rd, and sailing through the same narrow pass, which opened into a broad bay-like harbor beyond and a series of intricate channels, coves and islands, we at length reached Triangle harbor, another of those pirate-like coves in which the coast so profusely abounds. The harbor is well sheltered from the seas, but hard to enter, being narrow and shallow. High hills and cliffs are all about it, the highest point, on the right, being a hill with lofty sides extending perpendicularly nearly to its very crest, which is about three hundred and eighty feet above the sea. We threw stones from this crest into the sea and found that the top receded, from a point that overhung the water about midway of this height, so much that the stones we threw with all our force fell into the water behind the cliff and consequently out of our sight. Back from the hill grew a luxuriant growth of vegetation, while a small but deep pond, partially surrounded with high cliffs, afforded us a most excellent opportunity for a fine bath in not too cold fresh water. The pond was one of a series, doubtless extending way into the interior and forming the head waters of some stream that flowed to the sea in one of the neighboring fiord valleys, abundant here also. At this, our final post north, we secured capital results with the dredge, though we found a clayey and muddy bottom, which, I recollect, gave us great trouble to strain in our sieves. Black bears are abundant in these parts, I was told, and the very morning after our arrival one was seen perched on the summit of a huge cliff above us. It was pursued by the natives but not captured.

At length, on Friday the 25th, we started for home, as our time of absence had already nearly expired. We stopped at Fox harbor on our way back, and the next day had a most excellent run of about one hundred and ten miles to Bonne Esperance where we remained over Sunday and Monday.

At Bonne we found a new machine in operation for the conversion of the refuse of cod and other fish into a sort of fish guano. Several barrels had been sent to the United States to be analyzed and tried for mixture with other materials for a soluble guano for the land and crops, but I am not informed as to whether it was a success or not.

Monday night, for our benefit, the natives performed a Labrador, or rather Newfoundland dance, at one of the native cabins near by. A crowd of about thirty assembled and danced till nearly morning. Their main object seemed to be to "start the sweat, and see who could make the most noise." It seemed as if the very house would come down over our heads as they hammered on the floor with their top-legged boots pounding with the full force of their powers: this serenade to the departing guests closed our sight-seeing upon the Labrador Coast, while the hearty good-bye of Mr. Whiteley, the magistrate, compensated for all bad weather and mishaps that we had previously experienced as we slowly spread sail and started for home.

The following brief Indian vocabulary will give a slight clew to that most obscure yet interesting language of the Labrador Indians, as spoken all along the coast.

AMONG THE NUMERALS.

1 pay yuck.	7 nish wash.
2 nesh.	8 nursh wash.
3 nurst.	9 pay-er coush.
4 nao.	10 pay-er cannou.
5 pertater.	20 nesh ennou.
6 goot wash.	30 nurst ennou.

OTHER WORDS.

and,	ash-shoo.	no,	mar watch.
I, me,	nin.	yes,	topway.
you,	tin.	what,	chaquin.
he,	win.	water,	nee-pe.
that,	ne-ya.	spirits, liquor,	skutee-wabee.
all of us (we),	cassino.	an axe,	eustache.
money,	soumentish.	salmon,	oush-a-muck.
quick,	sellerpe.	trout,	meta-muck.
girl,	squish.	cod,	ohm-zhee.
boy,	nowpee.	seal,	ar-chook.
mother,	naga.	deer,	atchick.
give,	perta.	martin,	wabistan.
I go with you,	mu pou shoo.	meat,	mee-ash.
how much,	ten ash push.	butter,	tootoosh pimme.
ship,	jonne push.	milk,	tootoosh ackee.
come on,	stammetay.	pork,	coocoosh.
go on,	mate.	lard,	pimme.
canoe,	oushe.		

NOTE. The other important localities on the Labrador Peninsula are as follows: —

Hamilton Inlet (*Ivucktoke*) which extends about ninety navigable miles in a westerly direction. Its entrance is a wide bay which is succeeded by lake-like expansions of this same inlet connected by narrow passes or channels. In the first channel, or "the narrows," as it is called, are Indian Village and Rigoulette, — the latter the most important station hereabouts; and formerly, I believe, if not now, connected with the Hudson's Bay Company. The river, which flows into this inlet and is called by the natives Esquimaux river, is the largest and most important in all Labrador. It is the terminus of the French and English settlements on the coast: below it the Dutch and Esquimaux are the chief and more often the only inhabitants, to Ungava Bay itself which borders the entrance to Hudson's Bay.

These almost mongrel inhabitants are known chiefly by the names of their villages, as the people of *Umiakkoviktanuk* or Cape Strawberry, which is some 1200 feet above the sea, in the background of which is *Altagaiyaivik* or Monkey Hill, said to be over 2000 feet high. Next comes a post of the Hudson's Bay Company at *Aillik*, and one on the opposite side of the bay at *Kaipokok*. Towards the sea are the Gull rocks, called by the musical (?) name of *Nanyaktikiluk*, and farther along Gull island or *Nanyaksigaluk*. On the mainland nearly opposite Gull island comes the important Mission station of Hopedale. Below this is Nain, the next important Moravian mission. East of Nain is *Tunnulusoak* or Pownal or Paul Island, the place so often quoted as abounding in Labradorite. *Okkuk*, followed by Port Manvers and Hebron, other missionary stations follow while Cape Chudleigh (or Chidley as some give it) forms the northern terminus, from which this promontory descends to Ungava Bay the northern boundary of the Labrador Peninsula. Of the interior of this vast plateau little or nothing is known. The blackflies and mosquitoes form an almost impassable barrier to investigation; try it *once* and you will thoroughly believe it.

www.ingramcontent.com/pod-product-compliance
Lightning Source LLC
Chambersburg PA
CBHW031249250426
43672CB00029BA/1386